Library of
Davidson College

Trends Affecting the U.S. Banking System

Trends Affecting the U.S. Banking System

By
Cambridge Research Institute

Paul V. Teplitz,
Principal Author

Ballinger Publishing Company • Cambridge, Mass.
A Subsidiary of J.B. Lippincott Company

332.1
C178t

 This book is printed on recycled paper.

Cambridge Research Institute provides services to help executives understand the future, plan for it, and manage change. CRI provides these services through research, consulting, and education.

Copyright © 1976 by Cambridge Research Institute, Incorporated, and Western Union Corporation. All rights reserved. No part of this publication may be reproduced, stored in a retrieval system, or transmitted in any form or by any means, electronic mechanical photocopy, recording or otherwise, without the prior written consent of the publisher.

International Standard Book Number: 0-88410-291-2

Library of Congress Catalog Card Number: 75-37754

Printed in the United States of America

Library of Congress Cataloging in Publication Data
Cambridge Research Institute.
    Trends Affecting the U.S. Banking System
    "Principal author of the report is Paul V. Teplitz. Principal contributors are Bertrand Fox . . . [et al.]"
    Sponsored by Western Union Teleprocessing, Inc.
    Bibliography: p.
    1. Banks and banking–United States. 2. Banks and banking–United States–State supervision. I. Teplitz, Paul V. II. Title.
HG2491.C35   1975a   332.1'0973   75-37754
ISBN 0-88410-291-2

Contents

List of Tables   vii

List of Figures   xi

Preface   xiii

Chapter One
Introduction   1

Financial Intermediaries	2
The Commercial Banking System	5
Branch Banking, Mergers, and Holding Companies	9
Organization of the Report	10
Notes	41

Chapter Two
The Banking System and Its Economic Environment   13

The Banking System	13
Postwar Trends in the U.S. Economy	21
Trends in the Economics of Banking	33
Trends in the Financial Needs and Habits of Bank Customer Groups	52
Summary and Conclusions	61
Notes	64

Chapter Three
The Competitive Environment of Commercial Banks   65

The Markets in Which Banks Compete   66

vi Contents

Major Competitor Groups	72
Proposals to Reform the Financial System	94
Summary and Conclusions	104
Notes	106

Chapter Four
The Regulatory Environment of Commercial Banks — 109

Federal Banking Regulation	109
State Banking Regulation	118
Prospects for Changes in Financial Regulations	125
Notes	129

Chapter Five
The Technological Environment of Commercial Banks — 131

The Delivery of Banking Services	132
Recent Technological Innovations in Banking	135
Regulatory Issues Raised by EFTS	140
Conclusions	154
Notes	155

Chapter Six
Conclusions — 157

Banks' Position in the Financial System	157
The Shortage of Funds	159
The Regulation of Banks	161

Appendix
Potential Effects of the 1971 Statewide Branching Law on New York State's Banking Industry — 165

History of New York State's Banking Industry	165
Analysis of Possible Effects of Statewide Branching in 1976 on the Structure and Characteristics of New York's Banking Industry	172
Conclusions	183
Notes	185

Bibliography	187
Index	203

List of Tables

1-1	Supply and Demand for Credit, Calendar Year 1972	3
1-2	Deposits of Banks and Thrift Institutions, End of Calendar Year 1974	5
1-3	Regulation and Organization of the Banking Industry	7
2-1	Income Velocity of Money, 1929-1972	17
2-2	Growth of U.S. Gross National Product	22
2-3	Projections of Gross National Product and Employment	23
2-4	Number of Births and Birth Rate in the U.S., 1940-1973	24
2-5	Average Annual Rate of Productivity Change by Sector, 1955-1985	25
2-6	Percent Distribution of Employment, by Major Occupational Group—1960 and 1972, and Projected 1980 and 1985	26
2-7	Total Employment by Major Sector, Selected Years 1955-1972 and Projected 1980 and 1985	27
2-8	Gross Product Originating in Various Sectors of the Private Economy, Selected Years 1955-1972 and Projected to 1980 and 1985	29
2-9	Types of Investment in the United States, 1929-1974	32
2-10	Bond Yields and Interest Rates, 1929-1974	34
2-11	Money Stock Measures, 1947-1974	36
2-12	Net Public and Private Debt, 1929-1973	38
2-13	Financial Assets and Liabilities of U.S. Commercial Banks	40
2-14	Growth of Bank Balance Sheet Items, 1945-1972	42
2-15	Ownership of Demand Deposits and Currency	43
2-16	Ownership of Time Deposits and Savings Accounts at Commercial Banks	44
2-17	Comparisons of Gross National Product, Bank Debits, and Turnover of Demand Deposits	50
2-18	Trends in Income Ratios	51

viii List of Tables

2-19	Financial Assets and Liabilities of Corporate Non-Financial Businesses	54
2-20	State and Municipal and Corporate Securities Offered, 1934-1974	58
2-21	Financial Assets and Liabilities of State and Local Governments	60
2-22	Financial Assets and Liabilities of U.S. Households, 1945-1974	62
2-23	Consumer Attitudes Toward Installment Debt	63
3-1	Comparison of Financial Assets in Financial Intermediaries versus Direct Market Instruments, by Sector—1945-1974	69
3-2	Total Assets of Financial Intermediaries, 1945 versus 1972	73
3-3	Characteristics of Commercial Banks and Thrift Institutions	76
3-4	Location of Time and Savings Deposits—1950, 1960, 1974	80
3-5	Annual Change in Depository Savings and Direct Investments of Households, 1960-1974	81
3-6	Total Mortgage Credit Outstanding, by Supplier—1950, 1960, 1974	83
3-7	Mortgage Credit Outstanding, Supplier and Type of Mortgage—1972	85
3-8	Characteristics of Other Financial Institutions	86
3-9	Percentage Composition of Short-Term Business Debt, 1945-1974	90
3-10	Consumer Credit Outstanding, by Type of Credit and Institution—1950, 1960, 1974	92
3-11	Number of Foreign Branches of U.S. Commercial Banks	93
3-12	Comparison of Recommendations for Financial Reform—The Hunt Commission versus President Nixon	97
3-13	Summary of Competitive Position of Commercial Banks in Some Major Markets	105
4-1	Nonbanking Activities Under Section 4(c)(8)	116
4-2	Effect of Branching Regulation on Concentration of Commercial Bank Deposits	121
4-3	Impact of Holding Company Acquisitions on Concentration in States with Different Levels of Concentration	124
4-4	Growth of Multibank Holding Companies	126
5-1	Sample Framework for Comparing Characteristics of Banking Services	136
5-2	Possible Scheme for Evaluating the Impacts of EFTS	139
5-3	Some Viewpoints of Interested Parties on Questions Raised by EFTS	142
A-1	Percentage of Deposits Held by the Three Largest Banks in Metropolitan Areas of New York State—1950 and 1960	167

A-2	Number of Commercial Bank Offices in Nassau and Westchester Counties, New York–1959 versus 1968	168
A-3	Proportion of Commercial Bank Deposits in New York Held by Bank Holding Companies–1965, 1970, 1971	172
A-4	Comparison of Demographic, Economic, and Regulatory Environments of the Banking Industries in California, New York, and Florida	174

List of Figures

1-1	Regulatory Framework	6
2-1	Federal Funds Purchases, 1959-1972	19
2-2	Educational Attainment of the Civilian Labor Force, March 1972 and Projected 1980 and 1985	26
2-3	Employment in Finance, Insurance and Real Estate, 1959-1985	31
2-4	Net Public and Private Debt—1947, 1960, 1972	37
2-5	Nondeposit Sources of Funds	47
2-6	Corporate Liquidity Positions	55
3-1	Sources and Uses of Credit	67
4-1	Number of Banks by State Branching Law	122
5-1	Examples of Check Movements	132
5-2	Clearing Process for Bank Credit Card Purchases	134
5-3	Wire Transfer of Funds Among Banks	134
5-4	Number of Banks by Status of Automation	137
A-1	Holders of Commercial Bank Deposits in New York State—December 31, 1973	172
A-2	Holders of Commercial Bank Deposits in California—December 31, 1973	177
A-3	Holders of Commercial Bank Deposits in Florida—December 31, 1973	179
A-4	Holders of Commercial Bank Deposits in Florida—December 31, 1969	180

Preface

This report, initially published in softcover, makes its appearance in book form thanks to the suggestions of several friends of Cambridge Research Institute who, having a lively interest in the field of commercial banking, have encouraged its wider circulation. Occasioned by the rapid changes taking place in the economic, competitive, regulatory and technological environment of this industry, this report provides decision-makers and planners in both industry and government with a factual, objective and future-oriented view of where commercial banking is headed. The report is one of several covering different industries by Cambridge Research Institute.

Just what forces are at work that shape and constrain banking in this country, and what future directions and outcomes are anticipated—especially as regards the various types of financial institutions and service offerings—is what this book is all about. Two distinct groups are likely to find this book of interest: First, those directors and managers who are intimately concerned with strategy and planning for commercial banks; Second, active onlookers such as legislators, banking regulators, and marketers to banks.

Thanks are due to the officers and staffs of Teleprocessing Industries, Inc., and of National Sharedata Corporation, subsidiaries of Western Union Corporation, for their sponsorship and assistance.

Principal author of the report is Paul V. Teplitz. Principal contributors are Bertrand Fox, Elizabeth Huard, Dominique C. Poussin, Dan Throop Smith, and James B. Webber. John Desmond Glover provided overall direction. All are members of the Cambridge Research Institute.

                                            Gerald A. Simon
                                            Managing Director
                                            Cambridge Research Institute

November 1975

Chapter One

Introduction

When we undertook this project, we sought to study recent technological innovations in banking and the opportunities they might create for selling information services to banks. As the project developed it became apparent, to us and to the client, that something broader was called for. The range of innovations in banking was broad, and the variety of reactions from banks, consumers, the regulatory agencies, and the Congress was broader still. Banking seemed to be caught up in a tide of events, of which technological progress was only a part. It was difficult to evaluate technical innovations without some understanding of the broader forces which were acting on the banking industry.

During the last three decades the banking industry (by this term we mean, principally, the commercial banks) has undergone considerable change. To some extent, the changes have been a recovery from the double shocks of the Depression and World War II. In other respects, some of the recent events in banking represent evolutionary changes, as banks adapt to the lifestyles and financial needs of their customers. Through all of the recent changes there has been a strong influence of public policy. The U.S. has evolved an unusually complex array of statutory controls and regulatory agencies around which the financial industry and banking especially have molded themselves. The regulations pervade almost every aspect of the banking business, and many bank activities which at first seemed illogical can be explained by the peculiarities in public policy.

This report attempts to provide an analytical framework for viewing the ongoing developments in banking. It attempts this by examining the interactions between the banking industry and its environment, in the same way that a biologist, in order to understand an organism, looks at its interactions with its environment. The underlying assumption is that the external forces acting on an industry are fundamental constraints. In a sense they are its "givens." No matter what the internal changes that might occur, in structure or in particulars, the industry must always cope with these external forces. Understanding those forces allows us to reduce the range of speculation about the future.

Throughout the report, we have tried to keep in mind that its purpose is to help formulate a strategy for products or acquisitions related to banking. This concern has influenced our choice of material. For example, we have focused on issues relating to the banking structure rather than on particulars. We have devoted considerable discussion to the functions of commercial banks and relatively little to their operations. We have emphasized causes rather than mechanics, and we have made no effort to be exhaustive in our coverage. The environmental segments we have examined are those we feel are the principal determinants of the structure and functions of the banking industry. These are the regulatory environment, the economic environment, the competitive environment, and the technological environment of commercial banks.

FINANCIAL INTERMEDIARIES

Commercial banks are one of the major types of financial intermediaries in the United States at the present time. The term *intermediary* is usually associated with financial businesses such as banks, savings institutions, insurance companies, and investment companies, whose function is to borrow for the purpose of lending rather than for nonfinancial outlays. These intermediaries serve as collection centers for the surplus funds people have and as distribution centers for people who need to borrow funds.

Intermediaries tend to specialize in the forms of debt they accept or the forms of credit—including new issues of stock—they extend, or both. Insurance companies, for example, raise funds primarily through policy premiums but invest broadly in credit markets, whereas savings and loan associations are specialists both in borrowing through savings accounts and in lending through mortgages. Intermediaries fill a gap between the types of claims that people prefer to hold as assets, including demand deposits, and the very different forms of claims that borrowers owe, such as bank loans to business, consumer credit, and mortgages. With or without intermediaries, the total claims held as assets by nonfinancial transactors are nearly equal to the total of their debts, because directly or indirectly they owe the debt to one another. But with intermediation, the composition of their assets becomes very different from the composition of their debts. The intermediaries thus perform a transformation process within the financial markets between the asset and the liability sides of the public's balance sheet. Their presence in the market broadens enormously the forms of financial investment and borrowing available to the public. There is no question that capital formation, saving, income and consumption are all higher than they would be without the influence of intermediaries in raising financial flows.[1]

In the U.S. economy, a large part of all credit goes through intermediaries. Table 1-1 shows in matrix form a tabulation of the supply and demand for

Table 1-1. Supply and Demand for Credit, Calendar Year 1972 (Billions of Dollars)

	U.S. Government Securities		Mortgages		Corporate Securities		State & Local Government Securities	Consumer Loans	Business Loans	Open Market Paper	Other Bank Loans	Foreign Securities	Total
	Direct	Agency	Home	Other	Bonds	Stocks							
Life Insurance Company	-0.1	—	-2.6	3.8	6.7	3.6	—	0.9	—	0.8	—	0.3	13.4
Fire and Casualty Insurance	—	-0.1	—	—	0.3	2.6	3.3	—	—	—	—	0.1	6.2
Savings and Loan Association	1.6	1.7	24.2	7.9	—	—	—	0.1	—	0.3	—	—	35.8
Mututal Savings Banks	0.1	1.5	2.8	2.7	2.2	0.5	0.5	0.3	—	—	—	—	10.6
Credit Unions	1.2	—	0.1	—	—	—	—	2.1	—	—	—	—	3.4
Commercial Banks	1.7	1.5	7.8	8.6	1.6	—	8.1	10.1	20.2	-0.8	11.2	—	70.0
Corporate Pension Funds	0.2	0.2	—	-0.7	-0.3	6.7	—	—	—	—	—	—	6.1
State and Local Pension Funds	0.2	-0.3	—	-0.1	4.4	2.8	-0.3	—	—	—	—	0.5	7.2
Mutual Funds	—	—	—	—	0.2	-1.6	—	—	—	—	—	—	-1.4
Nonfinancial Corps	1.0	0.5	—	—	—	—	-0.4	3.3	—	0.8	—	—	5.2
Financial Companies	—	—	3.3	—	—	—	—	3.2	1.4	—	—	—	7.9
Foreigners	8.6	0.1	—	—	0.2	1.9	—	—	—	-0.2	—	—	10.6
State and Local Government	2.8	1.0	—	—	—	—	—	—	—	0.3	—	—	4.1
Individuals and Miscellaneous	-3.3	3.6	-3.0	3.8	4.1	-2.7	1.3	—	—	-0.4	—	—	3.4
Totals	14.0	9.7	32.6	26.0	19.4	13.8	12.5	20.0	21.6	0.8	11.2	0.9	182.5

Source: Salomon Brothers; Supply and Demand for Credit in 1973, as derived from Flow of Funds data of the Federal Reserve.

credit (including net new stock issues) for the calendar year 1972. The various suppliers of funds, mainly financial intermediaries, which play the major role in supplying credit to the U.S. economy are listed down the left-hand side of the Table. The dollar totals in the far right-hand column indicate the amounts of credit supplied by each of these various financial intermediaries. (It should be noted that these are net figures—new credits supplied less repayments or retirements.) The various users of credit and the types of credit instruments involved in obtaining credit from the various financial intermediaries are indicated across the top of the table. The total amount of credit of that particular type demanded in the year 1974 is indicated at the bottom of each column.[2]

No attempt will be made at this point to draw conclusions about the many features of our financial system revealed by Table 1-1. Such conclusions are drawn systematically in later chapters. Initially, however, one can note that the key suppliers of credit are the banks and thrift institutions, other financial intermediaries, and nonfinancial units which participate only partially as credit suppliers. The relative importance of each type of supplier can be noted from the right-hand column of figures where it is indicated that commercial banks were the largest credit supplier in 1974 by a wide margin. Also, the types of credit supplied by financial institutions are indicated by the figures recorded across each row of data. For example, the specialization in lending by savings and loan associations, in home mortgages, contrasts with the wide participation in credit markets by commercial banks. Finally, by examining the various columns of data, one can ascertain which institutions compete in supplying credit to particular markets and the relative success of that competition. These competitive features are developed further in later sections of this report.

It should be emphasized that the data for nonfinancial corporations, state and local governments, foreigners, and individuals and miscellaneous differ from the other categories because these groups are not financial institutions as such. In this table, only investments in direct credit instruments are shown. The major investments of nonfinancial corporations are in plant and equipment and in inventories, but these are not financial instruments and hence are not shown here. Similarly, state and local governments acquire buildings, roads, schools, hospitals, etc., and these physical assets are not shown. For individuals, only those portions of savings which individuals invest directly in financial instruments are covered. Their acquisitions of real estate and durable goods are not shown, and in fact, only a fraction of the investment of their personal savings are shown in this table. The great bulk of personal savings are invested in one or another of the financial intermediaries. Indeed, they constitute the principal source of funds for the intermediaries.

An important segment of individuals' savings and the liquid balances of businesses are kept as *deposits* in banks and thrift institutions. Table 1-2 shows the relative importance of commercial banks among these institutions as holders of deposits in 1974.

Commercial banks are the only institutions allowed to accept demand deposits

Table 1-2. Deposits of Banks and Thrift Institutions, End of Calendar Year 1972 (Billions of dollars)

Commercial Banks	
Demand Deposits	$215.2
Large Negotiable Certificates of Deposit	44.5
Other Time and Savings Deposits	271.1
Savings and Loan Associations—Savings Deposits	207.3
Mutual Savings Banks—Savings Deposits	91.6
Credit Unions—Savings Deposits and Shares	21.7
Total	$851.4

Source: Board of Governors of the Federal Reserve System, *Flow of Funds Accounts, 1945-1972* (Washington, D.C.: August 1973), pp. 94-6 and 111-113.

which are transferable to third parties by check. These checking deposits constitute the major part of our money supply, and because of this special role played by commercial banks, they are subject to special forms of regulation by the board of governors of the Federal Reserve System, our central banking system.

The banks also are in direct competition with the other three kinds of thrift institutions in providing savings and time deposit facilities to individuals and businesses. There are differences among the various institutions as to the kinds of time deposits that can be provided and to whom they can be provided, but it is clear that in 1974 the commercial banks held almost as great a volume of time and savings deposits as the other thrift institutions combined.

THE COMMERCIAL BANKING SYSTEM

The commercial banking system today consists of slightly more than 14,000 separate banks. About 4,500 of these banks are chartered by the federal government as national banks; the other banks, just under 10,000, are chartered by the states. These are the banks doing business with the public, accepting deposits and lending to individuals, businesses, and governments. In addition, there are 12 Federal Reserve Banks, which are bankers' banks, holding deposits of other banks (and of the federal government) and lending to member commercial banks. These 12 central banks are in turn controlled by the Board of Governors of the Federal Reserve System, a semiautonomous agency of the government.

In addition to the dichotomy of our banking system between national and state banks, a second division exists between banks which are members of the Federal Reserve System and those which are not. All "national" banks *must* be members and state banks *may* be members. At present, slightly more than 1,000 state banks are members of the Federal Reserve System. Altogether, member banks account for nearly 80 percent of all deposits in the commercial banking system.

Another distinction among banks is whether or not their deposits are insured

6 Trends Affecting the U.S. Banking System

by the Federal Deposit Insurance Corporation. All member banks are insured, and practically all state banks have elected to become insured. Only about 200 commercial banks are not insured by the FDIC.

These distinctions are important because the various classes of banks are subject to differing statutory restrictions and to differing regulatory jurisdictions. The regulatory framework of the various types of banks is indicated in Figure 1-1.

The more important regulatory differences relate to size of capital, the kinds of deposits, levels of reserves against deposits, the composition and location of reserves, the types and characteristics of assets that can be held or credit that can be extended, and the identity of the body conducting periodic examinations. These differences have considerable significance for the safety of the deposits of individual banks and the control of the volume of deposits which comprise the major component of our money supply.

Table 1-3 summarizes the different types of commercial banks and thrift institutions and their regulatory environment.

Chartering by states was the original form by which banks were created after the adoption of the Constitution. At that time, in addition to specie, the principal means of payment consisted of bank notes, and these circulating notes were created by the state banks in the process of making loans. Presumably the notes were redeemable in specie at the issuing banks, but in fact many banks overissued notes which became irredeemable and subject to severe depreciation. For a time two federally chartered banks, the First and Second Banks of the United States, acted to control state bank note issues by systematically presenting such notes for redemption. The enmity of state banks resulting from this process led to the demise of the Second Bank by President Jackson's veto in 1832 of the bill to extend the charter of that bank. This ushered in a chaotic period of rapid bank chartering, marked overissue and depreciation of the note currency, and widespread bank failures known as the era of "wildcat" banking.

This era came to an end with the creation of the National Banking System in 1863 and 1864. The purpose of the legislation was to create a safe note currency and to assist the government in financing the Civil War. The new sound

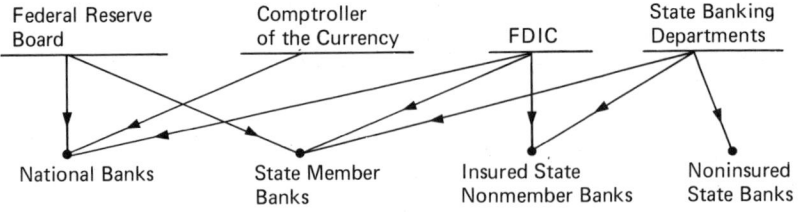

Figure 1-1. Regulatory Framework

Table 1-3. Regulation and Organization of the Banking Industry

Type of Bank	Commercial Banks			Thrift Institutions				
	National	State Member of FRS	State Non-member of FRS	Mutual Savings Banks	Savings and Loans		Credit Unions	
					Federal	State	Federal	State
Regulated by	FRB; Comptroller; FDIC	FRB; Comptroller; FDIC; States	FRB; FDIC (some); States	FDIC (some); FHLBB (some); States	FHLBB; FDIC (some); FRS (some)	States	National Credit Union Administration	States
Insured by	FDIC	FDIC	FDIC (some)	FDIC (most); FSLIC (few)	FSLIC	FSLIC (some)	Internal (some)	Internal (some)
Examined by	Comptroller; FRB; FDIC	FRB; FDIC; States	FDIC (some); States	States	FHLBB	FHLBB (some); States	NCUA	States
Chartered by	Comptroller	States	States	States	FHLBB	FHLBB (some); States	NCUA	States
Mergers or Branches Authorized by	Comptroller; FRB	FRB; States	FDIC (some); States	States	FHLBB	FHLBB (some); States	NCUA	States
Principal Laws Pertaining to	National Banking Act; Bank Merger Act; Bank Holding Act and Amendment; Federal Reserve Act; FDIC Act	Federal Reserve Act; FDIC Act; Bank Merger Act	FDIC Act; Bank Merger Act	Federal Home Loan Bank Act; FDIC Act	Federal Home Loan Bank Act; Federal Reserve Act; FDIC Act	Federal Home Loan Bank Act	NCUA Act	—
Trade Associations	American Bankers Association (ABA)	ABA; Independent Bankers Association of America	ABA; Independent Bankers Association of America	National Association of Mutual Savings Banks	National Savings and Loan League; U.S. League of Savings Associations	National Savings and Loan Association; U.S. League of Savings Associations	CUNA International, Inc.	CUNA International, Inc., State Organizations
Amount of Deposits in 1972 ($ Billions)	359.3	123.2	134.1	92.2	207.3		11.0	10.7
Number of Banks (1972)	4,612	1,092	8,223	486	5,445		12,734	10,400

Source: Federal Deposit Insurance Corporation, *Annual Report, 1972; Journal 74,* April 1974 (1973 Annual Report of the FHLBB).

Notes: Comptroller: Comptroller of the Currency (part of the U.S. Department of the Treasury)
FRB: Federal Reserve Board
FRS: Federal Reserve System
FDIC: Federal Deposit Insurance Corporation
FHLBB: Federal Home Loan Bank Board
FSLIC: Federal Savings and Loan Insurance Corporation

currency was National Bank Notes which were to be backed initially by 110 percent and later 100 percent U.S. Government Bonds. The currency banking, of course, generated a new demand for government bonds to help finance the war. Then, to stimulate the chartering of national banks, the circulating notes of state banks were taxed out of existence by a 10 percent tax levied on them. Consequently, many state banks converted their charters to become national banks.

The national banks were also required to maintain substantial reserves behind their deposits, 25 percent for central reserve and reserve city banks and 15 percent for other banks. Reserves were to be in specie or as deposits in central reserve or reserve city banks. Such requirements were to give a measure of safety to bank deposits. State banks generally were either not required to hold reserves behind deposits or to hold much lower levels of reserves. These differences in reserve requirements assumed greater significance in the years following the Civil War, as more and more people found it convenient to use checking accounts rather than currency to effect payments. The loans of banks, therefore, gave rise to demand deposits rather than bank note expansion, and the prohibition of state bank notes diminished in importance. Consequently, most banks preferred to remain state banks with their less restrictive regulations rather than shift to national charters. For example, by 1921 when there were 29,000 banks in the U.S., about 21,000 were state banks.

Unfortunately, although the National Bank Note currency proved to be eminently safe, it proved to be inflexible and did not expand and contract to meet the needs of trade. In addition, the pyramiding of reserves made the system subject to recurrent seasonal and cyclical financial crises and a less safe system than had been contemplated. The need was for a central bank which could provide a more elastic currency and which could alleviate the recurrent financial squeezes by providing a lender of last resort. The solution adopted by Congress was the Federal Reserve System, created in 1913.

Twelve Federal Reserve Banks were established that had the power to issue Federal Reserve Notes, hold the reserves of member banks, and lend to member banks to meet heavy demands on them for credit or deposit withdrawals. A Federal Reserve Board was established in Washington, but the powers of the system were shared between the Reserve banks and the board. At the time the system was established, its founders did not envisage a deliberately managed money supply, or the setting of monetary policy in Washington, or the present role of the board and the banks in helping to stabilize the economy. These changes developed gradually in the 1920s and especially in the 1930s with new legislation growing out of the Depression.

With the onset of the Depression in 1930 and 1931 there were waves of bank failures with which the Federal Reserve Banks could not cope. By April 1933 about half of the more than 24,000 banks which had been in existence in 1929 had failed. A national bank holiday, designed to break the wave of hysteria about the safety of banks and to permit various steps to restore confidence, was declared in March 1933 just after the inauguration of President Franklin D. Roosevelt. Then came the Glass-Steagall Act (the Banking Act of 1933) which, among other things, divorced investment banking from commercial banking and established the FDIC to insure the deposits of commercial banks. This latter reform especially alleviated fears about the safety of banks, especially small banks, and there has been no significant wave of bank failures since then.

The Banking Act of 1935 incorporated a number of additional reforms of the Federal Reserve System. These reforms centralized the power of the system to a far greater degree in the Board of Governors, and made clear that the system was to establish monetary policy and to control the money supply in the interests of a stable economy. Shortly before establishment of the 1935 Banking Act, all government bonds which had the circulation privilege were retired and all National Bank Notes were withdrawn. This step left Federal Reserve Notes as the major element of our circulating currency and thus gave the Federal Reserve key control of the U.S. money supply.

We still have a dual banking system—partially federally or state chartered, and partially member banks of the Federal Reserve System and state nonmember banks. The greater leniency of the banking regulations of most states and the freedom from the direct controls of the Fed have induced many state banks to remain outside the system. Fortunately, these are smaller banks, but the situation does make the control of the money supply by the Fed more difficult and raises questions of safety and equity among banks.

BRANCH BANKING, MERGERS, AND HOLDING COMPANIES

Branching was scarcely an issue before 1900. A few banks operated branches, and others tried and abandoned branches for lack of suitable return. By and large, state laws used singular nouns in referring to a bank's "place of business," but had no explicit prohibitions on branching.

The first serious moves toward branching began after the turn of the century, with the growth of the "streetcar" suburbs. By 1921, there were 1,281 branches maintained by 530 banks, but these banks accounted for 15 percent of U.S. bank deposits. By 1930, banks with branches accounted for almost half of all deposits. Since there were only 751 such banks and only 3,522 branches, branching was clearly an activity of the larger banks. A number of states in these early years passed antibranching legislation. Yet from about 1915 onward the overall trend has been toward liberalization of branching laws.

The Depression also brought several moves to strengthen the financial system by allowing more widespread branching of banks. During the 1930s nine states passed statewide branching laws (making a total of 18) and eight states allowed limited branching (making a total of 18).

The Depression, combined with World War II, effectively froze the formation of banks or branches for 15 years. After the war, the urban banks sought to follow their customers into the suburbs. One means of doing this was to acquire suburban banks, and the number of consolidations rose to more than 200 per year in the middle 1950s. This merger wave raised serious questions concerning the maintenance of competition and which authorities should control such mergers. Congress sought to resolve the issue with the Bank Merger Act of 1960. Also, in the following year the Justice Department brought suit against and blocked the proposed merger of the Philadelphia National Bank and the Girard Trust Corn Exchange Bank, the second and third largest banks in Philadelphia.

The Justice Department's position has been that banks should be free to enter markets in other cities, providing they do so by opening a *de novo* branch or by a "foothold acquisition" of a small existing bank and by expanding its activities. The department has, however, consistently opposed mergers between significant direct competitors in local markets.

In addition to direct mergers among banks, another mechanism to get around the restrictions against branch banking in many states was the development of bank holding companies. Such holding companies were created to acquire the stock of several banks in a state and thus to achieve some of the benefits of branching by establishing working relationships among these related banks. These holding companies have also been brought under regulatory control by several successive acts of Congress as well as by state regulations. These organizations have mushroomed, however, with an increasing proportion of banking resources in the various states coming under the control of sytems of banks in both branching and nonbranching states. In addition, these holding company organizations are expanding to carry on other approved lines of business.

It appears that additional changes in banking structure will take place in the future and one likely trend is the development of statewide or even economic-area-wide banking organizations either through branching mergers or holding companies.

ORGANIZATION OF THE REPORT

In the chapters that follow we will examine the effects of various aspects of the environment on commercial banking as well as the interactions between the banking industry and its environment. In Chapter Two we examine certain features of the economic environment. Initially we comment on the fundamental role of commercial banks in our monetary system and the constraints posed by that role. Then we discuss a few dominant economic trends that affect the banking industry, and some of the effects of these trends on banking. In addition, we comment on some of the other more important economic trends in commercial banking. Finally, we examine the trends in the financial needs of the key customer groups of commercial banks.

Chapter Three focuses on the competitive environment of commercial banks both in their activities to obtain funds for lending and investing and in their use of those funds to extend credit to borrowers. Major consideration is devoted to thrift institutions as a group, but competition with other intermediaries is also discussed. Because it is evident that the structure and behavior of our financial system is so dependent on the constraints of regulation, we also discuss a series of recent proposals for reform of our financial system.

In Chapter Four the regulatory system affecting commercial banking is discussed in detail. Both the rationale for and the impacts of the present patterns of federal and state regulation are examined, and the prospects for change are considered.

Chapter Five considers how the technological environment affects commercial banking services and functions. Special emphasis will be given to the opportunities for expanded or new services made possible by technological developments.

Finally, Chapter Six summarizes the key interrelationships of the various aspects of the environment on each other and on the commercial banking industry. In addition, a few broad projections are made of particular apsects of commercial banking.

NOTES

1. These two paragraphs are taken largely from the *Flow of Funds Accounts* (Washington, D.C.: Board of Governors of the Federal Reserve System, March 1970), pp. I. 13 and 14.

2. These data are preliminary estimates for 1972, prepared by the financial firm Salomon Brothers, from Flow of Funds data developed by the Federal Reserve System. The data were prepared shortly after the end of the calendar year before many of the figures were available in final form. This presentation has been developed from their figures to show the structure of the supply and demand for credit in the calendar year.

Chapter Two

The Banking System and its Economic Environment

Commercial banks stand at the crossroads of the nation's commerce. They create and hold the nation's money supply; they execute the transfer of funds arising from business or personal transactions; they hold a large part of the savings and supply a large part of the credit needed for our economy to function smoothly. Because of this central position, the activities and the health of commercial banks are determined to a very large extent by the patterns of activity in the economy generally. Indeed, most of the changes in banking in the past two decades have their origins in fundamental economic trends.

This chapter begins with some necessary groundwork in economic theory; the first section describes how money is created by banks and controlled by the Federal Reserve System. The next section adds further background by reviewing some overall trends in U.S. economic activity since World War II. The third section relates these trends to some specific changes (and innovations) in banking. The next section discusses some trends in the financial needs of banks' major customer groups, and the final section presents some overall conclusions.

THE BANKING SYSTEM

The Creation of Money

The United States (and most other countries) operates on a system of *fractional reserve banking*. Basically this means that banks keep only a fraction of their deposits in ready cash (or similar reserves) and lend out the rest to businesses or other borrowers. These loans create money for the banking system. When a bank makes a loan to a borrower, it does so by creating a deposit of that amount in his checking account.[1] As he spends that money by writing checks, these checks end as deposits in someone else's bank account and—after a portion has been set aside as reserves—can be loaned again. The ensuing chain of loans and deposits converges to a situation where the amount of money circulating in the banking system (currency plus demand deposits) is a constant multiple of the amount of reserves.[2] Thus the central bank (which in our case is the Federal Reserve System) can control the total money supply by controlling the quantity of reserves.

The whole concept of fractional reserve banking relies upon a strong statistical regularity in the way people hold and spend their money. If people "freeze" their money—(e.g., by withdrawing it as cash and hiding it in a mattress—the use of that money is lost to the banking system, and the money supply will contract by a multiple (in the U.S. about 6.0) of the amount frozen. This happened on a massive scale during the Depression, when the money supply contracted by 27 percent from June 29, 1929 to June 30, 1933, while the amount of cash held by the public grew by 31 percent as a result of currency hoarding.

Another way to upset the statistical regularity would be, simply, to use more cash for transactions instead of checks. Currently checks account for more than 90 percent of the dollar volume of transactions in this country. If people were to hold more of their money in the form of currency, then banks would have fewer deposits and would be forced to contract their loans and investments.[3]

Another leakage of money from the banking system arises from a balance of payments deficit, either through imports exceeding exports or through foreign investments by U.S. businesses. To the extent that Arab oil nations do not repatriate their "petrodollars" by depositing them in U.S. banks (or spending or investing them in the U.S.), banks will be forced to contract their loans and investments. The effect would be the same as if people were to withdraw the equivalent billions of dollars as cash and stuff them into a mattress. Fortunately, the Arab nations have chosen to "recycle" their petrodollars by depositing them in banks and by direct investments.

The Federal Reserve System and Control of the Money Supply

In the United States, most bank reserves are kept as deposits with the Federal Reserve Banks. Banks that are not members of the Federal Reserve System (which represent only about 20 percent of all banks deposits) normally keep their reserves in the form of Treasury bills or as deposits in large member banks. The "Fed" was established in 1913 for three principal functions:

1. to hold member bank reserves;
2. to serve as a "lender of last resort" for banks in temporary need of liquidity. This is frequently called "borrowing at the discount window," because the Fed simply rediscounts loans the banks have made to their own customers.

3. To provide a more orderly process for the clearing of checks, particularly over long distances.

As we have said, the Fed has the ability to control the money supply by controlling the quantity of bank reserves. Since World War II this has emerged as a major function of the Fed, as a means of stabilizing the economy. The Fed employs two principal mechanisms for controlling the quantity of bank reserves:

1. It can raise or lower the percentage of deposits that member banks must keep as reserves. This device has been used sparingly because it disrupts the member banks' own planning.
2. It can increase or decrease its own holdings of government (or other) securities through trading in the open market. The Fed pays for these securities with checks drawn upon itself which, when deposited by the seller, constitute new bank reserves. The Federal Open Market Committee (FOMC), which decides the level of open market activity, has come to be the principal agent of Fed monetary policy.

The Velocity of the Circulation of Money

The principal uses of money are as a means of payment and as a temporary store of liquid funds. Every transaction, except those involving barter, involves a transfer of funds either by check or by cash. The frequency of transfer depends on personal and business customs. People and corporate treasurers find it convenient to keep balances of deposits and currency related to various factors, perhaps equal to a certain number of days of ordinary expenditures.

The habits regarding the desirable size of money balances to be kept on hand change with circumstances. A shift from payment of wages from weekly checks to a monthly one, for example, would increase the average amount of money in the hands of wage earners and, given the same total expenditures, decrease the frequency of transfer of each unit of money. In other words, the velocity of circulation of money would decrease. More frequent payment of bills—e.g., weekly instead of monthly—would increase the velocity of circulation. (In periods of hyper-inflation abroad, to take an extreme example, when prices rose daily or even hourly, no one wanted to hold currency more than momentarily, and increases in velocity became proportionately greater than increases in the supply of money, large though the latter were. Thus large increases in velocity of circulation can become an inflationary force.)

Money is an idle asset; it produces no income. (Keep in mind that "money" includes only demand deposits and currency. Funds which are put to interest-bearing use—e.g., savings deposits—constitute a different kind of asset.) If the income foregone is negligible, there is little inducement to modify habitual patterns regarding the amount of money held in relation to ordinary expenditures. But as interest rates rise or as the sums involved become larger, the opportunity cost of holding funds idle in checking accounts becomes substantial. If an individual were to reduce the average balance in his checking account by $1,000 and transfer the funds to a savings account yielding 5 percent, he would earn an additional $50 per year. Many people would regard such a yield as too small to justify the inconvenience of occasionally running their checking balances low or even bouncing a check. For a large corporation, however, with access to the commercial paper markets, even overnight interest on $10 million may amount to $2,200 at an 8 percent yield. Accordingly, many corporations with good financial controls have developed methods to minimize the opportunity costs of holding idle cash. With rising interest rates, small companies and individuals also are becoming more alert to the possibilities of earning interest.

The simplest action to secure income from idle funds is to shift from a demand deposit to a time deposit. With daily interest available, a time deposit may be very temporary and constitute "near money." A temporary time deposit of this sort is quite different than the traditional savings account in which funds are accumulated for long periods—e.g., for an annual vacation. The velocity of circulation of time deposits thus varies with their intended use which ranges from simply another form of money to a long-term investment.

The search for higher returns on liquid assets may involve a different shift of funds. U.S. Treasury bills are also a very liquid asset and may be regarded by corporate treasurers or individuals as "near money" earning interest. No part of Treasury bills is included in any definition of the money supply. But to the extent they function as a replacement for bank deposits, they permit the remaining bank deposits to "do more work" in handling payments. The velocity of circulation of deposits is thereby increased.

Changes over the years in the velocity of circulation of money are shown in Table 2-1. The velocity calculated for this purpose is defined as the income velocity of money and is measured by the relationship between the gross national product and the money supply, defined as demand deposits (other than interbank deposits) plus currency. Another measure of velocity relates total debits to the money supply, but the income velocity shown here is in a sense a more fundamental measure of the efficiency in use of money because it ignores the rapid and distorting changes occurring in bank debits associated with flurries of activity in the financial markets themselves.

If one takes the 1929 figures as a pre-Depression and prewar norm, the decline in velocity from 4.0 to 2.9 in 1935 and 2.5 in 1940 indicates the general slackness in the economy. Interest rates became very low and the opportunity cost of holding idle demand deposits was negligible. After a small decline, the money supply actually increased, though the GNP declined.

The period of World War II saw a further decline in velocity to 2.1 in 1945, as the money supply expanded much more rapidly than did the GNP. The expansion in the money supply arose primarily because the banks became the residual suppliers of finance for the government deficits. Taxes fell far short of covering government expenditures. Sales of government securities

Table 2-1. Income Velocity of Money, 1929-1974

	M_1 Demand Deposits plus Currency ($ billion)	GNP ($ billion)	Income Velocity (Ratio: GNP/M_1)
1929	26.2	103.8	4.0
1935	25.0	72.2	2.9
1940	39.2	99.7	2.5
1945	102.3	211.9	2.1
1950	114.1	284.8	2.5
1955	134.4	398.0	3.0
1960	140.9	503.7	3.6
1965	167.5	684.9	4.1
1970	214.9	977.1	4.5
1971	228.2	1,055.5	4.6
1972	245.4	1,155.2	4.7
1973	271.5	1,294.9	4.8
1974	283.8	1,396.7	4.9

Sources: Economic Report of the President (Washington, D.C.: U.S. Government Printing Office) 1952, 1961 and 1975. Tables C-1, C-52, *Supplement to Banking and Monetary Statistics, Section 1* (Washington, D.C.: Board of Governors of the Federal Reserve System), 1962.

to individuals and institutions failed to cover the deficits and the banks became the lenders of last resort, supported by the Federal Reserve System which might be thought of as the "ultimate last resort." The Federal Reserve Banks expanded their credit by purchasing government securities; the banks on the basis of the newly created reserves purchased government securities and thereby built up total demand deposits.

During the war period, the scarcity of consumer goods meant that individuals built up idle bank balances. The scarcity of capital equipment except for war production, and the prompt payments on war production, meant that business deposits became high relative to business activity. Interest rates were frozen substantially at the low levels developed during the preceding Depression, ranging from three-eighths of 1 percent on Treasury bills to 2.5 percent on bonds. The velocity of circulation declined further until at the end of the war; it was only slightly more than half of that in 1929.

It then took 20 years, from 1945 to 1965, for the velocity of circulation to build back up to the pre-Depression level, rising from 2.1 to 4.1. The period can be described as one in which the country grew up to its inflated money supply. There were some increases, but substantial stability, from 1966 through 1970. Another upward movement started in 1971 as the opportunity cost of holding idle balance began to rise in the tight money situation. A continuation of high interest rates would doubtless induce more and more holders of demand deposits to reduce their opportunity costs by seeking temporary uses of excess funds, thereby further increasing the income velocity of money.

The Federal Funds Market

The search for income from idle deposits has spread to the banks themselves as well as to those who keep deposits in banks. In a tight money market, the member banks attempt to keep their reserves at the Federal Reserve Banks fully employed—that is, to extend their own loans (and expand their own deposits) to the maximum. But there are inevitable daily fluctuations around a position which, on the average, just meets the required legal reserves. Any momentary excess reserves thus represent an opportunity cost to the banks which hold them.

A market has developed for overnight loans of excess reserves between banks. Such loans are referred to as Federal Funds. Originally the market existed only among large banks in financial centers, but by 1974 it had been extended to smaller banks throughout the country. The rates offered by banks for such loans had come to be regarded as a particularly sensitive indicator of the tightness in the money markets.

As Figure 2-1 shows, activity in the Federal Funds market has increased dramatically since 1967, with some $35 billion outstanding now. This trading was initially among larger, more sophisticated banks but the last two or three years has seen the entry of banks in the $10-25 million deposit class. The net effect has been to soak up excess reserves from the banking system. Excess reserves have declined from $1.5 billion in 1945, almost a 10 percent excess, to only $35 million in June of 1974, a 0.1 percent excess for the system as a whole.[4]

The rapid increase in activity in the Fed Funds market has prompted some concern by persons close to the banking industry.[5] The concern centers on the possibility of smaller banks placing their money in Fed Funds at inflation boosted rates—around 12.5 percent in the late summer of 1974—rather than accommodating the credit needs of their customers.

Money Supply and the Price Level

The amount of money needed to permit a smooth functioning of a nation's economy thus depends on habits regarding cash balances and the use of money. A useful way to indicate the interrelationship among relevant factors is given in the familiar equation used to describe the quantity theory of money,

$$MV = PT,$$

in which M represents the amount of money, V the average velocity of circulation of money, P a composite price index of all transactions, and T a composite quantitative index of all transactions. The equation is a truism, since each side equals the total amount of money spent. MV equals tha amount spent measured in terms of units of money and its use; PT equals the amount spent measured in terms of prices and the quantity of goods and services exchanged.

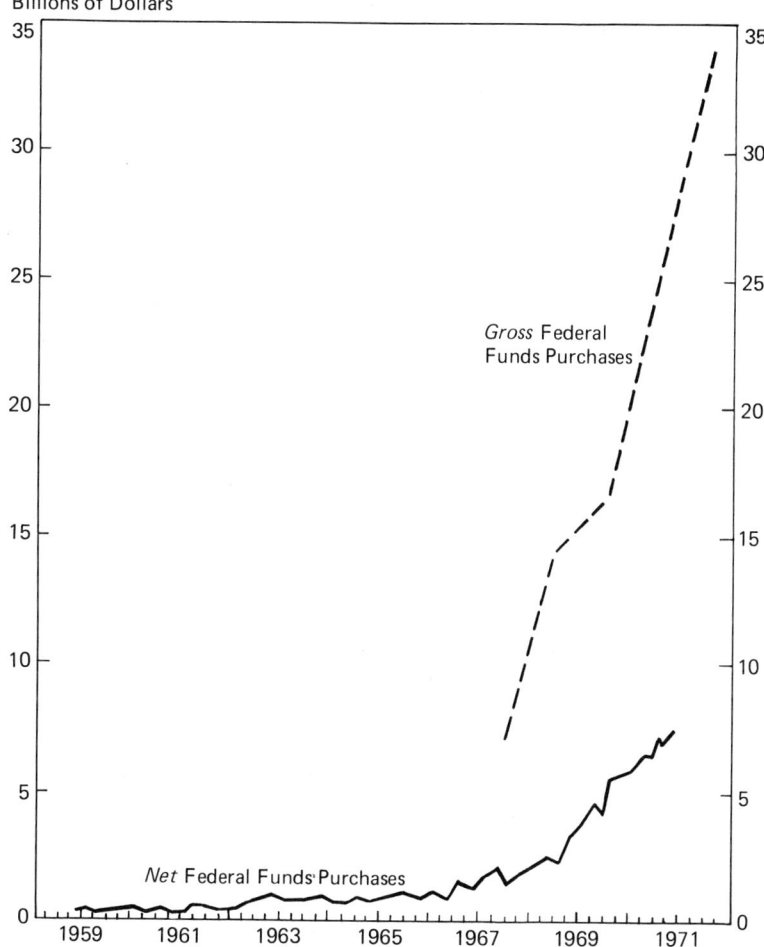

Figure 2-1. Federal Funds Purchases, 1969-1972

Sources: Federal Deposit Insurance Corporation, *Annual Report 1972* (Washington, D.C.: FDIC, 1972), p. 251; Donald M. DePamphilis, *A Microeconomic Econometric Analysis of the Short-Term Commercial Bank Adjustment Process* (Boston: Federal Reserve Bank of Boston, April 1974), p. 15.

In its crudest form, the quantity theory of money assumed that V was relatively stable and that T was either constant or led to proportionate increases in M. The conclusion was that fluctuations in the price level, P, were determined by fluctuation in the quantity of money, M. In fact, the velocity of circulation of money, V, has changed substantially over time for reasons previously noted. The number of transactions involved, even for a given level of real gross national product, may also change independently with, for example, a shift in the number of intermediate steps in the distribution process or the degree of vertical integration in production.

Conceptually, it is useful to think of the four factors M, V, P, and T as separate elements, each subject to change by independent forces, but so interrelated that a change in any one must be offset by a change in one or more of the others. Much of the analysis in monetary theory consists of attempts to determine causal sequences among these factors. Numerous hypotheses have been advanced on causation, many of which are oversimplified or related to a particular set of circumstances, as was the quantity theory of money. It is indeed true that the amount of money spent is always equal to the amount of money spent, but each of the four factors—money supply, velocity of circulation of money, prices, and the volume of transactions—are subject to independent forces and there is no agreement on a simple set of causal relations among them.

Asset Management versus Liabilities Management

With changing conditions, the emphasis in bank management may shift from seeking the best *use* of funds which are plentiful (asset management) to seeking additional *sources* of funds to meet the plentiful profitable uses which are available (liabilities management). Neither aspect, to be sure, is ever ignored. At all times, good management requires attention to both the best uses of whatever funds are available and acquisition of funds at minimum cost. But the emphasis may change dramatically.

During World War II, for example, bank credit was greatly expanded in the process of financing the war in the manner described previously. Deposits were created by the banks' purchases of government securities, supported by increases in Federal Reserve credit. The principal objective in bank management was to secure the most profitable mix of assets consistent with safety. In the absence of adequate loans of traditional sorts, banks shifted their security portfolios to the higher-yielding longer-term securities, in the belief that the pegged pattern of interest rates made them equally liquid.

In 1974, by contrast, banks were subject to demands for business loans far in excess of available funds. Emphasis and ingenuity were directed to the development of sources of additional funds through such devices as negotiable certificates of deposit, daily interest time deposits, and active markets in Federal Funds.

As a general proposition, when conventional loans and investments are inadequate to absorb available funds, emphasis will be directed to asset management by developing new and more profitable uses. When conventional demands for banks funds exceed available funds, emphasis will be directed to developing new sources. The rest of this chapter gives many details on asset and liability management. These brief comments merely introduce the concepts.

One final set of points relates activities and data of individual banks to those of the total banking system. To an individual bank its ability to lend and invest depends on the magnitude of its reserves in relation to its required reserves. If it has excess reserves it can expand its loans and investments. Consequently, one dimension of its competitive activities centers around attempts to acquire additional reserve funds. The major source of new reserve funds comes from new deposits, and individual banks are continuously seeking new deposits, in part by attracting depositors from other commercial banks and from the various thrift institutions. From what has been stated earlier, however, deposits attracted from other banks and thrift institutions do not change the total volume of deposits in the financial system. They simply represent transfers within the system and the banks gaining reserves acquire the capacity to expand their loans and investments only at the expense of the banks losing reserves which are then forced to contract credit.

For the banking system as a whole the volume of deposits depends on (1) the volume of reserves, (2) the required reserve ratios, and (3) the mix among types of deposits which have different reserve requirements. The Federal Reserve authorities determine both the volume of reserves of banking system and the required reserve ratios. In addition, through the control of these two elements they can offset independent changes in the third factor to the extent desired. Consequently, the total volume of deposits is determined by actions of the Federal Reserve. Thus, we have a managed money supply, and the relationship between total deposits, or total demand deposits, or the money supply and other economic variables such as total production or GNP is a managed relationship. The actions of individual banks have little or no effect on these relationships. Consequently, it is critical to keep in mind the distinctions between individual banks or small segments of the banking system and the banking system as a whole. Total credit extensions or deposits of the one are determined by quite different factors than those for the system as a whole.

POSTWAR TRENDS IN THE U.S. ECONOMY

The period since World War II is one of the longest periods of unbroken growth in U.S. history. Except for a few relatively mild recessions, business activity has remained high and incomes have climbed steadily. Financial services and banking have been among the more rapidly growing sectors of the economy.

This section will review first the overall growth of the economy; second,

Table 2-2. Growth of U.S. Gross National Product (Dollars in billions)

Year	Total GNP (Current Dollars)	Total GNP (1972 Dollars)	Index (1945 = 100)
1929	$ 103.1	$ 297.5	57.3
1933	55.6	206.7	39.8
1940	99.7	331.9	64.0
1945	211.9	518.9	100.0
1950	284.8	519.1	100.0
1955	398.0	639.9	123.3
1960	503.7	712.5	137.3
1965	684.9	902.6	173.9
1970	977.1	1,055.6	203.4
1971	1,055.5	1,089.0	209.9
1972	1,155.2	1,155.2	222.6
1973	1,288.2	1,223.3	235.7
1974	1,396.7	1,176.0	222.6

Source: *Economic Report of the President* (Washington, D.C.: U.S. Government Printing Office, 1975), Tables C-1 and C-2.

the growth of the financial sector and some employment patterns within it; and third, the trends of interest rates in the money markets.

Overall Growth of the Economy

Table 2-2 shows the growth of the U.S. Gross National Product (GNP) since 1945 (with a few earlier years for comparison). In current dollars the total has increased from $211.9 billion to almost $1400 billion in 29 years. Adjusted for price changes, the growth is a factor of 2.27 over this period, a compound annual growth rate of about 2.9 percent. Part of this increase can be explained simply in terms of a larger population. Over the same period our population has increased from about 150 million to 210 million. Thus, per capita GNP has increased at a compound rate of 2.4 percent. This falls somewhat below the rate in other countries such as Japan or Germany, which have grown at 4 percent per year, or Iran at 7 percent per year, but it is higher than Great Britain which has grown at less than 2 percent.

Projections by the U.S. Bureau of Labor Statistics show our GNP increasing to almost $2 trillion by 1985 in 1972 dollars (Table 2-3). There is an interesting pattern in this timing. Between 1972 and 1980 the growth is projected to be fairly rapid—4.6 percent per year—whereas the following five years, from 1980 to 1985, are projected to grow at a somewhat slower rate—3.2 percent. The explanation for this is a similar kink in the pattern of our population growth. In the years just after World War II the annual number of births in the U.S. increased by almost 50 percent (Table 2-4). This increase constituted the so-called "baby boom." The high rates continued for about 15 years and then fell off sharply during the middle 1960s. Births have now fallen to almost a replacement rate (about 2.1 children per family), which would mean that the U.S. population

Table 2-3. Projections of Gross National Product and Employment

Year	Total GNP (Billions of 1972 dollars)	Employment (Jobs concept)*
Actual		
1955	$ 645.9	69,252
1960	717.1	71,792
1968	1,038.6	84,873
1972	1,155.2	88,506
Projected		
1980	$1,657.9	104,076
1985	1,942.5	110,109
	Total GNP (percent)	Employment (percent)
Average Annual Rate of Growth		
1955-68	3.72	1.54
1968-72	2.69	1.05
1972-80	4.62	2.05
1980-85	3.22	1.13

*Employment using a persons concept is a count of the number of persons holding jobs or looking for them. Employment based on a jobs concept is a count of the number of jobs held by people. Therefore, if persons hold more than one job, they are counted more than once.

Source: U.S. Bureau of Labor Statistics, *The U.S. Economy in 1985*, Bulletin 1809 (Washington, D.C.: U.S. Government Printing Office, 1974), p. 28.

would stabilize at about 300 million by the year 2030. The children born during this baby boom are now reaching the age where they are entering the labor force, and this accounts for the projected higher rate of growth in GNP between now and 1980. After the early 1980s fewer people will be entering the labor force each year, and this will cause the lower rate of increase in our economy.

A changing age distribution has significant effects on particular industries or particular sectors of the economy. For example, some baby food manufacturers, distressed by recent declines in sales, are making plans to enter other lines of business. Many suburban elementary schools, which were expanding rapidly during the late 1960s, now find that they have excess classrooms and teachers. The wave of postwar babies was responsible for a large part of the so-called youth market of the late 1960s and it has resulted in a fairly rapid increase in the demand for apartments over the last several years. As these people become older they will increase the demand for single family homes in the early 1980s.

For banks, changing age distributions has particular significance because people's financial resources and requirements change as they pass through successive stages of life. Specifically, along with a demand for homes will come a need for mortgages and installment loans for cars and appliances. If previous

24 Trends Affecting the U.S. Banking System

Table 2-4. Number of Births and Birth Rate in the U.S., 1940-1973

Year	Number of Births (thousands)	Birth Rate (per thousand of midyear population)
1940	2,570	19.4
1945	2,873	20.5
1950	3,645	23.9
1955	4,128	24.9
1956	4,244	25.1
1957	4,332	25.2
1958	4,279	24.5
1959	4,313	24.3
1960	4,307	23.8
1965	3,801	19.6
1967	3,555	17.9
1968	3,535	17.6
1969	3,605	17.8
1970	3,725	18.2
1971	3,559	17.2
1972	3,256	15.6
1973	3,141	15.0

Source: U.S. Department of Commerce, *Statistical Abstract of the United States: 1973* (Washington, D.C.: 1973), p. 11.

patterns of behavior continue, the build-up of savings should begin toward the latter half of the 1980s.

A projected slowing in the rate of productivity increase, if it actually occurs, will contribute to the slowing of economic growth in the middle 1980s. Over the period 1955 to 1968, overall productivity increased at a rate of 3 percent per year in the private economy (Table 2-5). This was paced by agricultural activity increasing at 5.5 percent per year. During the same time there was a massive shift of low productivity agricultural workers off the farm into higher productivity jobs in manufacturing. It is believed that this shift is essentially completed. Also, manufacturing employment is growing more slowly than the work force as a whole (see Table 2-7). Thus, future increases in manufacturing productivity will have less effect on the overall productivity of the economy than in the past. Many of the newest jobs are in wholesale and retail trade and government enterprises, areas which have shown relatively slow gains in productivity.

White collar workers will gradually increase as a percentage of the labor force (see Table 2-6). Pacing this growth will be increases in professional, technical, and clerical workers. Farm workers as a percentage of the total will decline by more than half, from 3.8 percent of the work force to 1.6 percent by 1985.

The educational attainments of U.S. workers continue to increase at a rate faster than the growth of jobs requiring higher education (see Figure 2-2).

Table 2-5. Percent Average Annual Rate of Productivity Change by Sector, 1955-1985*

	Actual		Projected	
Sector	1955-68	1968-72	1972-80	1980-85
Total Private	3.0	2.3	3.2	2.8
Agriculture	5.5	4.5	6.1	5.5
Nonagriculture	2.6	2.2	3.0	2.7
Mining	3.6	1.0	.9	.8
Contract Construction	–	–	1.5	.7
Manufacturing	2.7	3.8	2.7	2.6
Transportation	3.5	2.4	4.1	3.1
Communication	5.9	5.0	5.6	4.9
Public Utilities	5.1	3.5	4.7	4.3
Retail and Wholesale Trade	2.9	1.9	3.1	2.5
Finance, Insurance, Real Estate	–	–	2.8	1.9
Other Services	–	–	3.6	2.4
Government Enterprises	–	–	2.6	2.9

*Productivity data are GNP per man-hour with the GNP stated in constant 1972 prices.
Source: U.S. Bureau of Labor Statistics, *The U.S. Economy in 1985*, Bulletin 1809 (Washington, D.C.: U.S. Government Printing Office, 1974), p. 37.

Table 2-6. Percent Distribution of Employment, by Major Occupational Group—1960 and 1972, and Projected 1980 and 1985

Occupational Group	1960*	1972	1980	1985
Total	100.0	100.0	100.0	100.0
White Collar Workers	43.1	47.8	51.5	52.9
Professional and Technical Workers	11.0	14.0	15.7	16.8
Managers and Administrators	11.2	9.8	10.5	10.3
Sales Workers	6.4	6.6	6.6	6.4
Clerical Workers	14.5	17.4	18.7	19.4
Blue Collar Workers	36.3	35.0	33.1	32.3
Craft and Kindred Workers	13.3	13.2	12.8	12.8
Operatives**	17.3	16.6	15.6	15.1
Nonfarm Laborers	5.7	5.2	4.7	4.4
Service Workers	12.7	13.4	13.3	13.2
Private Household Workers	3.0	1.8	1.3	1.1
Other Service Workers	9.7	11.6	12.0	12.1
Farm Workers	7.9	3.8	2.1	1.6

*Data for 1960 were adjusted to reflect the occupational classification in the 1970 census to make it comparable to the 1972 and projected 1980 and 1985 data.
**Includes the 1970 census classification "operatives," except transport and transport equipment operatives.
Source: U.S. Bureau of Labor Statistics, *The U.S. Economy in 1985*, Bulletin 1809 (Washington, U.S. Government Printing Office, 1974), p. 19.

Educational Attainment of the Civilian Labor Force, March 1972 and Projected 1980 and 1985

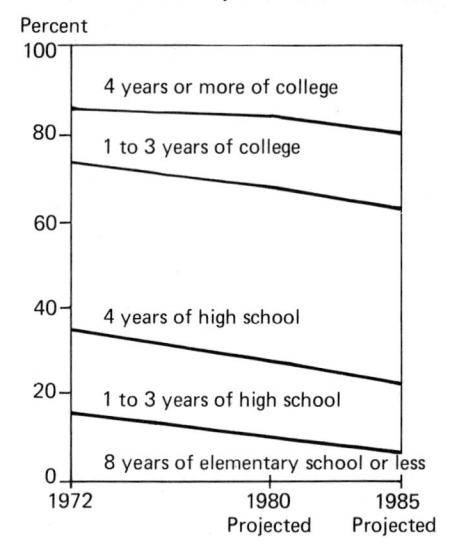

- 4 years or more of college
- 1 to 3 years of college
- 4 years of high school
- 1 to 3 years of high school
- 8 years of elementary school or less

Figure 2-2. Educational Attainment of the Civilian Labor Force, March 1972 and Projected 1980 and 1985
Source: U.S. Bureau of Labor Statistics, *The U.S. Economy in 1985*, Bulletin 1809 (Washington, D.C.: U.S. Government Printing Office; 1974), p. 13.

In fact, the supply of college graduates between now and 1985 is projected to be almost one million greater than the job requirements for college graduates.[6] The implications of such a trend are difficult to assess. On the one hand, social values in the U.S. are likely to continue to cause a large percentage of high school graduates to seek higher education, though perhaps with some shift to two year community colleges and technical training institutions. On the other hand, the entry of college graduates into jobs requiring less than their education, if this occurs, may build job dissatisfaction and increase job switching.

Changes in the Types of Economic Activity

As most people recognize, the U.S. is becoming increasingly a service economy. Manufacturing now represents less than 30 percent of the GNP and less than one-quarter of all jobs (see Tables 2-7 and 2-8). Services, broadly defined here to include retail trade, transportation, utilities, finance, and other services account for 50 percent of the GNP and about half of all jobs. Actually, the overall pattern of manufacturing versus nonmanufacturing has been relatively stable, but changes within the nonmanufacturing area have been substantial. Major growth has occurred in such sectors as retail trade, financial services, health care, education, and other specialized "pure" services. These have in-

Table 2-7. Total Employment* by Major Sector, Selected Years 1955-1972 and Projected to 1980 and 1985 (Thousands of jobs)

	Actual				Projected	
Sector	1955	1960	1968	1972	1980	1985
Total	65,745	68,369	80,926	85,597	101,576	107,609
Government[a]	6,914	8,353	11,845	13,290	16,610	18,800
Total Private	58,831	60,516	69,081	72,307	84,966	88,809
Agriculture	6,434	5,389	3,816	3,450	2,300	1,900
Nonagriculture	52,397	55,127	65,265	68,857	82,666	86,909
Mining	832	748	640	645	655	632
Construction	3,582	3,654	4,038	4,352	4,908	5,184
Manufacturing	17,309	17,197	20,138	19,281	22,923	23,499
Durable	9,782	9,681	11,828	11,091	13,629	14,154
Nondurable	7,527	7,516	8,310	8,190	9,294	9,345
Transportation, Communication, and Public Utilities	4,353	4,214	4,519	4,726	5,321	5,368
Transportation	2,918	2,743	2,863	2,842	3,250	3,266
Communication	832	844	986	1,150	1,300	1,312
Public Utilities	603	624	665	734	771	790
Trade	13,201	14,177	16,655	18,432	21,695	22,381
Wholesale Trade	3,063	3,295	3,894	4,235	4,946	5,123
Retail Trade	10,138	10,882	12,761	14,197	16,749	17,268
Finance, Insurance, and Real Estate	2,652	2,985	3,720	4,303	5,349	5,932
Other Services[b]	10,468	12,152	15,555	17,118	21,815	23,913
	\multicolumn{6}{c}{Percent distribution[c]}
Total	100.0	100.0	100.0	100.0	100.0	100.0
Government[a]	10.5	12.1	14.6	15.5	16.4	17.5
Total Private	89.5	87.9	85.4	84.5	83.6	82.6
Agriculture	9.8	7.8	4.7	4.0	2.3	1.8
Nonagriculture	79.7	80.0	80.6	80.4	81.4	80.3
Mining	1.3	1.1	0.8	0.8	0.6	0.6
Construction	5.4	5.3	5.0	5.1	4.8	4.8
Manufacturing	20.3	25.0	24.9	22.5	22.6	21.8
Durable	14.9	14.1	14.6	13.0	13.4	13.2
Nondurable	11.5	10.9	10.3	9.6	9.2	8.7
Transportation, Communication, and Public Utilities	6.6	6.1	5.6	5.5	5.2	5.0
Transportation	4.4	4.0	3.5	3.3	3.2	3.0
Communication	1.3	1.2	1.2	1.3	1.3	1.2
Public Utilities	0.9	0.8	0.8	0.9	0.8	0.7
Trade	20.1	20.6	21.6	21.5	21.4	20.8
Wholesale Trade	4.7	4.8	4.8	4.9	4.9	4.8
Retail Trade	15.4	15.8	15.8	16.6	16.5	16.0
Finance, Insurance, and Real Estate	4.0	4.3	4.6	5.0	5.3	5.5
Other Services	15.9	17.6	19.2	20.0	21.5	22.2

Table 2-7 continued

Table 2-7. (continued)

Sector	Actual 1955	Actual 1960	Actual 1968	Actual 1972	Projected 1980	Projected 1985
	\multicolumn{6}{c}{Average annual rate of change[d]}					
	1955-68	1968-72	1968-85	1968-80	1972-80	1980-85
Total	1.6	1.4	1.7	1.9	2.2	1.2
Government[a]	4.2	2.9	2.8	2.9	2.8	2.5
Total Private	1.2	1.2	1.5	1.7	2.0	0.9
Agriculture	-3.9	-2.5	-4.0	-4.1	-4.9	-3.7
Nonagriculture	1.7	1.4	1.7	2.0	2.3	1.0
Mining	-2.0	0.2	-0.1	-0.2	-0.4	-0.7
Construction	0.9	1.9	1.5	1.6	1.5	1.1
Manufacturing	1.2	-1.1	0.9	1.1	2.2	0.5
Durable	1.5	-1.6	1.1	1.2	2.6	0.8
Nondurable	0.8	-0.4	0.7	0.9	1.6	0.1
Transportation, Communication, and Public Utilities	0.3	1.1	1.0	1.4	1.5	0.2
Transportation	-0.1	-0.2	0.8	1.0	1.7	0.1
Communication	1.3	3.9	1.7	2.3	1.5	0.2
Public Utilities	0.8	2.1	1.0	1.2	0.8	0.5
Trade	1.8	2.6	1.8	2.2	2.1	0.6
Wholesale Trade	1.9	2.1	1.6	2.0	2.0	0.7
Retail Trade	1.8	2.7	1.8	2.3	2.1	0.6
Finance, Insurance, and Real Estate	2.6	3.7	2.8	3.1	2.8	2.1
Other Services	3.1	2.4	2.6	2.9	3.1	1.9

*Employment is on a jobs concept and includes wage and salary workers, the self-employed, and unpaid family workers. Persons holding more than one job are counted in each job held.
[a]Government employment used in this table is based on the BLS concept to be consistent with other employment data. It is different from the government employment shown in table 1 because of inclusion of government enterprise employees as well as other statistical and coverage differences.
[b]Includes paid household employment.
[c]Components may not add to totals because of rounding.
[d]Compound interest rate between terminal years.
Source: U.S. Bureau of Labor Statistics, *The U.S. Economy in 1985*, Bulletin 1809 (Washington, D.C.: U.S. Government Printing Office, 1974), p. 39.

creased from 40 percent of all jobs in 1955 to 46.5 percent in 1972 and are projected to increase further to 48.5 percent by 1985. The finance, insurance, and real estate sector has increased from 4 percent of all jobs in 1955 to 5 percent now and is projected to continue to 5.5 percent by 1985. The government sector of the economy has increased from 10.5 percent of all jobs in 1955 to 15.5 percent in 1972 and is projected to continue to 17.5 percent in 1985. These shifts are perhaps among the most significant structural changes going on in the economy. Manufacturing continues to occupy a near constant

Table 2-8. Gross Product Originating* in Various Sectors of the Private Economy, Selected Years 1955-1972 and Projected to 1980 and 1985

Sector	1955	1960	1968	1972	1980	1985
	\multicolumn{6}{c}{Billions of 1972 dollars}					
Total	555.2	620.6	904.3	1,019.7	1,500.6	1,767.6
Agriculture	29.2	30.0	32.6	34.4	35.3	37.1
Nonagriculture	526.0	590.0	871.7	985.3	1,465.3	1,730.5
Mining	13.7	14.0	17.4	18.2	20.2	20.4
Contract Construction	47.1	49.3	54.0	56.0	71.5	77.9
Manufacturing	159.6	168.1	261.9	290.7	428.6	490.1
Durable	98.2	98.5	160.4	170.7	268.5	313.5
Nondurable	61.4	69.6	101.5	119.9	160.1	185.6
Transportation, Communication and Public Utilities	46.6	53.7	84.5	102.3	164.7	202.0
Transportation	27.9	28.5	42.1	45.8	71.8	83.6
Communication	8.2	11.0	20.3	28.5	50.5	64.8
Public Utilities	10.5	14.2	22.1	28.0	42.4	53.6
Trade	100.5	115.0	167.8	194.5	281.1	318.9
Wholesale	34.5	42.1	67.0	77.7	116.0	132.6
Retail	66.0	72.9	100.8	116.7	165.1	186.3
Finance, Insurance, and Real Estate	82.1	99.9	148.4	163.8	250.5	303.5
Other Services	72.0	88.0	123.8	135.9	223.6	269.9
Government Enterprises	8.9	9.3	15.3	18.0	25.8	30.9
Rest of World plus Statistical Discrepancy	-4.5	-7.3	-1.4	6.0	-0.7	7.8
	\multicolumn{6}{c}{Percent distribution}					
Total	100.0	100.0	100.0	100.0	100.0	100.0
Agriculture	5.3	4.9	3.6	3.4	2.4	2.1
Nonagriculture	94.7	95.1	96.4	96.6	97.6	97.9
Mining	2.5	2.3	1.9	1.8	1.3	1.2
Contract Construction	8.5	7.9	6.0	5.5	4.8	4.4
Manufacturing	28.7	27.1	29.0	28.5	28.6	28.2
Durable	17.7	15.9	17.7	16.7	17.9	17.7
Nondurable	11.1	11.2	11.2	11.8	10.7	10.4
Transportation, Communication, and Public Utilities	8.4	8.7	9.3	10.0	11.0	11.4
Transportation	5.0	4.6	4.7	4.5	4.8	4.7
Communication	1.5	1.8	2.2	2.8	3.4	3.7
Public Utilities	1.9	2.3	2.4	2.7	2.8	3.0
Trade	18.1	18.5	18.6	19.1	18.7	18.0
Wholesale	6.2	6.8	7.4	7.6	7.7	7.5
Retail	11.9	11.7	11.1	11.4	11.0	10.5
Finance, Insurance, and Real Estate	14.8	16.1	16.4	16.1	16.7	17.2
Other Services	13.0	14.2	13.7	13.3	14.9	15.3
Government Enterprises	1.6	1.5	1.7	1.8	1.7	1.7
Rest of World plus Statistical Discrepancy	-0.8	-1.2	-0.2	0.6	0.0	0.4

(continued)

30 Trends Affecting the U.S. Banking System

Table 2-8. (continued)

Sector	1955	1960	1968	1972	1980	1985
	\multicolumn{6}{c}{Average annual rate of change†}					
	\multicolumn{2}{c}{Actual}	\multicolumn{4}{c}{Projected}					
	1955-68	1968-72	1968-85	1968-80	1972-80	1980-85
Total	3.8	3.0	4.0	4.3	4.9	3.3
Agriculture	0.9	1.4	0.8	0.7	0.3	1.0
Nonagriculture	4.0	3.1	4.1	4.4	5.1	3.4
Mining	1.9	1.1	0.9	1.3	1.3	0.2
Contract Construction	1.1	0.9	2.2	2.4	3.1	1.7
Manufacturing	3.9	2.6	3.9	4.2	5.0	3.1
Durable	3.8	1.6	4.0	4.4	5.8	3.1
Nondurable	3.9	4.3	3.6	3.9	3.7	2.9
Transportation, Communication, and Public Utilities	4.7	4.9	5.3	5.7	6.1	4.2
Transportation	3.2	2.1	4.1	4.5	5.8	3.1
Communication	7.2	8.9	7.1	7.9	7.4	5.1
Public Utilities	5.9	6.1	5.4	5.8	5.3	4.8
Trade	4.0	3.8	3.8	4.4	4.7	2.6
Wholesale	5.2	3.8	4.1	4.7	5.1	2.7
Retail	3.3	3.7	3.6	4.2	4.4	2.4
Finance, Insurance, and Real Estate	4.7	2.5	4.3	4.5	5.5	3.9
Other Services	4.3	2.4	4.7	5.1	6.4	3.8
Government Enterprises	4.3	4.1	4.2	4.5	4.6	3.7

*The concept of gross product originating attributes to each industry only that part of income gross national product originating there.
†Compound interest between terminal years.
Source: U.S. Bureau of Labor Statistics, *The U.S. Economy in 1985*, Bulletin 1809 (Washington, D.C.: U.S. Government Printing Office, 1974, 1. 36.

percentage of the total GNP but its percentage of jobs is predicted to decline slightly.

Within the finance, insurance, and real estate sector, banking has been growing slightly faster than other financial and real estate institutions. Employment in banking in 1959 was 640,000, about 25 percent of that employment sector (see Figure 2-3). By 1972 it increased to 27 percent (1,150,000) and it is projected to increase further to 31 percent of the sector by 1985. During the same time, the insurance industry has grown at a rate about half that of banking.

If the contribution to GNP of the finance, insurance, and real estate sector is pro rated on the basis of employment, banking can be estimated as approximately a $46 billion industry. (compare Table 2-8 and Figure 2-3).

The pattern of U.S. investment shows some interesting changes in the postwar period (see Table 2-9). In the early 1950s the nation was building the suburbs and new homes absorbed about a third of private domestic investment. By the late 1960s this proportion had dropped off to one-quarter or less. By contrast,

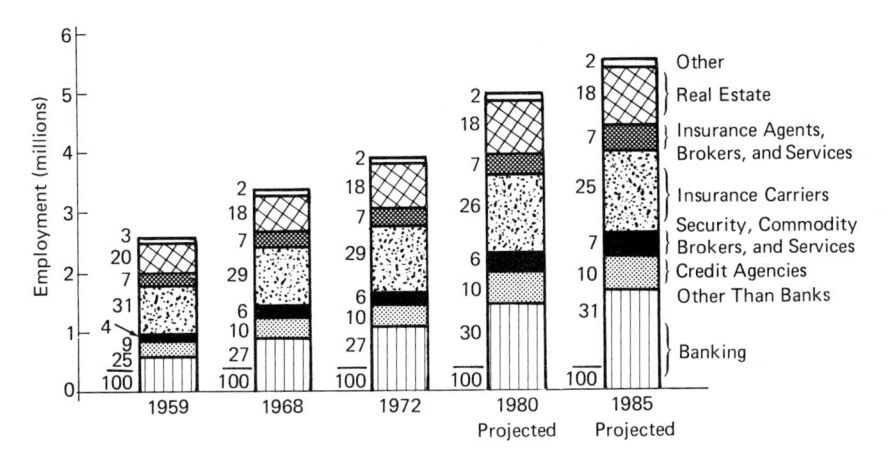

Figure 2-3. Employment in Finance, Insurance, and Real Estate, 1959-1985

Note: Detail may not add to totals because of rounding.
Source: U.S. Bureau of Labor Statistics, *The U.S. Economy in 1985*, Bulletin 1809 (Washington, D.C.: U.S. Government Printing Office; 1974), p. 61.

nonresidential structures took about one-fifth in the early 1950s and moved up close to one-fourth in the late 1960s and early 1970s. Producers durable equipment—that is, manufacturing plant and equipment—moved from slightly above 35 percent of investment in the early 1950s to about 45 percent 20 years later. These changes have had some impact on the patterns of public and private debt, as will be discussed shortly.

Trends in the Financial Markets

A key characteristic of the financial markets in postwar years has been the rise in interest rates (see Table 2-10). From a wartime low of 0.5 percent, Treasury bill rates have climbed steadily so that they were bringing 7 percent in 1973 and more than 9 percent at one time in 1974. In part, this trend represents a recovery to a more normal civilian economy after the combined impacts of the Depression and World War II. Longer-term government securities were pegged at low rates until 1951, and this control probably helped hold down other interest rates as well. The trend also reflects the phenomenon mentioned earlier of a large wartime expansion of the money supply. When the economy "caught up" to the money supply in the early 1960s (see Tables 2-11 and 2-1), demands for credit began to create stronger upward pressures on interest rates. Beginning in 1966 a series of credit "crunches" took place and interest rates rose sharply to their peak levels of 1973 and 1974. The Federal Reserve, in its efforts to control inflation, has not allowed the money supply to grow as fast as economic activity in general and the result has been both higher interest rates and a higher velocity of money.

During the war years, new issues of U.S. government securities dominated

Table 2-9. Types of Investment in the United States, 1929-1974
(Dollars in billions)

Year	Total Gross Private Domestic Investment (GPDI)	Nonresidential Structures $	Percent of Total GPDI	Producers Durable Equipment $	Percent of Total GPDI	Residential Structures $	Percent of Total GPDI
1929	16.2	5.0	30.9	5.6	34.6	4.0	24.7
1933	1.4	0.9	64.3	1.5	107.1	0.6	42.9
1940	13.1	2.3	17.6	5.3	40.5	3.4	26.0
1941	17.9	2.9	16.2	6.6	36.9	3.9	21.8
1942	9.8	1.9	19.4	4.1	41.8	2.1	21.4
1943	5.7	1.3	22.8	3.7	64.9	1.4	24.6
1944	7.1	1.8	25.4	5.0	70.4	1.3	18.3
1945	10.6	2.8	26.4	7.3	68.9	1.5	14.2
1946	30.6	6.8	22.2	10.2	33.3	7.2	23.5
1947	34.0	7.5	22.1	15.9	46.8	11.1	32.6
1948	46.0	8.8	19.1	18.1	39.3	14.4	31.3
1949	35.7	8.5	23.8	16.6	46.5	13.7	38.4
1950	54.1	9.2	17.0	18.7	34.6	19.4	35.9
1951	59.3	11.2	18.9	20.7	34.9	17.2	29.0
1952	51.9	11.4	22.0	20.2	38.9	17.2	33.1
1953	52.6	12.7	24.1	21.5	40.9	18.0	34.2
1954	51.7	13.1	25.3	20.6	39.8	19.7	38.1
1955	67.4	14.3	21.2	23.8	35.3	23.3	34.6
1956	70.0	17.2	24.6	26.5	37.9	21.6	30.9
1957	67.9	18.0	26.5	28.4	41.8	20.2	29.7
1958	60.9	16.6	27.3	25.0	41.1	20.8	34.2
1959	75.3	16.7	22.2	28.4	37.7	25.5	33.9
1960	74.8	18.1	24.2	30.3	40.5	22.8	30.5
1961	71.7	18.4	25.7	28.6	39.9	22.6	31.5
1962	83.0	19.2	23.1	32.5	39.2	25.3	30.5
1963	87.1	19.5	22.4	34.8	40.0	27.0	31.0
1964	94.0	21.2	22.6	39.9	42.4	27.1	28.8
1965	108.1	25.5	23.6	45.8	42.4	27.2	25.2
1966	121.4	28.5	23.5	53.1	43.7	25.0	20.6
1967	116.6	28.0	24.0	55.3	47.4	25.1	21.5
1968	126.0	30.3	24.0	58.5	46.4	30.1	23.9
1969	139.0	34.2	24.6	64.3	46.3	32.6	23.5
1970	136.3	36.1	26.5	64.4	47.2	31.2	22.9
1971	153.2	37.9	24.7	66.5	43.4	42.7	27.9
1972	178.3	41.7	23.4	76.5	42.9	54.0	30.3
1973	201.5	48.3	24.0	87.7	43.5	58.0	28.8
1974	208.9	52.2	25.0	97.4	46.6	46.0	22.0

Source: *Economic Report of the President* (Washington, D.C.: U.S. Government Printing Office, 1975), Table C-13.

the financial markets and the rates on such issues set the interest rate structure for all securities. At the end of World War II, the federal debt constituted more than 60 percent of all debt outstanding, in contrast to about 20 percent in 1940. However, since the war the government debt has increased by only about 35 percent while all other types of debt have grown by more than a factor of ten. (Indeed, in real terms and as a percentage of total debt the federal debt has declined.) Thus, by 1973, federal government issues represented less than one-sixth of all debt outstanding (see Figure 2-4 and Table 2-12) and there were many high grade alternatives for investors. To be competitive, the government has had to increase its coupon rates on bonds and notes to more closely match the yields established in the private sector.

TRENDS IN THE ECONOMICS OF BANKING

Among the many developments in banking during the three decades since the end of World War II, a few stand out as especially significant:

1. a large growth in the aggregate assets and liabilities of banks;
2. shifts in the composition of both assets and liabilities;
3. Changes in the emphasis by bank managements from finding profitable uses for funds toward finding new sources of funds;
4. a decline in the ratio of bank capital to deposits;
5. a margin squeeze between the rates banks must pay for funds and the rates they can earn on them;
6. a persistent inflation which reinforces some of the above trends and creates problems in its own right.

Most of these developments are consequences of the economic and demographic trends described above and in this section we will try to show this relationship. Table 2-13 is the basic source of data from which much of the following discussion is taken. It shows the trends in financial assets and liabilities of U.S. commercial banks since World War II.

Aggregate Growth of Banking

Total assets of commercial banks grew between 1945 and 1974 about 5.5 times from $142 to $785 billion. This is a somewhat slower rate of growth than GNP in current dollars of about 6.6 times. As indicated above, this pace of growth of banks is determined largely by the Federal Reserve authorities in controlling the amounts of reserves provided to the banking system and in setting the levels of reserve requirements as percentages of various classes of deposits. The banking system itself also influences its growth, however, by affecting the mix of deposits between demand and time deposits and to a

Table 2-10. Bond Yields and Interest Rates, 1929-1974 (Percent per annum)

Year or Month	U.S. Government Securities				Corporate Bonds (Moody's)		High Grade Municipal Bonds (Standard & Poor's)	Average Rate on Short-Term Bank Loans to Business Selected Cities	Prime Commercial Paper, 4 to 6 Months	Federal Reserve Bank Discount Rate	FHA New Home Mortgage Yields[e]
	3 Month Treasury Bills[a]	9-12 Month Issues[b]	3-5 Year Issues[c]	Taxable Bonds[d]	Aaa	Baa					
1929	—	—	—	—	4.73	5.90	4.27	—	5.85	5.16	—
1933	0.515	—	2.66	—	4.49	7.76	4.71	—	1.73	2.56	—
1940	0.014	—	0.50	—	2.84	4.75	2.50	2.10	0.56	1.00	—
1941	0.103	—	0.73	—	2.77	4.33	2.10	2.00	0.53	1.00[f]	—
1942	0.326	—	1.46	2.46	2.83	4.28	2.36	2.20	0.66	1.00[f]	—
1943	0.373	0.75	1.34	2.47	2.73	3.91	2.06	2.60	0.69	1.00[f]	—
1944	0.375	0.79	1.33	2.48	2.72	3.61	1.86	2.40	0.73	1.00[f]	—
1945	0.375	0.81	1.18	2.37	2.62	3.29	1.67	2.20	0.75	1.00[f]	—
1946	0.375	0.82	1.16	2.19	2.53	3.05	1.64	2.10	0.81	1.00[f]	—
1947	0.594	0.88	1.32	2.25	2.61	3.24	2.01	2.10	1.03	1.00	—
1948	1.040	1.14	1.62	2.44	2.82	3.47	2.40	2.50	1.44	1.34	—
1949	1.102	1.14	1.43	2.31	2.66	3.42	2.21	2.68	1.49	1.50	4.34
1950	1.218	1.26	1.50	2.32	2.62	3.24	1.98	2.69	1.45	1.59	4.17
1951	1.552	1.73	1.93	2.57	2.86	3.41	2.00	3.11	2.16	1.75	4.21
1952	1.766	1.81	2.13	2.68	2.96	3.52	2.19	3.49	2.33	1.75	4.29
1953	1.931	2.07	2.56	2.94	3.20	3.74	2.72	3.69	2.52	1.99	4.61
1954	.953	0.92	1.82	2.55	2.90	3.51	2.37	3.61	1.58	1.60	4.62
1955	1.753	1.89	2.50	2.84	3.06	3.53	2.53	3.70	2.18	1.89	4.64
1956	2.658	2.83	3.12	3.08	3.36	3.88	2.93	4.20	3.31	2.77	4.79
1957	3.267	3.53	3.62	3.47	3.89	4.71	3.60	4.62	3.81	3.12	5.42

Year									
1958	1.839	2.09	2.90	3.43	3.79	4.73	3.56	4.34	2.46	2.15	5.49
1959	3.405	4.11	4.33	4.07	4.38	5.05	3.95	5.00g	3.97	3.36	5.71
1960	2.938	3.55	3.99	4.01	4.41	5.19	3.73	5.16	3.85	3.53	6.18
1961	2.378	2.91	3.60	3.90	4.35	5.08	3.46	4.97	2.97	3.00	5.80
1962	2.778	3.02	3.57	3.95	4.33	5.02	3.18	5.00	3.26	3.00	5.61
1963	3.157	3.28	3.72	4.00	4.26	4.86	3.23	5.01	3.55	3.23	5.47
1964	3.549	3.76	4.06	4.15	4.40	4.83	3.22	4.99	3.97	3.55	5.45
1965	3.954	4.09	4.22	4.21	4.49	4.87	3.27	5.06	4.38	4.40	5.46
1966	4.881	5.17	5.16	4.66	5.13	5.67	3.82	6.00	5.55	4.50	6.29
1967	4.321	4.84	5.07	4.85	5.51	6.23	3.98	6.00g	5.10	4.19	6.55
1968	5.339	5.62	5.59	5.25	6.18	6.94	4.51	6.68	5.90	5.17	7.13
1969	6.677	7.06	6.85	6.10	7.03	7.81	5.81	8.21	7.83	5.87	8.19
1970	6.458	6.90	7.37	6.59	8.04	9.11	6.51	8.48	7.72	5.95	9.05
1971	4.348	4.75	5.77	5.74	7.39	8.56	5.70	6.32g	5.11	4.88	7.78
1972	4.071	4.86	5.85	5.63	7.21	8.16	5.27	5.82	4.69	4.50	7.53
1973	7.041	7.30	6.92	6.30	7.44	8.24	5.18	8.30	8.15	6.44	8.08
1974	7.886	7.71	7.81	6.99	8.57	9.50	6.09	11.28	9.87	7.83	9.47

[a]Rate on new issues within period. First issued in December 1929.

[b]Certificates of indebtedness and selected note and bond issues.

[c]Selected note and bond issues.

[d]First issued in 1941. Series includes bonds which are neither due nor callable before a given number of years as follows: April 1953 to date, 10 years; April 1952–March 1953, 12 years; October 1941–March 1952, 15 years.

[e]Data for first of the month, based on the maximum permissible interest rate (8.5 percent beginning August 25, 1973). Through July 1961, computed on 25 year mortgages paid in 12 years and thereafter, 30 year mortgages paid in 15 years.

[f]From October 30, 1942 to April 24, 1946 a preferential rate of 0.50 percent was in effect for advances secured by government securities maturing in one year or less.

[g]Series revised. Not strictly comparable with earlier data.

Source: Economic Report of the President (Washington, D.C.: U.S. Government Printing Office, 1975), Table C-58.

Table 2-11. Money Stock Measures, 1947-1974 (Averages of daily figures; billions of dollars, seasonally adjusted)

Year and Month	M_1 (Currency plus demand deposits)	M_2 (M_1 plus time deposits at commercial banks other than large CDs)	M_3 (M_2 plus deposits at nonbank thrift institutions)
1947: December	113.1	–	–
1948: December	111.5	–	–
1949: December	111.2	–	–
1950: December	116.2	–	–
1951: December	122.7	–	–
1952: December	127.4	–	–
1953: December	128.8	–	–
1954: December	132.3	–	–
1955: December	135.2	–	–
1956: December	136.9	–	–
1957: December	135.9	–	–
1958: December	141.1	–	–
1959: December	143.4	210.9	299.4
1960: December	144.2	217.1	314.4
1961: December	148.7	228.6	336.5
1962: December	150.9	242.8	362.9
1963: December	156.5	258.9	393.2
1964: December	163.7	277.1	426.3
1965: December	171.3	301.4	462.7
1966: December	175.4	317.8	485.2
1967: December	186.9	349.7	532.8
1968: December	201.5	382.4	577.1
1969: December	208.6	392.1	593.8
1970: December	221.2	425.2	641.2
1971: December	235.2	473.0	726.9
1972: December	255.7	525.5	822.4
1973: December	270.4	570.7	893.2
1974: December (preliminary)	283.8	613.9	955.0

Source: *Economic Report of the President* (Washington, D.C.: U.S. Government Printing Office, 1975), Table C-52.

small extent by acquiring additional equity and long-term debt funds. The deposit mix itself reflects the results of competition for funds between commercial banks and other deposit institutions.

For the postwar period as a whole the Fed provided new reserves to the commercial banking system at a slower rate than the growth of GNP. In aggregate, commercial bank reserves only slightly more than doubled. At the same time, however, reserve requirement percentages were reduced to a modest extent so that each dollar of reserves could support a larger volume of deposits and in consequence a larger volume of earning assets.

Reserves and bank deposits and assets did not grow at a uniform rate, how-

Figure 2-4. Net Public and Private Debt—1947, 1960, 1973

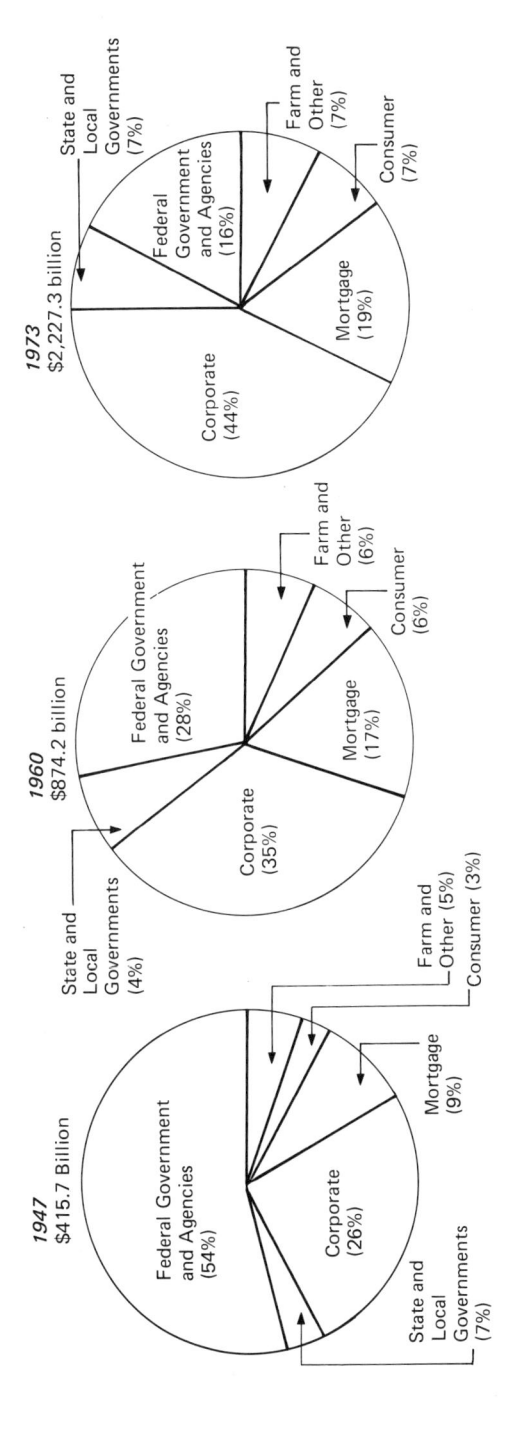

Source: Economic Report of the President (Washington, D.C.: U.S. Government Printing Office, 1975), Table C-63.

Table 2-12. Net Public and Private Debt, 1929-1973* (Billions of dollars)

		Public				Private						
									Individual and Noncorporate			
											Nonfarm	
End of Year	Total	Federal Govern- ment[a]	Federal Finan- cial Agen- cies[b]	State and Local Govern- ments	Total	Corporate	Total	Farm[c]	Total	Mort- gage	Com- mercial and Fi- nancial[d]	Consumer
1929	191.9	16.5	—	13.6	161.8	88.9	72.9	12.2	60.7	31.2	22.4	7.1
1933	168.5	24.3	—	16.3	127.9	76.9	51.0	9.1	41.9	26.3	11.7	3.9
1940	189.8	44.8	—	16.4	128.6	75.6	53.0	9.1	43.9	26.1	9.5	8.3
1941	211.4	56.3	—	16.1	139.0	83.4	55.6	9.3	46.3	27.1	10.0	9.2
1942	258.6	101.7	—	15.4	141.5	91.6	49.9	9.0	40.9	26.8	8.1	6.0
1943	313.2	154.4	—	14.5	144.3	95.5	48.8	8.2	40.5	26.1	9.5	4.9
1944	370.6	211.9	—	13.9	144.8	94.1	50.7	7.7	42.9	26.0	11.8	5.1
1945	405.9	252.5	—	13.4	140.0	85.3	54.7	7.3	47.4	27.0	14.7	5.7
1946	396.6	229.5	—	13.7	153.4	93.5	59.9	7.6	52.3	31.8	12.1	8.4
1947	415.7	221.7	0.7	15.0	178.3	108.9	69.4	8.6	60.7	37.2	11.9	11.6
1948	431.3	215.3	0.6	17.0	198.4	117.8	80.6	10.8	69.7	42.4	12.9	14.4
1949	445.8	217.6	0.7	19.1	208.4	118.0	90.4	12.0	78.4	47.1	13.9	17.4
1950	486.2	217.4	0.7	21.7	246.4	142.1	104.3	12.3	92.0	54.8	15.8	21.5
1951	519.2	216.9	1.3	24.2	276.8	162.5	114.3	13.7	100.6	61.7	16.2	22.7
1952	550.2	221.5	1.3	27.0	300.4	171.0	129.4	15.2	114.2	68.9	17.8	27.5
1953	581.6	226.8	1.4	30.7	322.7	179.5	143.2	16.8	126.4	76.7	18.4	31.4
1954	605.9	229.1	1.3	35.5	340.0	182.8	157.2	17.5	139.7	86.4	20.8	32.5

The Banking System and Its Economic Environment

Year											
1955	665.8	229.6	2.9	41.1	392.2	212.1	180.1	18.7	161.4	98.7	24.0	38.8
1956	698.4	224.3	2.4	44.5	427.2	231.7	195.5	19.4	176.1	109.4	24.4	42.3
1957	728.3	223.0	2.4	48.6	454.3	246.7	207.6	20.2	187.4	118.1	24.3	45.0
1958	769.6	231.0	2.5	53.7	482.4	259.5	222.9	23.2	199.7	128.1	26.5	45.1
1959	833.0	241.4	3.7	59.6	528.3	283.3	245.0	23.8	221.2	141.0	28.7	51.5
1960	874.2	239.8	3.5	64.9	566.1	302.8	263.3	25.1	238.2	151.3	30.8	56.1
1961	930.3	246.7	4.0	70.5	609.1	324.3	284.8	27.5	237.3	164.5	34.8	58.0
1962	996.0	253.6	5.3	77.0	660.1	348.2	311.9	30.2	281.7	180.3	37.6	63.8
1963	1,070.9	257.5	7.2	83.9	722.3	376.4	345.8	33.2	312.6	198.6	42.3	71.7
1964	1,151.6	264.0	7.5	90.4	789.7	409.6	380.1	36.0	344.1	218.9	45.0	80.3
1965	1,243.6	266.4	8.9	98.3	870.0	454.3	415.7	39.3	376.4	236.8	49.7	89.9
1966	1,338.7	271.8	11.2	104.8	950.8	506.6	444.2	42.4	401.8	251.6	53.9	96.2
1967	1,438.7	286.5	9.0	113.4	1,029.9	553.7	476.2	48.3	427.9	266.9	60.2	100.8
1968	1,582.5	291.9	21.4	123.9	1,145.4	631.5	513.9	51.8	462.1	284.9	66.4	110.8
1969	1,735.0	289.3	30.6	132.6	1,282.6	734.2	548.4	55.5	492.9	303.9	67.9	121.1
1970	1,854.1	301.1	38.8	144.8	1,369.4	793.5	575.9	58.7	517.2	320.9	69.1	127.2
1971	2,018.3	325.9	39.8	163.0	1,489.6	858.6	631.0	63.2	567.8	352.6	76.9	138.4
1972	2,227.3	341.2	42.6	176.5	1,667.0	952.3	714.7	67.8	646.9	397.8	91.5	157.6
1973	2,525.8	349.1	59.8	184.5	1,932.4	1,111.1	821.3	77.3	744.0	480.1	83.4	180.5

*Net public and private debt is a comprehensive aggregate of the indebtedness of borrowers after eliminating certain types of duplicating governmental and corporate debt.

[a] Net federal government and agency debt is the outstanding debt held by the public, as defined in the "Budget of the United States Government, or the Fiscal Year ending June 30, 1975."

[b] This comprises the debt of federally sponsored agencies, in which there is no longer any federal proprietary interest. The obligation of the Federal Land Banks are included beginning with 1947, the debt of the Federal Home Loan Banks is included beginning with 1951, and the debts of the Federal National Mortgage Association, Federal Intermediate Credit Banks, and Banks for Cooperatives are included beginning with 1968.

[c] Farm mortgages and farm production loans. Farmers' financial and consumer debt is included in the nonfarm categories.

[d] Financial debt is debt owed to banks for purchasing or carrying securities, customers' debt to brokers, and debt owned to life insurance companies by policy holders.

Source: *Economic Report of the President* (U.S. Government Printing Office 1976) Table C-63.

Table 2-13. Financial Assets and Liabilities of U.S. Commercial Banks (Dollars in millions)

	1945 $	%	1950 $	%	1955 $	%	1960 $	%	1965 $	%	1970 $	%	1972 $	%	1974 $	%
Assets																
U.S. Government Securities	91,484	64	63,896	43	64,274	35	63,264	28	65,341	19	75,149	15	88,820	14	88,700	11
State and Local Obligations	4,170	3	8,317	6	12,898	7	17,569	8	38,725	12	69,637	14	89,534	14	100,400	13
Corporate Bonds	2,226	2	2,219	1	1,681	1	1,045	—	798	—	2,664	1	5,348	1	6,800	1
Home Mortgages	2,866	2	9,390	6	14,931	8	19,172	9	30,115	9	41,760	9	56,306	9	73,700	9
Other Mortgages	1,895	1	4,159	3	5,882	3	9,540	4	19,186	6	30,732	6	42,084	7	56,300	7
Consumer Credit	1,420	1	7,374	5	13,236	7	20,556	9	35,652	11	53,867	11	70,640	11	84,000	11
Business and Other Loans	12,484	9	27,683	19	42,132	23	61,897	27	104,866	31	153,739	31	193,337	31	273,300	35
Open Market Paper	277	—	984	1	1,363	1	2,718	1	3,631	1	6,745	1	7,327	1	9,100	1
Security Credit	6,823	5	2,861	2	5,037	3	5,117	2	8,489	3	12,136	2	17,581	3	13,000	2
Interbank Claims	17,790	12	19,867	13	21,710	12	20,433	9	23,335	7	31,531	6	37,068	6	45,800	6
Miscellaneous	973	1	1,456	1	1,881	1	3,826	2	6,216	2	12,704	3	16,449	3	34,100	4
Total Assets	142,408	100	148,206	100	185,025	100	225,137	100	336,354	100	490,664	100	624,494	100	785,300	100
Liabilities																
Demand Deposits	101,444	75	95,691	69	114,202	67	123,743	60	146,990	47	181,997	40	215,175	37	226,800	31
Large Negotiable CDs	0	—	0	—	0	—	1,095	1	16,251	5	26,074	6	44,519	8	93,000	13
Other Time Deposits	30,355	23	36,938	27	50,257	29	72,241	35	130,946	42	205,608	45	271,071	46	329,600	44
Interbank Liabilities	803	1	1,577	1	1,976	1	2,342	1	3,227	1	10,154	2	12,184	2	16,200	2
Corporate Bonds	0	—	0	—	0	—	0	—	1,590	—	2,359	1	4,127	1	4,300	1
Security RPs	0	—	0	—	0	—	0	—	1,686	1	676	—	3,470	1	3,700	—
Profit Tax Liability	338	—	453	—	565	—	1,468	1	702	—	957	—	730	—	900	—
Miscellaneous Liability	1,481	1	3,078	2	4,429	3	6,100	3	11,499	4	31,802	7	36,599	6	66,500	9
Total Liabilities	134,421	100	137,737	100	171,429	100	206,989	100	312,841	100	459,627	100	587,875	100	741,000	100

Notes: Detail may not add to totals because of rounding.
— indicates less than 0.5 percent.

Source: Board of Governors of the Federal Reserve System, *Flow of Funds Accounts, 1945-1972* (Washington, D.C.: August 1973), pp. 94-96 and *Flow of Funds, Assets and Liabilities Outstanding, 1974*.

ever, during the years since 1945. Growth was very modest in the first five years, as banks liquidated government securities to acquire the funds to expand business and other loans. The retirement of outstanding debt issues by the Treasury offset the effects of bank liquidation of such securities so that there was little effect on total bank assets. Then in the next 15 or so years until about 1965, the Fed kept the level of growth of bank reserves well below the level of GNP growth in order to restore a more normal relationship of the money supply and GNP. In these years the level of income velocity of money that had prevailed before the Depression was restored.

After 1965 the Fed followed a very erratic policy in regard to expansion of the money supply. At times it expanded reserves and the money supply faster than real GNP, and this created inflationary pressures, and at other times it restricted growth in attempts to curb inflationary trends. In these years, 1965 to 1972, demand deposits grew by 46 percent, which exceeded the growth of real GNP of 28 percent. Total bank assets grew even faster at 86 percent.

The central concern of the Fed is in the growth of demand deposits, which is the major component of the money supply. These deposits increased only 2.1 times from 1945 to 1972. In contrast, time deposits (including large negotiable CDs) increased about nine times. This differential growth reflects the competition for time and savings deposits by commercial banks with the thrift institutions and with investments in U.S. Savings Bonds. The strong move by commercial banks, and especially by the large banks in metropolitan centers, into retail as well as wholesale banking initiated the drive for savings accounts beginning around 1950. This participation of commercial banks in the huge growth of savings and time deposits of individuals, and the fact that such deposits require a much lower level of reserves, account in large part for the faster growth of total bank assets than of bank reserves or the money supply. The nature of this competition is set forth at length in Chapter Three.

Shifts in Composition of Bank Assets and Liabilities

The principal change in the composition of bank liabilities since 1945 has already been mentioned above as the dramatic increase in both absolute and relative terms of time and savings deposits. This increase, as shown in Tables 2-13 and 2-14, was about ninefold from 1945 to 1972 and from 23 percent to 54 percent of total liabilities. Included in this growth was the emergence of the large negotiable certificates of deposit (CDs) around 1960 and their expansion to 13 percent of total liabilities in 1974. These CDs as well as security repurchase agreements (RPs) and bond issues represent new sources of funds for banks in recent years and the increase in borrowings from other banks and from the Fed represent additional new developments in the competition for funds which will be discussed in the next section.

The ownership patterns of time and savings deposits have also changed

Table 2-14. Growth of Bank Balance Sheet Items, 1945-1972

Demand Deposits	2.12x
Time Deposits	8.92x
Total Deposits	4.03x
Total Assets	4.38x
Addendum:	
Current Dollar GNP	5.45x
Constant Dollar GNP	2.23x

Source: Calculated from Tables 2-2 and 2-13.

since 1945. Although the dollar amounts of the increase of deposits of households have accounted for the bulk of the total dollar increase of time and savings deposits, household accounts have decreased in relative importance. The marked increase in the relative importance of the accounts of state and local governments and of businesses are readily apparent in Table 2-16. The desire of these customers to secure some return on liquid assets and better cash management practices have led to their shifts from demand to time deposits and after 1960 especially to large negotiable CDs.

The pattern of ownership of demand deposits has also changed during the postwar years, as indicated in Table 2-15. The ownership distribution of 1945 was distorted by the exceptionally large balances of the U.S. government, which resulted from the heavy Treasury borrowing just before the end of the war and which was used later to retire outstanding debt. A more normal pattern in the early postwar period is shown for the year 1950. The change from that year to 1972 shows the relative increase in the household balances and the relative decrease in business balances. These trends reflect partly the alertness of businesses to minimize their idle funds and partly the growing affluence and the increased proportion of households owning checking accounts.

The principal change in the composition of bank assets since 1945 has been the decline in the relative and absolute amount of U.S. government securities and the tremendous increase in various categories of loans and in the build up of state and local securities (see Table 2-13). The situation in 1945 was abnormal, as previously noted, arising from the process of war finance. Banks in 1945 were primarily Treasury bond-holding institutions. In the early postwar years, banks redeemed almost $30 billion of their government bonds and returned to their traditional business of making loans (which increased more than $30 billion in the same five years), extending credit to the private sector of the economy. In the five years 1945 to 1950, banks expanded their loans and investments in municipals by an almost equal amount to their reduction in government security holdings. In the years after 1950 no further liquidation of government securities took place, but the then existing holdings decreased

Table 2-15. Ownership of Demand Deposits and Currency (Dollars in millions)

	1945 $	1945 %	1950 $	1950 %	1955 $	1955 %	1960 $	1960 %	1965 $	1965 %	1970 $	1970 %	1972 $	1972 %	1974 $	1974 %
Households	56,737	43	56,945	46	66,125	46	74,063	48	94,221	50	132,812	55	156,487	56	174,200	61
Corporate Business	18,959	14	24,222	20	29,282	20	27,376	18	28,915	15	35,246	14	35,962	13	36,300	13
Noncorporate Business	8,926	7	9,738	8	11,200	8	12,415	8	12,515	7	12,515	5	12,515	4	12,500	4
Farm Business	4,600	4	7,000	6	6,900	5	5,800	4	6,000	3	6,515	3	6,776	2	7,000	2
Financial Institutions	3,992	3	6,001	5	7,809	5	9,088	6	11,836	6	14,046	6	16,951	6	21,400	7
Mail Float	5,393	4	6,896	6	9,024	6	9,413	6	10,480	6	13,023	5	17,049	6	NA	—
Rest of the World	2,677	2	2,035	2	1,532	1	2,122	1	4,373	2	6,169	3	7,975	3	13,000	5
State and Local Governments	3,715	3	6,495	5	7,982	6	8,418	5	12,127	6	13,722	6	14,570	5	14,800	5
U.S. Government	27,774	21	4,767	4	4,870	3	6,807	4	6,953	4	9,525	4	13,075	5	8,100	3
Total	132,773	100	124,099	100	144,724	100	155,502	100	187,420	100	243,573	100	281,360	100	287,300	100

Note: Detail may not add to totals because of rounding.

Source: Board of Governors of the Federal Reserve System, *Flow of Funds Accounts, 1945–1972* (Washington, D.C.: August 1973), pp. 111–113 and *Flow of Funds, Assets and Liabilities Outstanding, 1974*, pp. 1 and 6.

Table 2-16. Ownership of Time Deposits and Savings Accounts at Commercial Banks (Dollars in millions)

	1945 $	1945 %	1950 $	1950 %	1955 $	1955 %	1960 $	1960 %	1965 $	1965 %	1972 $	1972 %	1974 $	1974 %
Households	27,165	89	32,428	88	43,768	87	61,953	84	115,911	78	248,647	78	325,700	77
Corporate Business	900	3	900	2	1,000	2	3,867	5	13,131	9	20,195	6	28,100	7
State and Local Government	529	2	1,391	4	2,356	5	4,557	6	12,186	8	37,161	12	50,100	12
U.S. Government	104	—	190	1	357	1	262	—	250	—	606	—	500	—
Mutual Savings Banks	140	—	168	—	224	—	125	—	211	—	365	—	800	—
Foreign	1,578	5	1,958	5	2,799	6	2,859	4	6,006	4	9,822	3	19,400	5
Total Time Deposits	30,416	100	37,031	100	50,504	100	73,623	100	147,695	100	316,796	100	424,600	100

Notes: Detail may not add to totals because of rounding.
— indicates less than 0.5 percent.

Source: Board of Governors of the Federal Reserve System, *Flow of Funds Accounts, 1945-1972* (Washington, D.C.: August 1973), pp. 111-113 and *Flow of Funds, Assets & Liabilities Outstanding, 1974.*

steadily in relative importance. The importance of government security holdings as a source of hard liquidity diminished in importance.

In prewar times, bank loans to businesses were most commonly made to finance seasonal peak requirements for inventories or customer receivables. Self-liquidating loans (e.g., to finance an international transaction) were considered especially attractive. After the war, the growth of retail banking and the consequent marked expansion of time and savings deposits has led to the rapid growth of consumer loans and home and commercial mortgages, to substantial increases in investments in state and local government securities and to longer-term loans to businesses. Banks needed to cater to their individual depositors and also were considered better able to make longer-term loans because of their growth in longer-term deposits.

This presumption of shorter- or longer-term availability of different categories of deposits is questionable, but it has traditionally been a significant influence on bank loan and investment policies. Business loans themselves also have been lengthened to three years, five years, or even longer, especially in the last few years. "Composite" loans, with a seasonal portion to be periodically reduced and a long-term portion to be paid down gradually, have also become a common form of business financing.

Changes in Emphasis from Uses of Funds to Source of Funds

The overwhelming preponderance of federal government securities among the assets of banks in 1945 indicated an opportunity for initiative and activity to seek more profitable uses of funds. Bank managements were eager to secure business loans as business became less liquid and in need of funds. Longer-term business loans, consumer loans, and mortgages also provided more profitable uses of funds. The tax-exempt status of state and local securities offered higher returns, though with less liquidity, as new municipal issues came on the market to finance the postwar expansion. Expertise in lending (particularly to large corporate accounts) and portfolio management were considered especially important. The rapid growth of certificates of deposit after 1960, noted above, reflects the shift toward active solicitation for new funds. With established business loan customers being turned away because of an absence of funds, banks' efforts to secure funds from all conceivable sources are understandable.

Banks have turned to quite an array of new sources of funds. The times of greatest innovation have been the tight credit periods in 1966, 1969, and 1973-1974. Some of the new sources are as follows:

1. Large negotiable certificates of deposit (CDs) which are issued in amounts of $100,000 or more, for relatively short maturities (an average of aobut six months), and carry interest yields comparable to commercial paper.

2. Borrowings of Eurodollars from overseas branches by U.S. parent banks.
3. Issuance of commercial paper by bank holding companies. Originally the proceeds of this paper were used to buy loans from the subsidiary banks, but a regulation change by the Federal Reserve Board stopped the practice. Now, the proceeds are used to finance nonbank subsidiaries, freeing the bank from this demand on its funds.
4. Variable interest ("floating rate") bond issues, another source used by holding companies for their nonbank subsidiaries, relieving their demands on the banks themselves.
5. Sales of government securities under agreements to repurchase them at a specified price at a later date ("security RPs").
6. Extensive purchases of Federal Funds from smaller "country" banks by the major money center banks.
7. Growing use of bankers acceptances, a scheme whereby the bank underwrites the credit of its customers, who borrow directly in the money markets.

Figure 2-5 shows the recent history of some of these new financing methods, with their large increases in 1969-1970 and again in 1973-1974.

All of these new financing methods carry relatively high costs. In fact, during recent months in 1974 the interest rate banks have offered on CDs has at times exceeded the prime rate they charge their corporate loan customers (who have been the heaviest borrowers during this period). To relieve the pressure on the limited supplies of funds, some banks have encouraged their most credit-worthy borrowers to issue commercial paper, with the bank providing a standby line of credit to underwrite the issue. This frees the bank's funds for loans (at higher interest rates) to its smaller customers who do not have access to the commercial paper markets.

Traditionally, banks have relied for liquidity to meet sudden deposit withdrawals on holdings of short-term money market instruments as supplements to their reserves. The most important of these instruments were short-term government securities, primarily Treasury bills. Increasingly during the postwar period the larger banks especially have relied less for liquidity on their holdings of liquid assets and more on their ability to acquire funds by borrowing. Thus, they have supplemented their asset management practices with the management of their liabilities. The effects of this change, with the decline in the percentage holdings of government securities and the increased relative importance of large negotiable CDs, interbank liabilities, and security RPs, are shown in Table 2-13. Not shown in the table is the extensive use of the Federal Funds market. It also appears that there is less reluctance to borrow from the Federal Reserve Banks than has been true in the past. This change in banking practice by the larger money market banks especially gives every indication of being a permanent change which will continue in the future.

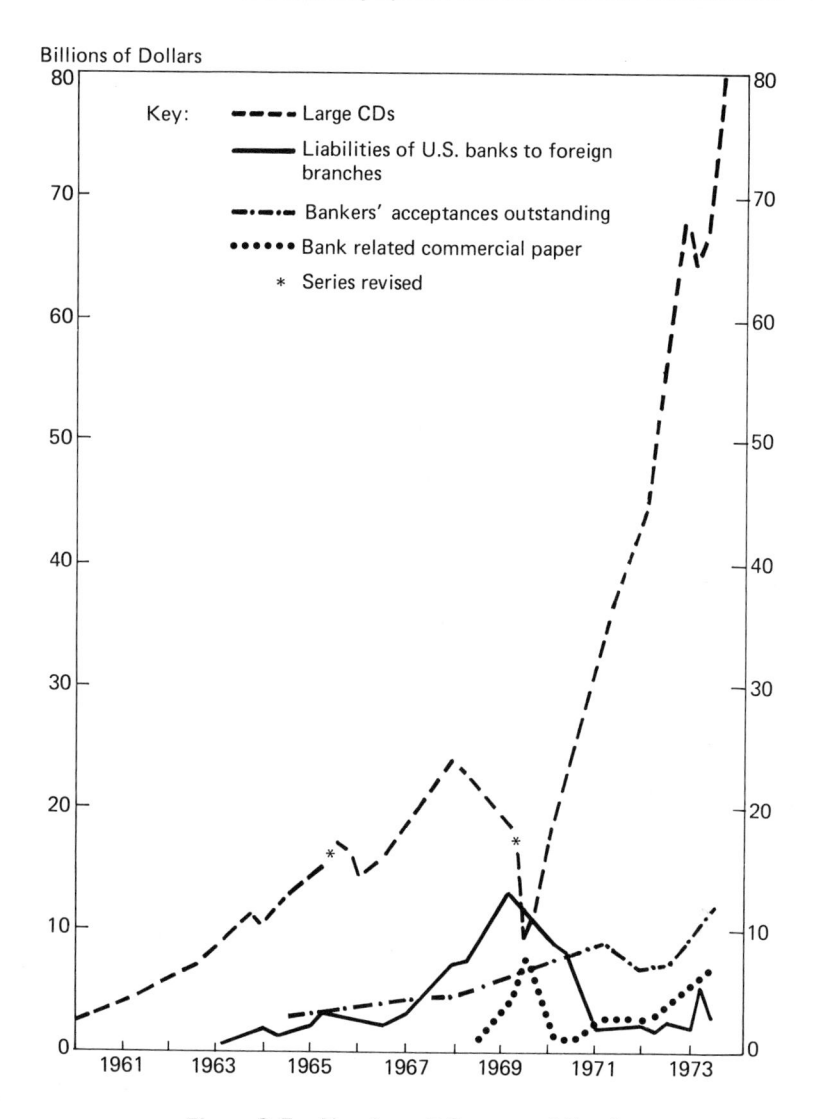

The Banking System and Its Economic Environment 47

Figure 2-5. Nondeposit Sources of Funds

Sources: Board of Governors of the Federal Reserve System, *Federal Reserve Bulletin* (Washington, D.C.: Board of Governors of the Federal Reserve System, July 1974), pp. A 14, A 27, A 72; Donald M. DePamphilis, *A Microeconomic Econometric Analysis of the Short-Term Commercial Paper Adjustment Process* (Boston: Federal Reserve Bank of Boston, April 1974), pp. 18, 21, 22.

Decline in Bank Capital Ratios

The equity of bank stockholders, represented by capital, surplus, and undivided profits, is a measure of the safety margin for depositors. It provides a cushion which the bank can fall back upon in adverse times. Traditionally, the ratio of capital funds to deposits has been used by the regulatory agencies as one indicator of a bank's soundness. A ratio of 10 percent or more was a familiar guideline during the 1920s. Bank failures followed by the injection of new capital by the Reconstruction Finance Corporation in the 1930s threw off conventional relationships. The large increases of deposits during World War II reduced the ratio of capital funds to deposits to a new low of about 6 percent. But, the banks' great increase in holdings of government securities was deemed to have reduced their exposure to risk. The composition of assets thus became a major factor in determining the appropriate level of capital funds to provide safe margins for depositors.

In the years since World War II, the concept of "risk" assets versus "safe" assets has received continuing study, and the test of bank soundness used by regulatory agencies has been changed several times.[7]

The new trends in the use of nondeposit sources of funds expose banks to a new form of risk, namely, a sudden drying up of the supply of funds. In 1969, for example, when open market interest rates rose sharply, banks experienced a considerable run-off of CDs until the Federal Reserve Board raised the allowable interest rates on them. In early 1974, the Franklin National Bank in New York saw almost 40 percent of its funds supply disappear within a few weeks after its financial problems became known. Although this new liquidity risk is no different in concept from the old-fashioned possibility of a "run" on a bank, it lacks the controls and stabilizing influences (e.g., FDIC insurance) which apply to ordinary deposits. Thus, the debate over the appropriate measures of capital-to-deposits or capital-to-risk assets, or whatever, has begun anew. Since some of the well-known New York City banks derive half their funds from nondeposit sources, public concern has been aroused.

Another concern over bank capital has arisen in recent years. During 1974, the prices of many bank stocks declined (along with the stock market generally) by almost half. At the same time, some large banks experienced large inflows of deposits from Arab oil nations, thus reducing their capital-to-deposit ratios to new lows. For example, by the middle of 1974, capital-to-deposit ratios for large banks had fallen to about 8.5 percent, a decline from about 10 percent in early 1970. At the current depressed stock prices new equity issues for these banks are unattractive. It remains to be seen whether the low capital-to-deposit ratios will become a new standard or whether banks will be forced to curtail their deposit growth.

The Margin Squeeze on Bank Profits

In the past two decades, banks have experienced a gradual narrowing of the margin between the interest rates they receive on loans and the rates they must pay for funds. Primarily, this squeeze has resulted from increased cost of funds. Nondeposit sources of funds such as CDs carry interest rates near (and occasionally exceeding) the prime rate on business loans. Also, as depositors have increasingly placed their funds in time deposits instead of interest-free checking accounts, the cost of deposits has risen. Finally, as the velocity of money has increased, the number of transactions per dollar of deposits has risen, with a consequent increase in processing costs. For example, in the past decade the turnover rate of demand deposits has nearly tripled (see Table 2-17).

Table 2-18 shows the effects of these trends on banks' profitability. In the period since World War II, banks' operating expenses have increased from 61 percent of operating income to almost 84 percent in 1973.[8] Interest expenses increased even more dramatically, from 9 percent to 46 percent. There have been some offsetting reductions in the proportions of salary and other expenses, but the overall result has been a reduction in banks' net profit margins by more than half.

It seems likely that the trend toward lower profit margins will continue, though perhaps at a slower rate. If it does, there are several predictable reactions of the banks' managements. First, there may be some movement to diversify into nonbanking (and non-funds-using) services. This phenomenon has already been observed in the activities of bank holding companies. Second, banks should find prime rate loans to large corporations less attractive, and move toward riskier, but higher yield loans. As we have said, banks have already encouraged some credit-worthy borrowers to issue their own commercial paper. Third, there should be some pressure for banks to expand, to spread their fixed costs over a larger operating base.

Implications of Persistent Inflation

Since the country has not previously operated under persistent inflation, one cannot foresee all the ramifications even as they may apply to banking. But it would be negligent not to recognize the probable new situation and at least suggest conjectures about its implications.

Persistent inflation will probably lead to higher interest rates than have been common under conditions of relatively stable prices. It is not feasible here to analyze the relative significance of a higher supply price of capital as savers and investors seek to protect the real value of their assets, and of higher demands as borrowers seek to buy assets before prices increase further. The two pressures reinforce each other and higher interest rates seem a probable fact under persistent inflation.

The existence of higher interest rates, in turn, increases the opportunity cost of holding idle funds. Business and individuals may be expected to seek to minimize non-interest-paying cash balances. Opportunities for other financial institutions to provide income on "near money" assets will continue and people's habits regarding the appropriate forms and amounts of cash in the form of demand deposits will change.

Table 2-17. Comparisons of Gross National Product, Bank Debits and Turnover of Demand Deposits

	1964	1965	1966	1967	1968	1969	1970	1971	1972	1974
Gross National Product ($ Billion)	$ 628.7	$ 684.9	$ 749.9	$ 793.5	$ 864.2	$ 930.3	$ 976.4	$ 1,050.4	$ 1,151.8	$ 1,396.7
Bank Debits to Demand Deposits in 233 SMSAs*	4,778.9	5,510.6	6,343.9	7,095.0	8,726.3	9,568.4	10,849.7	12,383.2	14,783.7	22,748.5
				Demand Deposit Turnover (Annual rate in percent)						
In New York City	90.5	102.9	120.2	123.2	143.1	145.1	169.2	196.1	215.7	333.9%
In Six Other Leading SMSAs	41.6	47.9	53.3	54.8	63.1	71.1	77.6	85.2	95.6	121.5
In 226 Other SMSAs	29.9	33.2	34.3	35.6	38.0	41.3	43.0	46.4	48.9	68.2
Overall Average Rate	45.1	50.6	56.4	58.4	65.9	69.8	76.9	83.7	90.7	129.3

*Seasonally adjusted annual rates, December of respective years.

Sources: GNP–*Statistical Abstract of the United States, 1973*, p. 319; *1970*, p. 311; *1966*, p. 320; *Survey of Current Business*, volume 54, no. 6, June 1974, p. S-1; *Federal Reserve Bulletin*, July 1972, pp. 634, 635; *Federal Reserve Bulletin*, December 1973, p. A14. *Economic Report of the President 1975*, p. 249.

Table 2-18. Trends in Income Ratios (Amounts per $100 of operating income)

Income or Expense Item	1945	1950	1955	1960	1965	1970	1973
Operating Income—Total	$100.00	$100.00	$100.00	$100.00	$100.00	$100.00	$100.00
Income on Loans	29.27	51.08	57.96	63.48	66.63	69.05	71.39
Interest on U.S. Treasury Securities	45.64	25.83	20.91	16.69	13.23	8.87	6.53
Interest and Dividends on Other Securities[a]	6.74	5.74	5.51	5.40	7.64	9.97	10.77
Service Charges on Deposit Accounts	4.42	5.40	5.33	5.50	5.01	3.39	2.50
Other Charges, Commissions, Fees, etc.	3.65	2.66	2.43	2.04	1.81	2.43	2.36
Trust Department Income					4.10	3.26	2.75
Other Operating Income	10.28	9.29	7.86	6.89	1.58	3.03	3.70
Operating Expense—Total[b]	$ 61.35	$ 62.19	$ 62.09	$ 64.65	$ 74.25	$ 79.47	$ 83.58
Interest on Time and Savings Deposits	9.40	8.73	10.63	16.65	30.15	30.20	37.40
Interest on Borrowed Money[c]					1.13	5.67	8.78
Salaries, Wages, and Fees	28.42	31.20	30.35	26.62	25.50	22.23	19.10
Recurring Depreciation on Banking House, Furniture, and Fixtures	1.62	1.51	1.70	1.98	6.80	6.23	5.62
Provision for Loan Losses[b]						2.03	2.38
Other Operating Expenses	21.91	20.75	19.41	19.40	10.67	13.11	10.30
Net Current Operating Income	$ 38.65	$ 37.81	$ 37.91	$ 35.35	$ 25.75	$ 20.53	$ 16.42

[a]Includes interest and dividends on securities of other U.S. government agencies and corporations and interest on state and local government obligations.
[b]"Interest on capital notes and debentures," which is included in "Interest on borrowed money" in 1969-1973, and "Provision for loan losses" were not included in "Operating Expense—Total" in 1968 and prior years.
[c]Includes interest on Federal Funds purchased. Beginning with 1969, also includes interest on capital notes and debentures.

Banks thus will be under increasing pressure to pay interest on demand deposits. But if they did so, interest expense would be very large and would put further pressure on profit margins. Some banks may devise additional ways to shift deposits back and forth between demand and time deposits to meet depositors' demands and the competition of NOW accounts described in Chapter Three.

Attitudes regarding indebtedness may also change, with reinforcement of the growing belief of the past decade that a large and expensive mortgage and residence is acceptable because the purchaser will be bailed out by continuing price rises. New balances between higher interest and new expectations of price increases will have to develop, with some increased acceptance of indebtedness by people who have thus far considered it imprudent. Such an attitude change would, of course, increase the demands for consumer credit and place further strains on banks' supply of loanable funds.

Inventory policies of business may not change greatly if higher interest costs involved in holding inventory offset the price advantages of earlier purchases. But conventional financial ratios may be modified in various ways.

With higher interest rates, lower price-to-earnings ratios seem probable for stock prices. Lower stock prices in turn increase the "cost" of new stock issues by business and increase the importance of retained earnings. The tax laws, especially with respect to last-in-first-out (LIFO) inventory accounting and the rules regarding depreciation, may perhaps be revised to improve corporate retained earnings. However, political and popular attacks on "excessive" profits tend to limit the potential of retained earnings as a source of funds. Thus, corporations probably will be increasingly dependent on bond issues and bank loans as sources of capital. This has been the pattern in 1971 and again in 1974. Banking, as we have said, is among the industries in need of new capital. As an industry, it must grow to provide and hold the cash balances necessary for the functioning of the entire economy. But changes in market prices, profit margins, or investor attitudes are necessary if the capital base is to be forthcoming.

These brief comments on the implications of persistent inflation do not purport to be predictions. They merely give perspective and call attention to one specific factor in the evolving environment in which banks operate.

TRENDS IN THE FINANCIAL NEEDS AND HABITS OF BANK CUSTOMER GROUPS

The foregoing major developments in banking reflect and are in response to developments in the financial needs and habits of the major categories of business and households. These evolving requirements and patterns of behavior are described in this section, along with details of some aspects of banking to which brief references have been made previously.

It is reasonable to expect that the prolonged period of economic expansion, characterized by rising incomes, higher interest rates and more diversity of economic activity, would produce some changes in the financial needs and behavior of both businesses and households. The proliferation of financial services and new financial firms indicates the existence of such changes. In this section we will look at each of these customer groups in turn.

Nonfinancial Businesses

The postwar period has been characterized by a tremendous growth in capital formation, increased interest rates, as noted above, and improvements in corporate financial management. Partly, the attention to financial management is a direct result of the higher costs of funds, and partly it can be attributed to better educated managers and the increasing number of security analysts and institutional investors looking over the shoulders of corporate treasurers. Technology has also played a role by increasing the ability of corporate headquarters to keep track of and manage corporation funds centrally. Many large corporations now have at their disposal an instantaneous presentation of the company's financial position as well as models for projecting cash flow under a variety of assumptions.

From the viewpoint of banks, the most dramatic change in corporate financing in postwar years has been the reduction in demand deposits as a proportion of financial assets. In 1945 demand deposits and currency holdings amounted to some 27 percent of corporate financial assets. By 1974 this proportion had dropped to only 7 percent. With rising interest rates, firms found it desirable to keep minimum bank balances and put their money to work in earning assets. Time deposits constituted some 5 percent of corporate financial assets in 1974 versus practically none in early postwar times. The growth has been particularly great in the large negotiable certificates of deposit offered by commercial banks, which are exempt from most federal limitations on interest rates. Banks have helped corporations minimize their demand deposit balances by offering wire transfer of funds, lockbox systems, and other services for moving funds quickly from one part of the country to another.

Even with the increase in time deposits, the proportion of corporate financial assets kept in banks or in other liquid forms such as Treasury bills has declined sharply (Table 2-19). It used to be common for businesses to keep a reserve of cash or government bonds to provide flexibility in times of unusual financial need. As interest rates have risen, this form of flexibility has become more costly, inasmuch as government securities typically pay relatively low interest rates and demand deposits pay none. Rather than keep idle assets, corporations are increasingly "buying" their flexibility in the form of open lines of credit with banks or other sources for borrowing on short notice. Also, they rely to some extent on better internal planning to avoid financial squeeze situations. The overall decline in corporate liquidity positions (as traditionally measured) is shown in Figure 2-6.

One source of flexible borrowing which corporations have used increasingly

Table 2-19. Financial Assets and Liabilities of Corporate Nonfinancial Businesses (Dollars in millions)

	1945 $	1945 %	1950 $	1950 %	1955 $	1955 %	1960 $	1960 %	1965 $	1965 %	1970 $	1970 %	1972 $	1972 %	1974 $	1974 %
Assets																
Demand Deposits & Currency	18,959	27	24,222	24	29,282	20	27,376	15	28,915	11	35,246	10	35,962	8	36,300	7
Time Deposits	900	1	900	1	1,000	1	3,867	2	13,131	5	13,485	4	20,195	5	28,100	5
U.S. Government Securities	18,508	27	17,870	18	21,581	15	16,868	9	12,693	5	7,325	2	6,975	2	8,900	2
Commercial Paper	7	–	340	–	1,100	1	2,532	1	6,725	3	19,363	5	23,462	5	32,800	6
Other Liquid Assets	339	–	652	1	1,219	1	2,402	1	6,286	2	2,409	1	6,863	2	7,200	1
Consumer Credit	1,664	2	4,632	5	7,066	5	9,679	5	13,151	5	15,000	4	17,145	4	20,300	4
Trade Credit	20,951	30	40,542	39	59,281	42	82,255	45	120,967	47	189,810	52	215,189	50	261,700	49
Foreign Direct Investment	7,227	10	11,788	12	19,313	13	32,744	18	49,233	19	72,966	20	83,345	19	110,400	21
Misc. Financial Assets	451	1	1,475	1	2,165	2	4,892	3	7,644	3	12,098	3	17,513	4	23,800	4
Total Financial Assets	69,006	100	102,421	100	142,007	100	182,615	100	258,745	100	367,702	100	426,649	100	529,500	100
Liabilities																
Bonds	23,527	33	35,734	29	53,286	31	75,312	32	97,800	28	167,306	30	198,300	30	227,100	27
Mortgages	8,540	12	14,419	12	20,334	12	32,024	13	52,821	15	77,046	14	104,115	16	131,200	16
Bank Loans	9,644	13	18,294	15	25,595	15	37,657	16	60,054	17	102,584	18	120,943	18	180,800	21
Commercial Paper Finance Company	162	–	344	–	528	–	1,186	–	1,242	–	10,558	2	8,561	1	14,200	2
Loans	1,338	2	1,138	1	2,471	1	5,558	2	7,586	2	13,704	2	18,365	3	24,800	3
Tax Liability	10,828	15	17,252	14	20,085	12	13,615	6	20,169	6	11,472	2	13,956	2	20,000	2
Trade Debt	14,125	20	32,788	26	46,318	27	64,135	27	98,124	28	157,485	28	174,545	27	216,700	26
Miscellaneous Liabilities	3,154	4	4,007	3	5,760	3	7,766	4	10,473	3	15,329	3	16,371	2	21,000	2
Total Liabilities	71,318	100	123,976	100	174,377	100	237,253	100	348,269	100	555,484	100	655,156	100	843,000	100

Notes: Detail may not add to totals because of rounding.
– indicates less than 0.5 percent.

Source: Board of Governors of the Federal Reserve System, *Flow of Funds Accounts, 1945-1972* (Washington, D.C.: August 1973), pp. 85–87 and *Flow of Funds, Assets & Liabilities Outstanding, 1974.*

Figure 2-6. Corporate Liquidity Positions

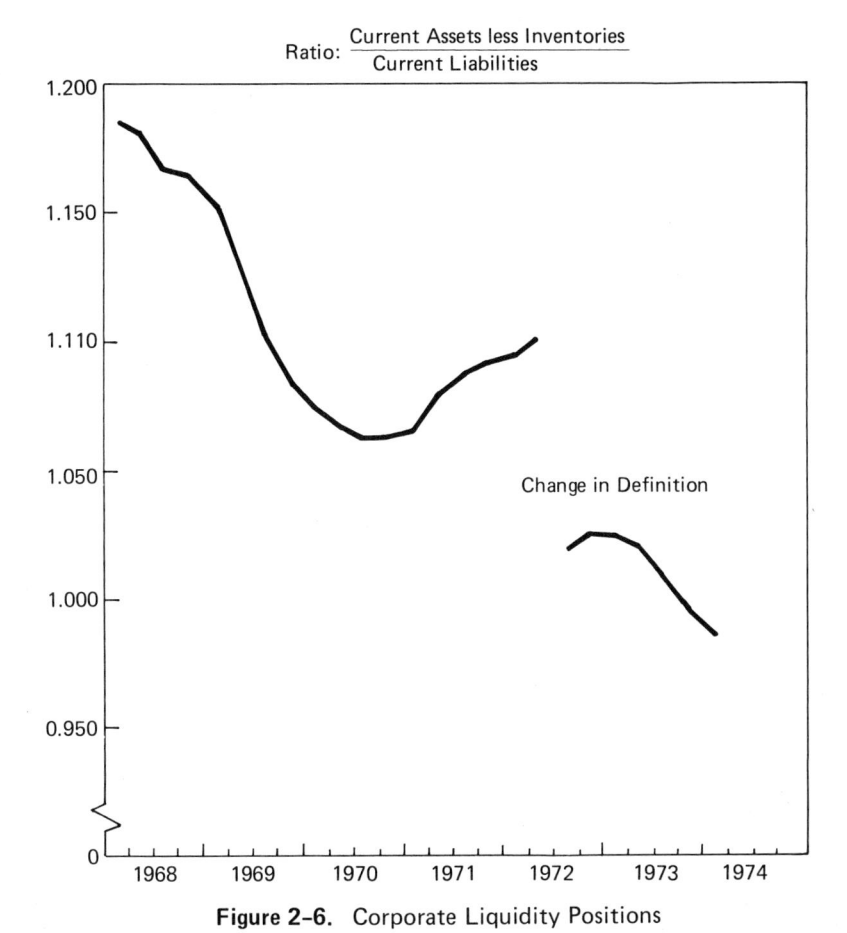

Ratio: Current Assets less Inventories / Current Liabilities

Source: Federal Reserve Bulletin (Board of Governors of the Federal Reserve System, Washington, D.C.), July 1974, (p. A 43), December 1973, (p. A 48), November 1972, (p. A 50), June 1971, (p. A 49), and March 1970, (p. A 49).

in recent years is the commercial paper market. Commercial paper is a form of debt issued by the most credit-worthy borrowers for terms ranging from 30 to 270 days. Interest rates are typically slightly below the so-called prime rate for business loans. It offers the added attraction of flexible timing in that the terms can be tailored exactly to the needs of the borrower or the lender. Slightly more than two-thirds of all commercial paper is negotiated directly between borrower and lender. However, it can be placed and bought through a few dealers who specialize in this service. Prior to 1965, the participants in this market were primarily finance companies, such as General Motors Acceptance Corporation, and a very few large corporations. However, during the credit crunches of 1966, and especially 1969, activity and participation in commercial paper increased greatly. To some extent, banks were responsible, since they often sent their most credit-worthy customers to the commercial paper market to save their scarce funds for smaller borrowers who did not have that option. Once these firms had learned the mechanics of the market and had become comfortable with it, they tended to stay as continuing participants. Since 1965 the volume of commercial paper outstanding has increased fivefold to approximately $52 billion in April 1975.[9]

Another new source of flexible borrowing or investment is the banker's acceptance, which has become more popular in very recent months as a method of extending credit without tying up bank funds. The banker's acceptance is a short-term note issued by a corporation in anticipation of some future receipt (e.g., payment for an overseas shipment of goods). After the note is "accepted" (i.e., underwritten) by the issuer's bank, it can be sold in the money markets just as any other security can. Banker's acceptances are considered quite safe since they are backed by a bank, the credit of the issuer, and, if all else fails, the shipment of merchandise that originally gave rise to the acceptance. Figure 2-5 has already documented the rise in the use of acceptances.

Still another source of financing tapped increasingly by corporations in recent years has been the leasing rather than outright purchase of equipment. There are several attractions to leasing. If nothing else, the lessee can achieve a certain amount of balance sheet cosmetics by showing the lease obligation as a footnote to the balance sheet, rather than purchasing the equipment and showing the corresponding debt (or decrease in liquid assets). Frequently, lease forms can offer more flexible repayment schedules than would be available on an equivalent loan. Finally, leasing firms often have specialized knowledge about the equipment and can offer installation, maintenance, and periodic upgrading of the equipment as part of the lease package.

A final characteristic of corporate financing to mention is the growth of equity issues from 1969 to 1972. Through the late 1950s and most of the 1960s, common stock averaged only 14 percent of new corporate securities issues. The predominant financing vehicles were bonds and retained earnings. However, in the late 1960s capital needs grew faster than internal sources of funds and corporations turned increasingly to the money markets for new funds. This period also saw a decrease in corporate liquidity and an increase in debt-to-equity ratios, both of which arose from the credit crunch of 1969-1970 (see Figure 2-6). Corporations made heavy use of short-term borrowing, primarily bank loans and commercial paper. During the stock market recovery of 1971 and 1972 they sought to refinance these short-term borrowings with longer term bonds or equity issues. In three of the past five years, common stock has represented more than 20 percent of corporate security issues. In 1972 and 1973 the proportion rose to 24 percent (Table 2-20). But with the decline in stock prices in 1974, the cost of equity issues became too great and new issues practically disappeared.

Governments

Through the postwar years, the activities of state and local governments have grown much faster than those of the federal government or of the economy generally. The growth of state and local activity reflects itself in state and local government finances: their financial assets grew by a factor of 5.8 but their debts grew by a factor of 8.4 between 1950 and 1974 (see Table 2-21). Like corporations, state and local governments have tended to reduce the percentage of demand deposits in their liquid asset portfolios, replacing them with higher yielding time deposits.

The growth of state and local government activities has had its impact on banks. State and local governments in 1972 held deposits of $65 billion in banks or thrift institutions, as compared to $9 billion for the U.S. government and $64 billion for nonfinancial businesses generally.

State and local governments have been consistent borrowers in the money markets for such capital projects as schools, sewers, bridges and highways, and mass transit. The total state and local bonds outstanding in 1974 was $203 billion as compared to about $330 billion for the federal government and $227 billion for nonfinancial businesses, and in 1974 new issues of state and local government bonds amounted to $22.8 billion, as compared with new corporate bond issues of $31.3 billion.

Households

From the viewpoint of banks perhaps the most pervasive change since World War II has occurred in the finances of households. Since 1945 their financial assets have increased from $372 billion to $2.2 trillion, a factor of 5.9. During the same time their liabilities have increased from $33 billion to $703 billion, a factor of 21 (see Table 2-22). Their financial assets have grown faster than the GNP, but their borrowing has grown even faster. This means that consumers are more leveraged, probably reflecting the overall security of employment during this period and a greater willingness to borrow against income. In fact, surveys of consumers show increasing tolerance for installment debt (see Table 2-23). Increasing purchases of automobiles caused a rapid rise in installment debt between 1945 and 1950, from $2.5 billion to $14.7 billion. Continued high demand for automobiles and other major appliances has increased installment debt almost tenfold since 1950 to $127 billion in 1972, and to almost $150 billion by June 1974.

More than half of all consumer indebtedness is in the form of mortgages. Homeownership has been historically a strong value in the U.S., but was discouraged somewhat by the Depression and the housing shortage of World War II. Since then it has risen to an all-time high of 63 percent of all families in 1970 and is estimated at 65 percent today.[10] The rate of increase slowed substantially during the 1960s for demographic reasons; as the baby boom children reached the age at which they would first set up households, their demand

Table 2-20. State and Municipal and Corporate Securities Offered, 1934–1974* (Millions of dollars)

Year or Quarter	State and Municipal Securities Offered for Cash (principal amounts)	Total Corporate Offerings	Type of Corporate Security			Industry of Corporate Issuer			
			Common Stock	Preferred Stock	Bonds and Notes	Manufacturing[a]	Electric, Gas, and Water[b]	Transportation[c]	Communication	Other
1934	939	397	19	6	371	67	133	176	—	21
1939	1,128	2,164	87	98	1,980	604	1,271	186	—	103
1940	1,238	2,677	108	183	2,386	992	1,203	324	—	159
1941	956	2,667	110	167	2,390	848	1,347	366	—	96
1942	524	1,062	34	112	917	539	472	48	—	4
1943	435	1,170	56	124	990	510	477	161	—	21
1944	661	3,202	163	369	2,669	1,061	1,422	609	—	109
1945	795	6,011	397	758	4,855	2,026	2,319	1,454	—	211
1946	1,157	6,900	891	1,127	4,882	3,701	2,158	711	—	329
1947	2,324	6,577	779	762	5,036	2,742	3,257	286	—	293
1948	2,690	7,078	614	492	5,973	2,226	2,187	755	902	1,008
1949	2,907	6,052	736	425	4,890	1,414	2,320	800	571	946
1950	3,532	6,361	811	631	4,920	1,200	2,649	813	399	1,300
1951	3,189	7,741	1,212	838	5,691	3,122	2,455	494	612	1,058
1952	4,401	9,534	1,369	564	7,601	4,039	2,675	992	760	1,068
1953	5,558	8,898	1,326	489	7,083	2,254	3,029	595	882	2,138
1954	6,969	9,516	1,213	816	7,488	2,268	3,713	778	720	2,037

The Banking System and Its Economic Environment 59

1955	5,977	10,240	2,185	635	7,420	2,994	2,464	893	1,132	2,757
1956	5,446	10,939	2,301	636	8,002	3,647	2,529	724	1,419	2,619
1957	6,958	12,884	2,516	411	9,957	4,234	3,938	824	1,462	2,426
1958	7,449	11,558	1,334	571	9,653	3,515	3,804	824	1,424	1,991
1959	7,681	9,748	2,027	531	7,190	2,073	3,258	967	717	2,733
1960	7,230	10,154	1,664	409	8,081	2,152	2,851	718	1,050	3,383
1961	8,360	13,165	3,294	450	9,420	4,077	3,032	694	1,834	3,527
1962	8,558	10,705	1,314	422	8,969	3,249	2,825	567	1,303	2,761
1963	10,107	12,211	1,011	343	10,856	3,514	2,677	957	1,105	3,957
1964	10,544	13,957	2,679	412	10,865	3,046	2,760	982	2,189	4,980
1965	11,148	15,992	1,547	725	13,720	5,417	3,936	1,013	947	5,680
1966	11,089	18,074	1,939	574	15,561	7,070	3,665	1,972	2,003	3,364
1967	14,288	24,798	1,959	885	21,954	11,058	4,935	2,067	1,979	4,759
1968	16,374	21,966	3,946	637	17,383	6,979	5,281	1,875	1,766	6,064
1969	11,460	26,744	7,714	682	18,348	6,356	6,736	2,146	2,188	9,319
1970	17,762	38,506	6,948	1,383	30,176	10,609	11,007	2,207	5,146	9,537
1971	24,370	44,907	9,315	3,677	31,915	11,682	11,778	2,442	5,819	13,190
1972	22,944	40,835	9,693	3,372	27,771	6,622	11,318	2,027	4,825	16,045
1973	22,760	33,110	7,905	3,390	21,816	4,845	10,246	1,711	4,898	11,411
1974	22,726	37,611	4,082	2,235	31,294	10,316	12,785	1,032	3,915	9,563

*Covers substantially all new issues of state, municipal, and corporate securities offered for cash sales in the United States in amounts over $100,000 and with terms to maturity of more than one year; excludes notes issued exclusively to commercial banks, intercorporate transactions, investment company issues, and issues to be sold over an extended period, such as employee purchase plans.

[a]Prior to 1948, also includes extractive, radio broadcasting, airline companies, commercial, and miscellaneous company issues.

[b]Prior to 1948, also includes telephone, street railway, and bus company issues.

[c]Prior to 1948, includes railroad issues only.

Source: *Economic Report of the President* (Washington, D.C.: U.S. Government Printing Office, 1975), Table C-80.

Table 2-21. Financial Assets and Liabilities of State and Local Governments (Dollars in millions)

	1945 $	1945 %	1950 $	1950 %	1955 $	1955 %	1960 $	1960 %	1965 $	1965 %	1970 $	1970 %	1972 $	1972 %	1974 $	1974 %
Assets																
Demand Deposits and Currency	3,715	31	6,495	36	7,982	30	8,418	26	12,127	24	13,722	19	14,570	17	14,800	14
Time Deposits	529	4	1,391	8	2,356	9	4,557	14	12,186	25	23,225	32	37,161	43	50,100	48
U.S. Government Securities	5,465	46	6,748	37	11,493	44	14,290	44	18,942	38	28,572	40	28,430	33	31,000	29
Other Financial Assets	2,239	19	3,489	19	4,560	17	5,414	17	6,365	13	6,092	8	6,542	8	9,200	9
Total Financial Assets	11,948	100	18,123	100	26,391	100	32,679	100	49,620	100	71,611	100	86,703	100	105,100	100
Liabilities																
Bonds Outstanding	14,818	93	24,381	93	45,870	95	70,766	95	100,278	94	144,473	93	173,029	93	203,300	92
Other Loans	505	3	555	2	451	1	1,240	2	2,777	3	4,816	3	5,526	3	6,700	3
Trade Debt	632	4	1,278	5	1,778	4	2,457	3	3,691	3	6,359	4	7,525	4	9,800	4
Total Liabilities	15,955	100	26,214	100	48,099	100	74,463	100	106,746	100	155,648	100	186,080	100	219,900	100

Note: Detail may not add to totals because of rounding.

Source: Board of Governors of the Federal Reserve System, *Flow of Funds Accounts, 1945-1972* (Washington, D.C., August 1973), pp. 88-90 and *Flow of Funds, Assets and Liabilities Outstanding, 1974.*

was largely for apartments. However, the demand for single family homes should rise strongly in the late 1970s and early 1980s, when these people reach the age of having children and moving to the suburbs. The Joint Center for Urban Studies forecast of 23 million new housing units between now and 1980 represents a 25 percent increase in the nation's housing stock after deducting for demolition and replacement.[11]

The volume of mortgages as reflected in Table 2-22 has risen faster than could be explained simply by the construction of new houses or the increase in home ownership. The principal cause has been a rise in the price of housing. Moreover, various studies show that as people's incomes rise they tend to spend an increasing proportion of that income on housing. Also, the tax laws favor homeownership and this has tended to keep prices of houses high.

Household assets, like those of businesses and governments, show a decline in the relative importance of demand deposits and an increasing emphasis on earning assets, particularly time deposits at banks and thrift institutions. Households have also built up substantial pension reserves over the years to a total $314 billion in 1974, about 14 percent of all their financial assets. Still, consumers in 1974 kept 40 percent of their financial assets in banks, 24 percent in stocks, and another 21 percent in insurance or pension reserves. Only 10 percent is invested in fixed dollar debt instruments and government bonds. Thus households, despite the rapid rise in their financial assets, still look to their banker, their broker and their insurance agent as the principal places to put their surplus funds.

SUMMARY AND CONCLUSIONS

1. A key characteristic of financial markets in the postwar period has been the strong increase in the demand for funds and especially since 1965 the growing scarcity of funds in relation to demands. This strong demand for funds stemmed from the growth of real GNP at a rate of about 4 percent per year, the rapid conversion of the economy from a wartime to a peacetime basis, and the increased velocity of circulation of money as the country grew up to a war-inflated money supply. The relative scarcity of funds after 1965 has been reflected in an accelerating pace of inflation and an unprecedented increase in interest rates.

2. Commercial banks play a unique role in the financial system because bank's demand deposits constitute the principal part of the country's money supply. Control of the amount of money in circulation (the essence of monetary policy) is the responsibility of the Federal Reserve authorities. Hence the growth of aggregate commercial bank assets or liabilities is determined at least in part by the Federal Reserve Board. Consequently, commercial bank growth has been and will continue to be strongly influenced by the country's monetary policies, and total commercial bank assets can be expected to grow in reasonably parallel fashion with GNP.

Table 2-22. Financial Assets and Liabilities of U.S. Households, 1945-1974 (Dollars in millions)

	1945 $	% of Total	1950 $	% of Total	1955 $	% of Total	1960 $	% of Total	1965 $	% of Total	1970 $	% of Total	1972 $	% of Total	1974 $	% of Total
Assets																
Demand Deposits and Currency	56,737	15	56,945	13	66,125	9	74,063	8	94,221	6	132,812	7	156,487	6	174,200	8
Time and Savings Accounts	50,115	13	67,295	15	106,307	15	165,272	17	287,525	20	422,284	22	568,565	24	695,300	32
U.S. Government Securities	68,078	18	68,554	15	68,868	10	73,431	8	81,789	6	100,795	5	92,207	4	120,800	6
State and Local Obligations	6,270	2	8,991	2	19,187	3	30,764	3	36,365	2	45,590	2	46,012	2	60,300	3
Corporate and Foreign Bonds	9,738	3	5,099	1	7,074	1	11,029	1	13,397	1	41,194	2	54,800	2	54,500	2
Mortgages	11,954	3	17,363	4	22,364	3	31,844	3	34,342	2	39,317	2	37,317	2	39,300	2
Mutual Funds	1,264	–	3,344	1	7,838	1	17,026	2	35,220	2	47,618	3	59,831	2	35,800	2
Corporate Stock	110,407	30	130,420	29	278,847	39	379,001	39	601,487	41	684,723	36	907,480	38	487,400	22
Life Insurance Reserves	39,560	11	55,049	12	69,254	10	85,184	9	105,876	7	130,265	7	143,747	6	157,500	7
Pension Fund Reserves	10,961	3	23,909	5	50,388	7	90,674	9	153,809	11	237,159	12	309,150	13	313,800	14
Other	6,866	2	9,604	2	12,329	2	14,473	1	19,519	1	35,298	2	37,469	2	43,700	2
Total Financial Assets	371,950	100	446,573	100	708,581	100	972,761	100	1,463,550	100	1,917,055	100	2,413,065	100	2,182,600	100
Liabilities																
Home Mortgages	18,000	55	42,564	56	84,607	58	136,745	61	206,338	59	272,539	57	334,789	57	411,500	59
Other Mortgages	500	2	2,353	3	5,198	3	9,184	4	14,228	4	20,450	4	23,088	4	25,900	4
Installment Consumer Credit	2,462	7	14,703	19	28,906	20	42,968	19	70,893	20	102,064	21	127,332	22	156,100	22
Other Consumer Credit	3,203	10	6,768	9	9,924	7	13,173	6	18,990	5	25,099	5	30,232	5	34,000	5
Other	8,886	27	9,949	13	16,114	11	24,073	11	38,282	11	59,399	12	74,550	13	75,900	11
Total Financial Liabilities	33,051	100	76,337	100	144,749	100	226,143	100	348,731	100	479,551	100	589,991	100	703,400	100

Notes: Detail may not add to totals because of rounding.
– indicates less than 0.5 percent.

Source: Board of Governors of the Federal Reserve System, *Flow of Funds Accounts, 1945-1972* (Washington, D.C.: August 1973), pp. 83-84 and *Flow of Funds, Assets and Liabilities Outstanding,* 1974.

Table 2-23. Consumer Attitudes Toward Installment Debt* (percent)

Appropriate Purposes for Borrowing	All Families 1959	All Families 1967	$7,500-9,999 1959	$7,500-9,999 1967	$10,000 or more 1959	$10,000 or more 1967
To Finance Purhcase of a Car	67	65	74	79	61	80
To Finance Purchase of Furniture	44	52	49	61	41	58
To Cover Living Expenses When Income is Cut	26	40	21	40	23	41
To Cover Expenses of a Vacation	5	9	8	10	5	13

*Proportion of families interviewed who agreed that borrowing was appropriate for specific purposes. Income in 1959 dollars.
Source: Lewis Mandell et al., *Survey of Consumers 1971-72: Contributions to Behavioral Economics*, (Ann Arbor: The University of Michigan, Institute for Social Research, 1973), p. 137.

3. Real GNP in the United States is projected to grow substantially in the decade ahead. This growth in itself will generate strong demands for funds. In addition, inflation will accentuate the demands for funds, particularly for business capital and for mortgages. A period of severe shortage of investment funds seems likely, and decisions on who should receive the scarce funds will be more difficult than in the past.

4. In the postwar years businesses, individuals, and financial institutions have reduced their proportions of money balances and liquid assets in relation to their total financial assets. In this sense they have reduced their liquidity markedly. This reduction has increased substantially the velocity of money. Pressures to economize on idle money balances have increased as interest rates (and thus the "opportunity costs" of these balances) have increased. The reduced levels of liquidity have also meant greater reliance on short-term borrowing to cover peak cash needs. Whether or not this trend can continue, in a period of tight credit, is uncertain. In any event, it seems unlikely that businesses will revert to their former levels of liquidity.

5. The increase in time deposits relative to demand deposits has increased the cost of banks' funds. The more recent competition for funds through large negotiable CDs, Eurodollar borrowing, and so forth has increased the costs of funds faster than the rates on loans. This has resulted in a margin squeeze and an overall decline in banks' rates of return to shareholders. These lower returns have contributed to a slower growth of bank capital in relation to deposits, so that capital-to-deposit ratios have declined. At the same time the asset mix of commercial banks has changed toward a higher risk portfolio. U.S. government securities have been reduced as a percentage of total assets, while loans, particularly those with longer maturities, have increased.

These trends have combined to raise some public concern about the adequacy of bank capital. The fear, seldom stated explicitly, is that banks are taking increased risks at the same time they are decreasing their own capacity to absorb losses. The problem applies particularly to the country's largest banks, which have tended to be among the most aggressive in using new sources of funds and making longer-maturity loans.

To what extent a real danger exists is difficult to say. The question is more subtle and complex than most public statements suggest, and it appears unlikely that capital ratios will return to their historical levels.

NOTES

1. Since none of the bank's other depositors is affected by this action, the bank's total deposits increase by the amount of the loan.

2. This multiplier is simply the reciprocal of the fraction kept in reserve. Thus, if banks hold back 17 percent of each new deposit as reserve, the total money supply will be about six times the amount of reserve.

3. Every year before Christmas, people do withdraw more currency than they normally hold. To prevent a contraction of bank credit, the Federal Reserve temporarily expands the amount of reserves.

4. *Federal Reserve Bulletin,* July 1974, p. A6.

5. See, for example, Paul Nadler, "Fed Funds Have Become a Threat to Both Borrower and Lender," *American Banker,* August 20, 1974, p. 4.

6. U.S. Bureau of Labor Statistics, *The U.S. Economy in 1985,* Bulletin 1809 (Washington, D.C.: U.S. Government Printing Office, 1974), p. 24.

7. Geoge J. Vojta, *Bank Capital Ratios* (New York: First National City Bank, 1973).

8. Because of definitional changes, these two figures are not strictly comparable. By present definitions, the 1945 figure would be about 64 to 65 percent.

9. *Federal Reserve Bulletin,* July 1975, p. A25.

10. *S&L Fact Book, 1971,* (Chicago: U.S. League of Savings Associations, 1971), p. 43.

11. David L. Birch et al., *America's Housing Needs: 1970-1980* (Cambridge: MIT-Harvard Joint Center for Urban Studies, 1974).

Chapter Three

The Competitive Environment of Commercial Banks

In Chapter One we discussed briefly the relationship between commercial banks and other financial institutions. In this chapter we will discuss further the types of firms that compete with banks and what forms the competition may take.

Banks, besides competing among themselves, face direct or indirect competition from a variety of other types of firms. The most familiar are the other institutions which accept deposits, namely, the mutual savings banks, savings and loan association, and credit unions. These are the so-called "thrift" institutions. Other financial firms which compete with banks, sometimes indirectly, are insurance companies, brokerage firms, mutual funds, finance companies, and others. Many nonfinancial firms such as retailers also compete with banks, particularly in the financing of consumer purchases.

These competitors operate in an environment which is regulated by governments in a complex and uneven way. Many laws, passed decades ago to deal with specific problems, remain today as artificial barriers to entry or prohibitions of traditional forms of competition. There is widespread agreement that some of the distinctions among financial institutions would disappear if existing regulations were relaxed. This does not imply, however, that competitive distinctions would disappear entirely. The market for financial services is segmented enough to support many firms that specialize in particular services. Moreover, the opportunities for specialization appear to be increasing as the market expands and becomes more mature. It seems quite likely that these specialized firms will continue to exist alongside commercial banks.

The first section of this chapter reviews the dual nature of competition among financial firms and some of the markets in which they compete. The second section examines specific competitor groups and their trends in market share. The next sections discuss the Hunt Commission's and other proposals to restructure the financial industry and present some conclusions.

THE MARKETS IN WHICH BANKS COMPETE

In most industries, competition normally relates to sale of the finished product—e.g., automobiles, or refrigerators, or whatever. The raw materials and supplies for these industries are simply purchased as needed to meet the demand for finished goods. Occasionally, shortages may occur or one firm may get a "corner" on the supply of some valuable ingredient, but the normal pattern of competition is along lines of product quality, price, and customer service.

Banks, in contrast, face competition on two fronts. Their finished product is loans or credit and in this market they face competition from anyone else with money to lend. As with other industries, the competition is along lines of price, customer service, and so forth. On the opposite front, the raw material for banks is money, and the total supply of money is carefully controlled by the government. Thus, banks must compete in a second market, the market for funds, as buyers of a scarce commodity. Their competitors in this market are any other firms who need money—that is, anyone else who is willing to pay interest (or other consideration) for the use of funds. Banks compete for funds on the basis of price (interest rate) and services performed (mainly check processing) for the person providing the funds.

The Role of Financial Intermediaries

Figure 3-1 is a schematic diagram of the flows of credit in our economy. Persons or organizations with surplus funds—that is, funds which exceed what they need for current expenditures—are at the bottom of the diagram, and persons or organizations which need funds (in excess of current cash flow) are at the top. One person or firm may simultaneously belong to both groups—for example, a family that keeps a savings account (source of funds) and at the same time owes money on a home mortgage (use of funds).

The holder of surplus funds has many options for investing them. He can provide funds directly to the users (as on the left side of the diagram) through direct loans or by buying stocks and bonds. Slightly more than half of the nation's financial assets are direct issues of this sort. Alternatively, the holder of funds can place his money in a financial institution (center and right side of the diagram) and that intermediary will channel the funds to the ultimate user. In effect, the financial institutions act as collection centers for surplus funds in the economy and as distribution centers which channel these funds to the end users. The institutions make their profit on the "point spread" between the interest rate they charge to funds users and the rates they pay to the suppliers of funds (i.e., depositors, in the case of banks).

As the diagram shows, slightly less than half the nation's savings pass through the financial intermediaries, and commercial banks are by far the largest of these institutions. Each type of institution specializes, to a certain extent, in some sector of the market. The institutions compete with each other on both

The Competitive Environment of Commercial Banks 67

Figure 3-1. Sources and Uses of Credit (Approximate Amounts Outstanding, in Billions of Dollars, as of December 31, 1974)[a]

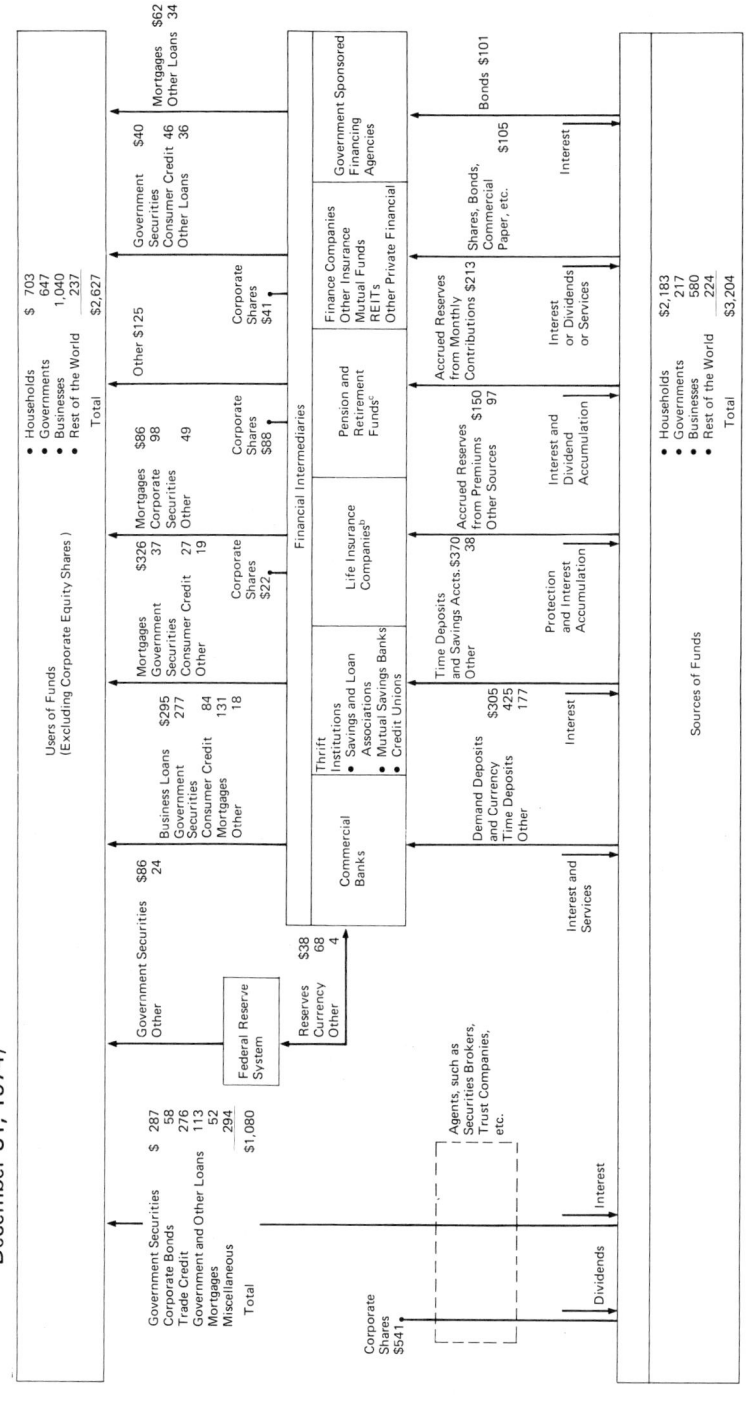

[figure content:]

Users of Funds (Excluding Corporate Equity Shares)
- Households $703
- Governments 647
- Businesses 1,040
- Rest of the World 237
- Total $2,627

Commercial Banks:
- Government Securities $86, Other 24
- Business Loans $295
- Government Securities 277
- Consumer Credit 84
- Mortgages 131
- Other 18

Thrift Institutions:
- Savings and Loan Associations
- Mutual Savings Banks
- Credit Unions
- Mortgages $326, Corporate Securities 37, Other 27, 19

Life Insurance Companies[b]:
- Corporate Shares $22

Pension and Retirement Funds[c]:
- Corporate Shares $88

Finance Companies, Other Insurance, Mutual Funds, REITs, Other Private Financial:
- Corporate Shares $41
- Other $125

Government Sponsored Financing Agencies:
- Government Securities $40
- Consumer Credit 46
- Other Loans 36
- Mortgages $62
- Other Loans 34

Federal Reserve System:
- Government Securities $86
- Other 24
- Reserves $38
- Currency 68
- Other 4

Sources of Funds:
- Demand Deposits and Currency $305
- Time Deposits 425
- Other 177
- Time Deposits and Savings Accts. $370, Other 38
- Accrued Reserves from Premiums $150, Other Sources 97
- Accrued Reserves from Monthly Contributions $213
- Shares, Bonds, Commercial Paper, etc. $105
- Bonds $101

Totals:
- Government Securities $287
- Corporate Bonds 58
- Trade Credit 276
- Government and Other Loans 113
- Mortgages 52
- Miscellaneous 294
- Total $1,080

Corporate Shares $541

Agents, such as Securities Brokers, Trust Companies, etc.

Sources of Funds Total:
- Households $2,183
- Governments 217
- Businesses 580
- Rest of the World 224
- Total $3,204

[a]To retain perspective of the relative sizes of financial intermediaries, some interinstitutional claims—e.g., bank loans to finance companies—have been included twice in this presentation. Hence, the amounts shown for sources and uses of funds do not balance. Many smaller claims have been submitted.

[b]Includes $7.5 billion in government life insurance programs.

[c]Includes state and local government retirement funds ($72 billion) and federal government pension funds ($33 billion).

Source: Board of Governors of the Federal Reserve System, *Flow of Funds, Assets and Liabilities Outstanding, 1974,* (Washington, D.C.: May 1975).

sides of the flow of funds. On the lending (credit) side, they compete in markets for business loans, mortgages, consumer credit, and so forth. On the collection (savings) side, they compete for funds by offering checking accounts, savings accounts, annuities, bonds, and so forth. Not all institutions compete on the same basis. For example, people's contributions to pension funds are usually arranged (or paid) by their employers. Hence these investments are nondiscretionary, and the pension funds don't "compete" for funds in the same way that banks and thrift institutions do. Similarly, the non-life insurance companies derive their funds by offering a service (protection from risk) and can't be considered direct competitors of the banks.

All financial intermediaries, of course, compete for funds with direct investments such as stocks and bonds, trade credit, and so forth. Table 3-1 shows that the balance in this competition has shifted slightly from direct investments toward financial intermediation since World War II (principally because of the declining role of government bonds). The table also shows that intermediaries capture about half of the surplus funds of households, but only a quarter or less of those of businesses and governments. A similar pattern exists in the competition for loans. Households obtain the majority of their loans from financial intermediaries, while businesses and governments derive most of their funds from direct issues of bonds and other securities. Here again, the proportion which passes through intermediaries has slightly increased since World War II (refer to Chapter Two, Tables 2-16 and 2-20).

Commercial Bank Services

Commercial banks possess the broadest depository and lending powers of all the financial intermediaries. Some of their services are exclusive privileges granted to commercial banks alone—for example, they are the only institution with the power to create money on the basis of cash reserves held against demand deposits of corporations and individuals. They also offer a variety of time and savings deposit accounts. Their credit-granting services include short- and long-term business loans, commercial and residential mortgage loans, consumer installment loans, farm loans, and bank credit cards. Because of the variety of their services, commercial banks have often been called the "department stores of finance."

At the end of 1974, *demand deposits* totaled $227 billion and their volume has been growing over the years. However, as a percentage of total commercial bank liabilities they have declined steadily, from 69 percent in 1950 to 60 percent in 1960 to 31 percent today, as depositors have shown increasing preference for interest-bearing time and savings accounts. Households are by far the largest holders of demand deposits and currency in commercial banks. They now account for more than half of such deposits (61 percent) and their share has been gradually increasing over the years. In comparison, businesses

Table 3-1. Comparison of Financial Assets in Financial Intermediaries Versus Direct Market Instruments, by Sector—1945-1974 (Amounts Outstanding in Millions of Dollars)

	1945		1950		1955		1960		1965		1970		1972		1974	
	$	%	$	%	$	%	$	%	$	%	$	%	$	%	$	%
Households																
Financial Intermediaries	158,637	42.7	206,542	46.3	299,912	42.3	432,219	44.4	676,651	46.2	970,138	50.6	1,237,780	51.3	1,376,600	63.1
Direct	213,313	57.3	240,031	53.7	408,669	57.7	540,542	55.6	786,899	53.8	946,917	49.4	1,175,285	48.7	806,000	36.9
Total	371,950	100.0	446,573	100.0	708,581	100.0	972,761	100.0	1,463,550	100.0	1,917,055	100.0	2,413,065	100.0	2,182,600	100.0
Businesses																
Financial Intermediaries	19,859	28.8	25,122	24.5	30,282	21.3	31,243	17.1	42,046	16.2	48,731	13.3	56,157	13.2	64,400	12.2
Direct	49,147	71.2	77,299	75.5	111,725	78.7	151,372	82.9	216,699	83.8	318,971	86.7	370,492	86.8	465,100	87.8
Total	69,006	100.0	102,421	100.0	142,007	100.0	182,615	100.0	258,745	100.0	367,702	100.0	426,649	100.0	529,500	100.0
Governments																
Financial Intermediaries	31,181	55.3	12,834	21.8	15,635	20.6	20,129	23.4	31,215	25.8	47,128	29.0	65,067	35.3	73,500	33.9
Direct	25,187	44.7	46,051	78.2	60,125	79.4	65,983	76.6	89,569	74.2	115,517	71.0	119,377	64.7	143,200	66.1
Total	56,368	100.0	58,885	100.0	75,760	100.0	86,112	100.0	120,784	100.0	162,645	100.0	184,444	100.0	216,700	100.0
All Sectors[a]																
Financial Intermediaries	209,677	42.2	244,498	40.2	345,829	37.3	483,591	39.0	749,912	40.7	1,065,997	43.6	1,359,004	44.9	1,491,500	51.3
Direct	287,647	57.8	363,381	59.8	580,519	62.7	757,897	61.0	1,093,167	59.3	1,381,405	56.4	1,665,154	55.1	1,414,300	48.7
Total	497,324	100.0	607,879	100.0	926,348	100.0	1,241,488	100.0	1,843,079	100.0	2,447,402	100.0	3,024,158	100.0	2,905,800	100.0

[a]Excludes incorporate business, forms, and rest of the world. The combined assets of these groups totaled $226 million in 1972.

Source: Calculated from Tables 2-16, 2-19, 2-20, and Figure 2-6.

hold 19 percent; federal, state, and local governments, 8 percent; and financial institutions, 7 percent.

Commercial banks also offer *time deposits and savings accounts* to households, corporate businesses, state and local governments, and others. Similar types of accounts are offered by the thrift institutions too, but mostly to a household clientele. In 1974 a total of $795 billion was held in time and savings accounts in all depository institutions, and more than half—$425 billion—was in commercial banks. Of this $425 billion, 77 percent was in passbook accounts or savings certificates owned by households, 12 percent was held by state and local governments, 7 percent by corporate business, and 4 percent by others. An important innovation in time deposits, introduced by banks in the early 1960s, is the *large negotiable certificate of deposit* (or simply, CD). This is a short-term security issued by banks in return for a deposit of $100,000 or more. It carries a higher yield than allowed on ordinary time deposits. For corporations, which previously were prevented by law from owning savings accounts in banks, it makes an attractive, liquid investment. The CD now accounts for the bulk of all corporate time deposits.

Commercial banks offer a complete line of credit to individuals, businesses, and farmers. They, along with finance companies and others, extend short- and long-term *business credit* on a local, regional, or national basis. In 1972 "business and other loans" of commercial banks totaled $193 billion, almost a third of all bank assets. This is the single most important item on the asset side of their balance sheet.

Commercial banks extend *mortgage credit* to households, farmers, and businesses. In this market their competitors are the savings and loan associations, life insurance companies, mutual savings banks, and some government-sponsored agencies. Competition is not always direct, since some institutions tend to specialize in particular segments of the market. In 1974 commercial banks supplied 19 percent ($131 billion) of the total mortgage credit outstanding. Their importance lies in commercial mortgages where they have captured nearly a third of the market. They also hold 18 percent of all single family residential mortgages, 8 percent of multifamily mortgages, and 13 percent of farm mortgages.

Banks (along with finance companies and credit unions) are important suppliers of *consumer credit*. In 1974 consumer credit held by commercial banks was valued at $84 billion, close to half of the total. Of this $84 billion, 36 percent was in automobile paper, 27 percent in other consumer goods paper (including bank credit cards), 18 percent in personal installment loans, 14 percent in single payment loans, and 5 percent in home improvement loans.

Banks also offer a range of services in which they are involved as an agent or as a manager rather than as a financial intermediary. By far the most important of these are the *trust services* in which the bank's trust department administers personal accounts (trusts and estates), employee benefit accounts (pension funds), and other agency accounts. In 1970 about 3,400 commercial banks in the United States had trust departments which administered more than one million accounts with an aggregate market value of $288 billion. By combining the assets of a number of small accounts and investing them as a unit, trust departments are able to achieve significant economies of scale. This has contributed to a high concentration of trust assets in the hands of a few large banks. In 1970, 52 banks accounted for 68 percent of total banks trust assets. One large trust department—Morgan Guaranty Trust Company in New York—alone held about 6 percent of total trust assets.

Recently there has been some concern over this accumulation of economic power and the potential conflict of interest situations arising from trust operations. Trust managers, through the sheer magnitude of their investments, hold large percentages of the common stock of some major corporations. For example, in 1967 Morgan Guaranty held 9.7 percent of Xerox Corporation's common stock, Chase Manhattan owned 8.7 percent of Boeing Aircraft, and the Mellon National Bank of Pittsburgh controlled more than a quarter of the common stock of Alcoa. Some people fear that such concentration of stock holdings can influence the corporate structure of our economy and have recommended closer government supervision of bank trust departments, or separation entirely. (See Table 3-12 for a synopsis of these recommendations.)

Equipment leasing services are being offered by increasing numbers of banks in an effort to provide their customers with more complete banking services and to take advantage of the improved profitability and tax benefits available through ownership and leasing. For several decades now, banks have been indirectly involved in the leasing industry as financiers of leasing firms. However, in 1963 the Comptroller of the Currency ruled that:

> A National Bank may become the owner or lessor of personal property acquired upon the specific request and for the use of a customer and may incur such additional obligations as may be incident to becoming an owner and lessor of such property.[1]

Since 1963, direct leasing by banks has grown substantially. By year end 1970, 390 national banks reported $790 million in equipment under lease. The movement gained momentum with the 1970 Amendments to the Bank Holding Company Act and subsequent decisions by the Federal Reserve Board which permitted holding companies to lease personal property. By June 1973, 557 national banks reported lease volume outstanding of $1.3 billion, and another 120 bank holding companies have established or acquired equipment leasing subsidiaries.

Since the middle 1960s, many banks have become part of bank holding companies, which can offer a broader range of financial services than the banks themselves can. Since many of these new services overlap the activities of other financial intermediaries, bank holding companies will be discussed in the next section of this chapter.

MAJOR COMPETITOR GROUPS

In the previous section we mentioned that banks face two forms of competition, one in acquiring funds and the other in lending them. During the 1960s the roles of these two forms reversed. As we have said in the second section of Chapter Two, the United States money supply expanded sharply during World War II and remained relatively plentiful until economic activity "caught up" to it in the 1960s. During this period, competition for funds was a minor matter. If banks needed more funds, they could simply sell off (or redeem) some of their government securities. Banks' attention was directed mostly toward competition in the lending of money to businesses (and, to a lesser degree, households). Generally, this competition was directed against other commercial banks, since by law most other types of institutions were excluded from this market.

By the late 1960s, economic growth had outpaced the money supply, and the availability of funds became a problem for banks. Banks turned their attention toward "liability management," which is another way of saying the competition for funds.

Banks' chief rivals in the competition for funds are the other institutions which can accept and pay interest on deposits, namely, the savings and loan associations, mutual savings banks, and credit unions. These so-called "thrift" institutions originated as mutual or cooperative associations of small savers, but in the postwar period have grown into an industry about half the size of commercial banking. Banks' other main competition for funds comes from direct investments, such as stocks and bonds. The remaining financial intermediaries—e.g., life insurance companies—obtain most of their funds in return for protection, or long-term annuities, or other services. Hence, they might be considered as indirect competitors for funds.

In the lending of funds, banks receive their most important competition from nonfinancial sources—e.g., commercial paper or trade credit extended by businesses to their customers. Thrift institutions concentrate most of their lending in mortgages, a market which (except for some specialties) is relatively unattractive to banks. Pension funds, insurance companies, and most of the other intermediaries put the bulk of their funds into mortgages, government bonds, or corporate debt issues—again an area relatively unattractive to banks. The most active competition lies in the area of consumer credit, where banks compete head-on with finance companies and direct lending by retail stores.

In the remainder of this section we will discuss some of these competitors in more detail. Readers who are interested only in the overall pattern of competition can glance at the summary in Tables 3-3, 3-6, 3-8, 3-9 and 3-11 and go on to the next section.

The Thrift Institutions

The thrift institutions—savings and loan associations (S&Ls), mutual savings banks (MSBs), and credit unions (CUs)—along with commercial banks are the nation's depository and lending institutions. Differences in their respective depository and lending powers and regulatory environments have helped to create the specialized institutions we know today, but not all of the specialization has been imposed by statute or regulation. While the thrifts have certainly become more sophisticated financial institutions over the years, they have also chosen to retain many of their original characteristics.

Savings and loan associations are the second largest financial intermediary in terms of total assets ($243.6 billion in 1972) and represent about 15 percent of all financial industry assets (see table 3-2). S&Ls have grown very rapidly over the years—in 1945 their assets amounted to only $8.7 billion, less than 4 percent of the industry total, and only about one-twenty-eighth of their recent level.

The first U.S. savings and loan association, organized in 1831 by a group of citizens in Frankford, Pennsylvania, was established as a neighborhood "building

Table 3-2. Total Assets of Financial Intermediaries, 1945 Versus 1972
(Dollars in billions)

Financial Intermediary	1945 $	1945 Percentage of Total	1972 $	1972 Percentage of Total
Commercial Banks	$160.3	66.2	$ 716.9	43.3
Thrift Institutions:				
Savings and Loan Associations	8.7	3.6	243.6	14.7
Mutual Savings Banks	17.0	7.0	100.6	6.1
Credit Unions	0.4	0.2	24.8	1.5
Other Financial Institutions:				
Life Insurance Companies	44.8	18.5	239.4	14.5
Pension Funds (private, state, local)	5.5	2.3	195.9	11.9
Finance Companies	4.3	1.8	73.7	4.5
Investment Companies	1.3	0.5	59.8	3.6
Total	$242.3	100.0	$1,654.7	100.0

Source: U.S. Savings and Loan League, *1973 Savings and Loan Fact Book* (Chicago: 1973), p. 53.

society" to lend money to its contributing members when their turn came up. As the name implies, most of its loans were used to buy homes. Since that time the operations of S&Ls have been formalized, and they have added nonborrowing savers as a principal source of funds. Their lending powers have been broadened somewhat, but regulations passed years ago to assure an adequate flow of funds to the home building industry still restrict the lending powers of S&Ls generally to real estate and passbook loans. S&Ls, like commercial banks, are both federally and state chartered (in approximately equal numbers) and some, accounting for about 20 percent of S&L assets, are organized as profit-making corporations. At the end of 1972, there were 5,448 S&Ls in the U.S., operating more than 11,000 offices.

Mutual savings banks are similar to S&Ls although they have somewhat more liberal loan and investment powers. Generally they may hold corporate debt and equity instruments. In 12 of the 18 states where they are chartered, they may make consumer loans; and in six states they may accept demand deposits. But still, like S&Ls they carry on a rather specialized business, deriving their funds from time and savings deposits and investing them in long-term obligations, especially mortgages. MSBs are much smaller than S&Ls in terms of total assets and have not grown as fast. They are located mostly in New England and the Middle Atlantic states, in part because there is no federal chartering of MSBs. Although MSBs supply only about one-eighth of the mortgage market, they rank first in holdings of FHA- and VA-guaranteed mortgages and are important sources of funds for special-purpose federal housing programs. Like S&Ls, they have retained many of their original characteristics, despite some broadening of their powers.

Credit unions are a tiny but fast-growing segment of the financial industry. Their assets in 1972 totaled $24.8 billion, only 3 percent of total commercial bank assets. Credit unions are characterized by a common-bond membership: that is, they are composed of individuals bound together by some common tie such as an employer; membership in a labor union, church, or fraternal organization; or residence in a well-defined geographic area. Members of CUs purchase shares resembling savings accounts and they may borrow from the association. Most CU loans are consumer installment loans with a relatively small face value and maturity of less than three years. Credit unions are estimated to supply about 15 percent of the automobile loans in the U.S. (see Table 3-9). Credit unions enjoy some advantages over other depository institutions. Occupational and associational CUs often operate in quarters provided by the host enterprise and are manned by volunteer workers. This results in low operating costs which allow the credit union to extend relatively low cost credit to its members. Members also enjoy the privilege of direct salary deductions for savings or loan payments.

Table 3-3 provides a summary of the characteristics of thrift institutions compared with those of commercial banks.

Thrift Institutions and the Competition for Funds

The thrift institutions have historically competed with commercial banks for time deposits and savings accounts largely on the basis of interest rates. Recently two developments within the thrift industry—NOW accounts and electronic funds transfer systems—have threatened the exclusive position of commercial banks in the demand deposit market. NOW accounts are a new type of savings account which permits the depositor to write negotiable orders of withdrawal payable to third parties. These accounts are presently being offered by a growing number of mutual savings banks in Massachusetts, New Hampshire, and New York and will very soon be offered by New Jersey MSBs. They differ from checking accounts in two respects: (1) interest is paid on the balance maintained in a NOW account whereas interest payments on demand deposits are prohibited by law, and (2) drafts written on NOW accounts are not technically demand instruments because withdrawal may be legally delayed for 30 days, although this is rarely exercised. Commercial banks have argued that NOW accounts are in effect interest-bearing checking accounts and that mutual savings banks which offer them have an unfair competitive advantage over commercial banks.

NOW accounts are growing rapidly in the states where they are allowed. As of July 31, 1974, 118 of the 167 MSBs in Massachusetts and 19 of the 34 MSBs in New Hampshire offered NOW accounts with total balances for the month of $162 million and $10 million respectively. Despite the growth of NOW balances, they are still small compared with total savings. For example, NOW balances in Massachusetts mutual savings banks were estimated to be only 1 percent of total savings deposits in the state.[2]

Electronic funds transfer technology, exemplified by the Transmatic Money Service (TMS) of the First Federal Savings and Loan Association in Lincoln, Nebraska, poses another potential threat to the exclusive demand deposit market of commercial banks. Through computer terminals which have been installed in supermarkets in the area, First Federal customers can deposit or withdraw on their savings accounts. This service was brought about in early 1974 by a new regulation of the Federal Home Loan Bank Board which essentially gave the S&Ls free rein in opening such electronic "branches". TMS touched off a storm of protest in the Nebraska banking community and three lawsuits were initiated to stop the service. Commercial banks in the area charged that the TMS outlets not only were branches (Nebraska is a unit banking state which prohibits branching) but also were performing a commercial bank function by allowing First Federal customers to use their savings accounts like checking accounts. Small banks opposed TMA because they feared that electronic banking would end unit banking; larger banks argued that they should be permitted to compete on equal terms. First Federal, on the other hand, argued that TMS was little more than an extension of banking by mail.

The thrift institutions compete directly with commercial banks for time

Table 3-3. Characteristics of Commercial Banks and Thrift Institutions

Item	Commercial Banks	Savings and Loan Associations	Mutual Savings Banks	Credit Unions
(1) Identifying Characteristics (Includes definition, chartering, number of firms, regionality, etc.)	Possess power to create money on the basis of cash reserves and in the process to expand credit in the form of loans and investments. Less specialized institutions that offer a department store of financial services. The only financial institution offering demand deposits to corporations and individuals. Offer savings and time deposits. Make business loans, consumer installment loans, other loans to individuals, real estate loans (commercial and residential), and farm loans. Operate throughout the country. In 1972, they numbered 13,950.	The largest of the specialized financial intermediaries. Channel savings into residential mortgages. Most are mutual organizations (where savers are shareholders). May also be stock associations. Offer savings and time deposits. Make residential mortgage loans. In 1972, they numbered 5,448, of which 3,404 were state chartered and 2,044 were federally chartered. Mutual associations numbered 4,783 and 665 were of stock form.	Unlike commercial banks, MSBs carry on a highly specialized business, stressing time and savings deposits and investment in long-term obligations, especially mortgages. Collect and channel savings of small investors into mortgages and other types of loans, government bonds, stocks and other securities. Do not generally accept demand deposits. Offer savings and time deposits. Make commercial and residential mortgage loans. All are state-chartered, nonstock depository institutions. Most located in New England and Middle Atlantic states. Important states are New York, Massachusetts, Connecticut, Pennsylvania, New Jersey. In 1972 they numbered 486.	Common-bond membership. Members own, control, and operate CU, either under Federal or state charter. Members purchase shares resembling savings accounts, and may borrow. Offer savings and time deposits. Make consumer installment loans. Located throughout country with high concentrations in California, Illinois, Michigan, New York, Ohio, Pennsylvania and Texas. In 1967, they numbered 23,200.

(2) Relative Importance	Hold about half of savings market, 17 percent of mortgages, and 45 percent of consumer credit. Share of credit card debt has grown from zero in 1965 to 35 percent today. Largest financial institution in terms of assets, time and savings deposits, commercial mortgages, installment and noninstallment credit.	The largest lenders in the home mortgage field. Also hold a large portion of all savings and time deposits (33 percent, 1972). Most important financial institution in terms of home mortgages and multifamily residential mortgages.	Important in mortgage market. Rank first in holdings of FHA and VA mortgages and are important sources of funds for special purpose federal housing programs. Important in local markets. Hold about one-third of savings accounts in savings bank states, but only 14 percent nationally.	Despite growth, are still relatively small.

(3) Source of Funds	1972 breakdown of total liabilities (percent):
	
	Demand deposits 28
	Time and savings deposits 38
	Government deposits (demand and time) 9
	Domestic interbank deposits 4
	Foreign government and bank deposits 2
	Other 2
	  Total deposits 83
	  Demand (38 percent)
	  Time (44 percent)
	Miscellaneous liabilities 9
	Reserves on loans and securities 1
	Capital accounts 7
	      100
		1972 breakdown of total liabilities (percent):
		
		Savings balances 85
		FHLB advances 4
		Reserves, undivided profits 6
		Loans in process 3
		Other 2
		  100
			1972 breakdown of total liabilities (percent):
			
			Savings deposits 91
			Surplus, undivided profits and other minor capital accounts 7
			Miscellaneous 2
			  100
				1967 breakdown of total liabilities (percent):
				
				Member shares 85
				
				Minor sources include reserves, retained earnings and borrowings from other CUs, banks, and other lenders.

Table 3-3 continued

		Thrift Institutions	
Item	Commercial Banks	Savings and Loan Associations	Mutual Savings Banks	Credit Unions
Percent of all time and savings accounts held (1945) (1972)	57 percent 50 percent	14 percent 33 percent	29 percent 14 percent	1 percent 3 percent
(4) Use of Funds (1972 breakdown of total assets) (percent)	Cash, bank balances, reserves, etc. reserves = 3 percent) Securities 15 Loans and discounts 25 Real estate loans (13 percent) Commercial and industry (18 percent) Automobile installment loans (4 percent) Other assets 53 — 7 100	Conventional mortgages 73 VA mortgages 6 FHA mortgages 6 Investment securities 9 Cash 1 Other 5 — 100	Cash and bank balances 2 U.S. government securities 8 Corporate stock 4 State, county, municipal obligations 1 Corporation bonds, notes, debentures 14 Real estate loans 67 Construction (1 percent) Farm (<1 percent) 1–4 family residential (46 percent) Multifamily (10 percent) Other (10 percent) Other assets 4 — 100	(1967 breakdown) Loans (mostly consumer) 78 Loans to other CUs, time deposits, government securities 22 — 100
Total assets 1945 (percent 1972 of all financial intermediaries)	$160.3 billions (66.2 percent) $716.9 billions (43.3 percent)	$8.7 billions (3.6 percent) $243.6 billions (14.7 percent)	$17.0 billions (7.0 percent) $100.6 billions (6.1 percent)	$0.4 billions (0.2 percent) $24.8 billions (1.5 percent)
Compound growth rate (percent): 1945–55, 1955–65, 1965–72	2.8, 6.0, 9.6	15.8, 13.1, 9.4	6.3, 6.4, 8.1	21.0, 14.7, 12.9
Percentage of all mortgage loans outstanding—1972	17.5	36.5	11.9	0

Percentage of 1–4 family nonfarm home mortgages—1972	16	48	12	0
Percentage of all multifamily nonfarm home mortgages—1972	7	27	20	0
Percentage of all commercial mortgage loans—1972	30	17	10	0
Percentage of all farm mortgage loans—1972	13	0	0	0
(5) Regulation and Supervision	FDIC supervises nonmember, insured, state chartered banks. FRS supervises state chartered member banks, which are also supervised by state agencies. Comptroller of Currency supervises national banks.	Federal Home Loan Bank Board supervises and examines all federal and state assns. insured by Federal Savings and Loan Insurance Corporation and noninsured state members of FHLB system if states do not supervise. State chartered associations usually supervised by state agency.	Supervised and examined by state banking departments. Those that belong to FDIC and FHLBS are also regulated by them.	State chartered CUs supervised by state superintendent of banks. Federal CUs, by National Credit Union Administration.
(6) Advantages to consumers	"One-stop banking" (offers a variety of savings and time accounts, checking accounts to corporations and individuals; offers variety of credit-granting services such as business loans, real estate loans, consumer installment loans, farm loans, credit cards, etc.).	Offer services to the small investor. High concentration in residential mortgages. Pay higher rates on time and savings accounts than commercial banks. Local orientation.		Convenience for small savers. Payroll deductions are often made. Cost of funds are reasonable and loans are made promptly. Offer free credit life insurance.

Sources: Robert P. Black and Doris E. Harless, *Nonbank Financial Institutions* (Federal Reserve Bank of Richmond, December 1969); Board of Governors of the Federal Reserve System, *Federal Reserve Bulletin* (Washington, D.C.: December 1973); Board of Governors of the Federal Reserve System, *Flow of Funds Accounts, 1945–1972* (Washington, D.C.: August 1973); U.S. Savings and Loan League, *1973 Savings and Loan Fact Book*, U.S. Savings and Loan League (Chicago: 1973).

deposits and savings accounts. Of the total $795 billion in such accounts at the end of 1974, half was in commercial banks, a third was in S&Ls, and the remainder in MSBs and CUs (see Table 3-4). In 1950 commercial banks held 52 percent of all time and savings deposits. Their share declined steadily to 42 percent in 1960, and has gained slightly since then because of the introduction of savings certificates. The portion in S&Ls increased rapidly from nineteen percent in 1950 to 35 percent in 1960 (Partly because S&Ls offered higher interest rates to depositors), and has since leveled off. MSBs have experienced a considerable decline over the years. Credit unions have increased somewhat, but they still account for only 3 percent of the total.

Disintermediation

It is important to remember that the comparisons above represent only one form of savings. People can, and do, invest their savings in a variety of other ways, such as purchases of U.S. savings bonds, corporate stocks and bonds, mutual funds, or investments in real assets, such as land, homes, antiques, or whatever. More than one-third of the personal wealth in America is in the form of real estate, and this proportion appears to be increasing.[3] Among financial assets, however, Table 2-20 showed that deposit accounts (checking or savings accounts) and corporate stock have remained, in relatively steady proportions, as the major repositories for surplus funds of households for more than two decades. Thus, it seems reasonable to say that time and savings deposits constitute a meaningful, separate market in which banks compete.

There is a relatively mobile segment of the savings market which will "disintermediate" during periods of tight credit. This segment consists of interest-

Table 3-4. Location of Time and Savings Deposits—1950, 1960, 1974
(Dollars in millions)

Financial Intermediary	1950 $	Percentage of Total	1960 $	Percentage of Total	1974 $	Percentage of Total
Commercial Banks	$37,031	52	$ 73,623	42	$924,600	53
Savings and Loan Associations	13,992	19	62,142	35	243,200	31
Mututal Savings Banks	20,025	28	36,343	21	99,500	13
Credit Unions	850	1	4,981	3	27,600	3
Total	$71,898	100	$177,089	100	$794,900	100

Source: Board of Governors of the Federal Reserve System, *Flow of Funds Accounts, 1945-1972* (Washington, D.C.: August 1973), pp. 111-113 and *Flow of Funds, Assets and Liabilities Outstanding, 1974.*

sensitive depositors who shift their funds to other assets when market interest rates rise above the interest ceilings allowed on savings deposits. Typically, these other assets are direct investments—e.g., government bonds—which do not involve a financial intermediary—hence the term *disintermediation*. Clearly, the greater the advantage of money market yields over the yield on savings accounts, the greater will be the amount of disintermediation. This has been manifested by the enthusiastic reception of recent high-yielding bond issues, accompanied by a net outflow of funds from savings institutions.

When money market yields have subsided to more traditional levels in the past, households have returned to savings deposits (see Table 3-5). Evidently, they have preferred the convenience and safety of the savings deposits to the more volatile, and generally less liquid, money market securities. The 1973-1974 credit crunch brought some institutional changes which may alter this historical pattern. First, and most visible, were the so-called "floating rate bonds" introduced by bank holding companies. These were bonds whose periodic interest payments varied according to formulas, based on current money market rates.[4] These bonds were offered in $1,000 denominations and could be redeemed at par every six months. Thus, they had many of the features of the very popular savings certificates issued by banks and thrift institutions, combined with a better yield. They do, however, lack the safety of federal insurance which savings deposits carry. Secondly, several forms of money market "mutual funds" were created which offered, to the small investor, yields which previously had been available only to large corporations and institutional investors. They

Table 3-5. Annual Change in Depository Savings and Direct Investments of Households, 1960-1972 (Billions of dollars)

	Year	Savings Deposits	Credit and Equity Instruments	
	1960	$12.4	$ 4.5	
	1961	17.4	3.0	
	1962	23.4	-0.8	
	1963	23.0	1.3	
	1964	23.9	4.0	
	1965	26.4	2.5	
	1966	19.1	11.9	← Disintermediation
Reintermediation →	1967	33.7	0.0	
	1968	28.6	5.8	
	1969	13.3	18.4	← Disintermediation
	1970	44.7	7.8	
Reintermediation →	1971	73.6	-16.8	
Reintermediation →	1972	79.0	0.4	

Source: U.S. Savings and Loan League, *1973 Savings and Loan Fact Book* (Chicago: 1973), p. 12.

featured low transaction costs and withdrawals on demand. Thus, they offered the features of savings accounts, except for federal insurance and guaranteed interest rates, again combined with a much better yield.

No one can predict confidently whether these new outlets for savings will attract a permanent following or whether people will continue to "reintermediate" as in previous cycles. The whole issue of disintermediation is created—in a sense, artificially—by federal and state regulations which prevent price competition. Without these restrictions, banks and thrift institutions could offer added incentives to savers to more accurately reflect market conditions and these new forms of investment would be much less likely to survive. Disintermediation is, however, a politically charged matter. Even though the mobile funds represent only 1 or 2 percent of the savings deposits in the country, these marginal shifts can have substantial short-term impacts. Thrift institutions, as already mentioned, invest the bulk of their funds in home mortgages. Furthermore, they rely upon deposit growth for about half the funds they lend every year. Thus, disintermediation which stops that growth or results in a new outflow of savings deposits can effectively dry up the availability of mortgages. That in turn tends to cause public pressure on Congress to alleviate the situation. Many of the measures proposed call for further government restrictions—e.g., placing the floating rate bonds of bank holding companies under control of the Federal Reserve Board. Other proposals call for releasing the interest ceilings on savings accounts.

Thrift Institutions and the Competition in Lending

As we have said, thrift institutions concentrate their lending activities in mortgages. Total mortgage credit outstanding was valued at $694 billion in 1974. Commercial banks supplied $131 billion, or 19 percent, of this total, savings and loan associations, 36 percent, and mutual savings banks, 11 percent. The remainder was held by life insurance companies (12 percent), households, government-sponsored credit agencies, and others (see Table 3-6).

Within the mortgage market, commercial banks and the thrift institutions specialize to some extent (see Table 3-7). Banks are important suppliers of mortgages on commercial properties. They account for nearly one-third of commercial mortgages, an increase from about 20 percent in the 1950s and 1960s. Similarly, life insurance companies focus their mortgages in apartment buildings and commercial properties. Government agencies and private individuals supply most of the farm mortgages. The largest segment—single family home mortgages—is now largely the province of the thrift institutions. This specialization in mortgage markets is partly a result of various laws which impose portfolio restrictions on the different institutions, particularly the thrifts. State usury laws tend to make home mortgages unattractive to the commercial banks and insurance companies, which have greater freedom in their investment choices.

Table 3-6. Total Mortgage Credit Outstanding, by Supplier—1950, 1960, 1974 (Dollars in millions)

Supplier	1950 $	Percentage of Total	1960 $	Percentage of Total	1974 $	Percentage of Total
Commercial Banks	$13,663	19	$28,806	14	$131,300	19
Thrift Institutions:						
Savings and Loan Associations	13,657	19	60,070	29	249,700	36
Mutual Savings Banks	8,262	11	26,935	13	75,400	11
Credit Unions	66	0	377	0	1,000	0
Other Financial Institutions:						
Life Insurance Companies	16,102	22	41,771	20	86,300	12
Pension Funds, Retirement Funds, and Other Insurance	281	0	2,900	1	9,900	1
Finance Companies	454	1	1,611	1	10,800	2
Real Estate Investment Trusts	0	0	0	0	15,800	2
Others:						
Households	17,363	24	31,844	15	39,300	6
Government-Sponsored Credit Agencies	952	1	5,467	3	61,900	9
Federal, State, and Local Governments (General Funds)	2,017	3	7,064	3	12,700	2
Total	$72,817	100	$206,845	100	$694,100	100

Source: Board of Governors of the Federal Reserve System, *Flow of Funds Accounts, 1945-1972* (Washington, D.C.: August 1973), pp. 117-119, and *Flow of Funds, Assets and Liabilities Outstanding,* 1974.

Other Forms of Competition for Banks

Many other firms compete with banks. Some of this competition is head on in specific markets—e.g., installment loans offered by consumer finance companies, or mortgages offered by life insurance companies. Other forms of competition are less direct; for example, the trade credit extended to small businesses by their suppliers helps to reduce their need for bank loans. Similarly, department store charge accounts are a form of competition to banks. In these cases, the extension of credit is ancillary to the main business of the firm.

Almost all of the other forms of competition relate to the lending of funds.

As already mentioned, banks' competition in obtaining funds comes largely from the thrift institutions or direct investments (see Figure 3-1).

In the past decade, banks have held or increased their market share in practically all the lending markets they serve. They have further invaded the markets of their competitors through holding company expansion. Most bank holding company affiliates are specialized subsidiaries which compete head on with the nonbank firms that already were competing, perhaps less directly, with banks. To explain this picture more clearly, this section looks briefly at the lending markets in question and the major participants in them. (See also Table 3-8 which summarizes the activities of other financial intermediaries.)

Historically, business loans have been the bread and butter of commercial banks. Originally, business loans were mostly loans for a few months to cover seasonal peaks in inventory or accounts receivable. Gradually they have expanded to cover a wide range of financing including loans of five to seven years for plant and equipment, construction loans, and term loans to new ventures. At year end, 1974, banks had $189 billion in business loans outstanding.

Aside from new issues of stocks and bonds, the alternate sources of (non-mortgage) credit for businesses have been the following:

1. finance companies, including "factors" who specialize in the financing of receivables ($25 billion in 1974);
2. trade credit extended by suppliers to their customers ($175 billion in 1972);
3. venture capital firms, individuals, and miscellaneous sources ($17 billion in 1972);
4. the commercial paper market, consisting of banks or large corporations with short-term (less than 270 days) funds to invest ($9 billion in 1972);
5. leasing firms, a comparatively recent source, which technically do not extend credit but offer its advantages (more than $20 billion in 1972).

Table 3-9 (calculated from Table 2-16) shows a relative increase in the importance of bank loans as a source of credit for businesses. During World War II, banks' funds were largely absorbed in the financing of the federal debt, and this table reflects their return to the banking business. Since 1960 the patterns have remained relatively stable. The principal changes in recent years have been the growth of the commercial paper market and the rise of leasing activities.

As mentioned in Chapter Two, banks and bank holding companies have become active participants in the leasing business. In a recent survey, bank holding companies accounted for $3 billion, an estimated 20 percent of the leases outstanding in August 1973. In addition, banks themselves had at least $1.3 billion in leases outstanding. This would imply that banks and their holding company affiliates account for about a quarter of the leasing market. Their principal competitors are investment banking firms, finance companies, and specialized lease packagers.

Table 3-7. Mortgage Credit Outstanding, Supplier and Type of Mortgage, 1974 (Dollars in millions)

Supplier	Residential Mortgages — Single Family $	Percentage of Total	Residential Mortgages — Multifamily $	Percentage of Total	Commercial Mortgages $	Percentage of Total	Farm Mortgages $	Percentage of Total	Total $	Percentage of Total
Commercial Banks	$ 74,400	18	$ 7,500	8	$ 43,500	32	$ 5,900	13	$131,300	19
Thrift Institutions:										
Savings & Loan Associations	201,900	48	23,700	25	24,100	18	0	0	249,700	36
Mutual Savings Banks	44,900	11	17,300	18	13,100	10	1	—	75,400	11
Credit Unions	1,000	—	0	0	0	0	0	0	1,000	—
Other Financial Institutions:										
Life Insurance Companies	22,400	5	20,000	21	37,600	28	6,300	14	86,300	12
Pension Funds, Retirement Funds and Other Insurance	2,700	1	7,000	7	200	—	0	0	2,700	—
Finance Companies	10,800	3	0	0	0	0	0	0	10,800	2
Real Estate Investment Trusts	4,400	1	3,900	4	7,500	6	0	0	15,800	2
Others:										
Households	10,000	2	2,200	2	10,300	8	16,800	38	39,300	6
Government-Sponsored Credit Agencies	41,300	10	6,700	7	—	—	13,900	32	61,900	9
Federal, State and Local Governments (General Funds)	6,600	2	5,300	6	—	—	900	2	12,700	2
Total	$420,300	100	$93,600	100	$136,300	100	$43,800	100	$694,100	100

Source: Board of Governors of the Federal Reserve System, *Flow of Funds, Assets and Liabilities Outstanding, 1974* (Washington, D.C.: May 1975).

Table 3-8. Characteristics of Other Financial Institutions

	Other Financial Institutions			
Item	Life Insurance Companies	Finance Companies	Investment Companies	Pension Funds
(1) Identifying Characteristics	Provide death benefits, and in the process accumulate vast amounts of policy reserves by charging premiums that exceed cost of benefit payments during early years of a policy. Reserves are invested, mostly in domestic corporate bonds and mortgages. Stock or mutual form of ownership. In 1967, they numbered 1,725.	Sales finance companies' major lending operation is financing of autos and other consumer durables primarily by purchasing consumer installment paper directly from dealers. Consumer finance companies mostly make personal cash loans.	A device for pooling and investing the funds of a number of investors in a wide range of securities to obtain diversification & portfolio management at a reasonable fee. Open- or closed-end form.	Noninsured funds are generally individual financial entities with assets separate from parent institution. Investments often handled by bank or banks. Some are funded by setting contributions, others are profit-sharing. Insured funds not a separate financial entity. Instead of investing to provide retirement benefits, they use contributions as premiums to buy retirement benefits.
(2) Relative Importance	Supply about 14 percent of mortgage credit, following S&Ls, 36 percent, and commercial banks, 17 percent.	Consumer installment credit. In 1972, they held 25 percent of total installment credit, second only to the 47 percent held by commercial banks.	Influence in the stock market—in 1967, their portfolios of common & preferred stocks equalled 7 percent of total market value of stocks outstanding and 40 percent of amt. owned by principal financial institutions.	Pension funds have grown much faster than other household assets. In 1945, they accounted for only 3 percent of household assets; today, 13 percent.
(3) Source of Funds (percent)	About 80 percent from policyholders' savings in the form of policy reserves; net worth, 9 percent. Limited funds from	sales / consumer Long term debt 38 41 Notes payable to banks 12 14 Commercial	Common stock Most used no borrowed funds. Net worth practically = total assets	Employer contributions 56 Employee payments 7 Investment income 27 Realized capital gains 10 100

	(Life insurance companies)	(Sales and consumer finance companies)	(Investment companies)	(Other)
(4) Use of Funds (percent)	bank loans, dividends accumulating at interest, and amounts set aside for policy dividends.	paper and other short-term notes 30, 16 Other liabilities 5, 7 Net worth 15, 21 —— 100, 100	Most channel all assets not needed for liquidity into common stock. Some also invest in preferred stock and bonds. Small percent kept in cash, bank balances, government securities. Some specialize in "growth stocks," others in "defensive issues," and others in "income stocks." Some confine purchases to particular industry or locality.	Recent in investment trends: (1) rapid buildup in common stock portfolios, (2) growing investments in real estate, (3) decrease in corporate bonds and government securities.
	(1967) Domestic corporate bonds 37 Other securities 12 Mortgages 38 Policy loans 6 Other 8 —— 100	*Sales finance companies* (1967) Retail passenger auto paper 37 Other consumer goods paper 21 Personal and other consumer loans 12 Retail commercial and wholesale auto paper 14 Other business credit 16 —— 100 *Consumer finance companies* Personal loans 84 Automobile paper 2 Other consumer goods paper 8 Other credit 6 —— 100		Common stock 47 Corporate bonds 36 Mortgages 6 U.S. government securities 3 Cash and deposits 2 Preferred stock 1 Other 6 —— 100
Total assets 1945 (percent of all financial intermediaries)	$44.8 billions (18.5 percent)	$4.3 billions (1.8 percent)	$1.3 billions (0.5 percent)	$5.5 billions (2.3 percent)
1972	$239.4 billions (14.5 percent)	$73.7 billions (4.5 percent)	$59.8 billions (3.6 percent)	$195.9 billions (11.9 percent)
Compound growth rate (percent): 1945–55, 1955–65, 1965–72	7.3, 5.8, 6.0	14.8, 9.1, 8.7	19.6, 16.3, 7.9	18.1, 13.9, 9.1
Percentage of all mortgage loans outstanding – 1972	14	2	0	2

Table 3-8 continued

Item	Life Insurance Companies	Finance Companies	Investment Companies	Pension Funds
Percentage of all 1–4 family mortgage loans outstanding—1972	6	3	0	1
Percentage of all multi-family mortgage loans outstanding—1972	22	0	0	9
Percentage of all commercial mortgage loans outstanding—1972	30	0	0	0
Percentage of all farm mortgage loans outstanding—1972	16	0	0	0
(5) Regulation and Supervision	Regulation by the states. Covers the licensing of companies and agents, incorporation, business practices, methods and assumptions used in calculating reserves,	In a number of states, sales financial companies regulated by state laws governing installment selling. In other states, no direct regulation. Consumer finance companies operate under state small loan laws.	Very tightly regulated. Subject to several Federal security laws including (1) Securities Act of 1933, (2) The Securities Exchange Act of 1934, (3) The Investment Company Act of 1940.	Federal regulatory legislation includes The Welfare and Pension Plans Disclosure Act and laws governing investments. IRS grants noninsured funds exemption from federal income taxes under certain conditions. 1974 Pension Act.

	permissible investments, etc. Subject to special income tax rules—must pay regular Federal corporate income tax rates, but only part of underwriting profits and investment income is taxable.	Both must conform to "truth-in-lending" legislation.	They are also subject to state acts governing sale of securities and the activities of brokers and dealers.
(6) Advantages to Consumer	Cash payments are made to beneficiaries in the event of death, on reaching a certain age, in case of disability, or for other reasons. Offers protection to the individual by spreading the economic risk.	Relative ease in acquiring installment credit and individuals often enabled to purchase goods they could not otherwise own because of small weekly or monthly payments.	Higher returns during periods of high market rates when ceiling rates at financial institutions lag behind. Relative safety of investments because of diversified portfolios, subject to stock market fluctuations.	Provide economic security in retirement years.

Sources: Robert P. Black and Doris E. Harless, *Nonbank Financial Institutions* (Federal Reserve Bank of Richmond: December 1969); Board of Governors of the Federal Reserve System, *Federal Reserve Bulletin* (Washington, D.C.: December 1973); Board of Governors of the Federal Reserve System, *Flow of Funds Accounts, 1945-1972* (Washington, D.C.: August 1973); U.S. Savings and Loan League, *1973 Savings and Loan Fact Book* (Chicago: U.S. Savings and Loan League, 1973).

90 Trends Affecting the U.S. Banking System

Table 3-9. Percentage Composition of Short-Term Business Debt[a], 1945-1974

	1945	1950	1955	1960	1965	1970	1971	1974
Bank Loans	25	25	25	29	30	33	33	37
Finance Company Loans	3	2	2	4	4	4	5	5
Deferred Taxes	28	23	20	10	10	4	4	4
Trade Debt	36	44	46	49	50	51	50	45
Commercial Paper	0	0	1	1	1	3	3	3
Miscellaneous	8	5	6	6	5	5	5	4
Total[b]	100	100	100	100	100	100	100	100

[a]Liabilities of corporate, nonfinancial businesses, excluding bonds, mortgages, and lease obligations.
[b]Detail may not add to total because of rounding.
Source: Calculated from Table 2-16.

The growth in the commercial paper market, if it becomes permanent, may represent a loss of customers for banks. During the 1960s, the number of firms issuing commercial paper doubled (to about 650 in 1969), and activity has increased sharply in the recent credit shortage. The volume of paper has increased more than one-third since the beginning of 1973. The number of institutions and investors who buy commercial paper (generally in quantities of $100,000 or more) has also expanded. With a broader, more stable market, commercial paper may continue to grow even if bank credit becomes easier to obtain. The growth of the use of commercial paper does not mean that banks lose their customer relationships altogether, though, because commercial paper issuers normally keep a matching line of bank credit as a guarantee for their paper.

Part of the growth in commercial paper has come from the bank holding companies themselves, as a device for financing their nonbank activities. At the end of 1973, holding companies were responsible for about 12 percent of the paper outstanding.

As Table 3-6 showed, banks hold about 19 percent of the mortgages outstanding; their principal competitors are the thrift institutions (47 percent) and life insurance companies (12 percent). There is another form of competition, however, which these statistics fail to show. That is the activity called mortgage banking. Many lenders, such as pension funds, trusts, and some insurance companies, have no facilities for originating mortgages, checking borrowers' credit, making certain payments are made on time, and so forth. Instead, they rely on firms called mortgage bankers which act as brokers in finding mortgages and as agents in servicing them. These firms tend to specialize in large, commercial or apartment mortgages or in "packages" of home mortgages (for example, in financing a Levittown development). Mortgage bankers may also finance some of the mortgages with their own capital.

This field has been a popular choice of the bank holding companies, which now operate more than 300 mortgage banking firms. Bank holding companies own six of the ten largest mortgage banking firms in the U.S., servicing some $10 billion in mortgages (more than half the total for these ten firms).

The move of bank holding companies into mortgage banking is competitively more significant than the dollar figures may suggest. First, commercial mortgages are a field in which banks have specialized; they hold about 30 percent of these mortgages. Operating a mortgage banking subsidiary allows a bank, in effect, to extend its mortgage department nationwide. Second, the arrangement opens up possibilities for combined financing packages that include the mortgage, construction financing, and other banking services.

Consumer loans are obtained principally from banks, finance companies, and credit unions. These sources account for more than three-fourths of the recorded consumer credit in the U.S. (see Table 3-10). The other significant sources are credit cards and retail stores.

About 30 percent of consumer credit is applied to the financing of automobiles and commercial banks supply well over half of this market (see Table 3-10). In earlier years, the captive finance companies of auto manufacturers played a bigger role, but as banks have become less conservative in their lending policies, they have gained in market share. Unsecured personal loans account for another fifth of consumer credit, though this proportion was much less (1/8) in 1950. Commercial banks' share of this market has remained about 35 percent.

The remaining consumer credit (about 50 percent), is divided among a diverse array of purposes: home improvements, boats, campers, mobile homes, homes appliances, charge accounts, and so forth. As Table 3-10 shows, banks' share of most of these markets has held steady or improved in recent times. Banks' overall share of consumer credit has advanced from 34 percent in 1950 to 44 percent in 1974, and it still is increasing.

Two recent trends are evident in the consumer credit markets. First is the declining importance of retail stores as a source of credit. In 1950 they provided 29 percent of the consumer credit; now they provide half of that share. Partly, the charge is a statistical fluke. Some large department store chains, notably Sears Roebuck, have reorganized their credit operations as captive finance companies. Others, particularly furniture and appliance dealers, have contracted their credit operations to firms such as CIT Financial Corp. or G.E. Credit Corp. Also important are the bank credit cards which have induced many smaller retailers to give up their own credit operations in favor of accepting the two nationwide bank cards.

Second, bank holding companies have started or purchased about 450 consumer finance companies in recent years, representing an additional lending

Table 3-10. Consumer Credit Outstanding, by Type of Credit and Institution—1950, 1960, 1974 (Dollars in millions)

Year and Institution	Automobile Paper $	%	Bank Credit Cards $	%	Mobile Homes $	%	Other Paper $	%	Home Improvement $	%	Personal Loans $	%	Total Installment Credit $	%	Single Payment Loans $	%	Charge Accounts $	%	Service Credit $	%	Total Noninstallment Credit $	%	Total Consumer Credit (Installment plus Noninstallment) $	%
1950																								
Commercial Banks	$ 2,471	41	$ 0	—	—	—	$ 1,456	30	$ 834	82	$ 1,037	37	$ 5,798	39	$ 1,576	87	0	0	0	0	$ 1,576	23	$ 7,374	34
Finance Companies	3,157	52	—	—	—	—	692	14	80	8	1,386	49	5,315	36	245	13	0	0	0	0	245	4	6,252	29
Thrift Institutions	159	3	—	—	—	—	40	1	102	10	391	14	692	5	0	0	3,291	98	0	0	3,291	49	6,189	29
Retail Outlets	287	5	—	—	—	—	2,611	54	0	0	0	0	2,898	20	0	0	76	2	0	0	76	1	76	0
Credit Cards[a]	0	0	—	—	—	—	0	0	0	0	0	0	0	0	0	0	0	0	0	0	0	0	0	0
Other Nonfinance Companies	0	0	—	—	—	—	0	0	0	0	0	0	0	0	0	0	0	0	$1,580	100	1,580	23	1,580	7
Total	$ 6,074	100	$ 0	—	—	—	$ 4,799	100	$1,016	100	$ 2,814	100	$14,703	100	$ 1,821	100	$3,367	100	$1,580	100	$ 6,768	100	$21,471	100
1960																								
Commercial Banks	$ 8,136	46	$ 0	—	—	—	$ 2,759	24	$2,200	70	$ 3,577	34	$16,672	39	$ 3,884	86	0	0	0	0	$ 3,884	29	$20,556	37
Finance Companies	7,703	44	—	—	—	—	2,553	22	173	5	5,006	47	15,435	36	623	14	0	0	0	0	623	5	20,624	37
Thrift Institutions	1,460	8	—	—	—	—	297	3	775	25	2,034	19	4,566	11	0	0	4,893	92	0	0	4,893	37	11,188	20
Retail Outlets	359	2	—	—	—	—	5,936	51	0	0	0	0	6,295	15	0	0	436	8	0	0	436	3	436	1
Credit Cards[a]	0	0	—	—	—	—	0	0	0	0	0	0	0	0	0	0	0	0	0	0	0	0	0	0
Other Nonfinance Companies	0	0	—	—	—	—	0	0	0	0	0	0	0	0	0	0	0	0	3,337	100	3,337	25	3,337	6
Total	$17,658	100	$ 0	—	—	—	$11,545	100	$3,148	100	$10,617	100	$42,968	100	$ 4,507	100	$5,329	100	$3,337	100	$13,173	100	$56,141	100
1974																								
Commercial Banks	$30,369	59	$8,242	100	$ 7,645	68	$ 6,414	20	$4,458	55	$15,382	35	$72,510	46	$11,500	89	0	0	0	0	$11,500	34	$84,010	44
Finance Companies	12,435	24	—	—	3,570	32	4,751	15	993	12	17,176	39	38,925	25	1,479	11	0	0	0	0	1,479	4	65,529	34
Thrift Institutions	8,599	17	—	—	—	—	2,200	7	2,711	33	11,706	26	25,216	16	0	0	8,012	79	0	0	8,012	24	27,485	14
Retail Outlets	286	1	—	—	—	—	19,473	60	0	0	0	0	19,473	12	0	0	2,122	21	0	0	2,122	6	2,122	1
Credit Cards[a]	0	0	—	—	—	—	0	0	0	0	0	0	0	0	0	0	0	0	0	0	0	0	0	0
Other Nonfinance Companies	0	0	—	—	—	—	0	0	0	0	0	0	0	0	0	0	0	0	10,884	100	10,884	32	10,884	6
Total	$51,689	100	$8,242	100	$11,215	100	$32,552	100	$8,162	100	$44,264	100	$156,124	100	$12,979	100	$10,134	100	$10,884	100	$33,997	100	$190,121	100

[a] Service station and miscellaneous credit cards and home heating oil accounts.

Detail may not add to totals because of rounding.

Source: U.S. Board of Governors of the Federal Reserve System, *Federal Reserve Bulletin* (Washington, D.C.: December 1973), pp. A54-55 and *Federal Reserve Bulletin*, Feb. 1975, pp. 446-47.

volume of at least $6 billion. No doubt there are some economies in combining banks with consumer finance companies in the same holding company, but the move is also viewed as a strategic positioning for the future world of electronic banking. Consumer finance companies presently have high costs of originating and servicing loans. These costs, not defaults, are the principal reason they must charge high interest rates. In an electronic environment, many of these costs should be greatly reduced and, the argument goes, the holding companies with their banking expertise can exploit these savings more quickly and profitably than other finance companies.

Foreign Banks

Over the past decade, many foreign banks have added branches and expanded their operations in the United States. About 60 foreign banks do business in this country, and they hold about $38 billion in assets, which is nearly 5 percent of all U.S. bank assets. In 1965, foreign banks held only about $7 billion in assets. These activities are still small in comparison to the overseas operations of U.S. banks. There are now 136 U.S. banks operating almost 700 foreign branches and holding approximately $125 billion in assets abroad.[5] As Table 3-11 shows, the number of branches has more than tripled since 1965.

The great majority of foreign bank activities in the U.S. are in New York City and in California. The foreign banks use several methods of establishing their presence here. The simplest way is to open a *representative office* ("Edge Act" office) which can discuss, but not conduct, banking operations. There are about 140 foreign representative offices in the U.S. A foreign bank can also open *agencies* which, under state laws, can conduct commercial banking operations—e.g., currency exchanges, money market transactions for the parent bank, etc.—but cannot accept deposits. At the end of 1972, foreign bank agencies held $11 billion in assets. *Branches* of foreign banks can accept deposits of the

Table 3-11. Number of Foreign Branches of U.S. Commercial Banks

Location	1945	1950	1955	1960	1965	1970	1973
Europe	12	15	17	19	43	116	157
Latin America and Caribbean	42	49	56	55	88	273	345
Near East	–	–	4	4	5	12	15
Far East	6	19	20	23	50	78	105
Africa	–	–	–	1	2	2	2
U.S. Possessions and Dependencies	12	12	14	22	23	41	52
Other	–	–	–	–	–	10	23
Total Foreign Branches	72	95	111	124	211	532	699

Source: Board of Governors of the Federal Reserve System, *Annual Reports*, respective years.

same sort as domestic banks, but they are ineligible for federal deposit insurance. A sizable proportion of their deposits comes from overseas sources. Finally, a foreign bank can establish U.S. *subsidiaries,* such as Bank of Tokyo Trust Co., in New York, or Sumitomo Bank of California, in San Francisco. These subsidiaries, of course, compete on an equal footing with domestic banks.

Most observers agree that the foreign banks have opened offices here to service international trade and to gain access to the New York money markets. Although some banks have entered directly into retail banking—e.g., Lloyds Bank in California—most of the foreign offices attend to international payments settlements, service for the parent bank, or services for foreign corporations doing business in the U.S. A study by the Federal Reserve Bank of New York said:

> Despite the marked expansion of foreign banking in this country in recent years, the overall role of foreign-owned institutions in the U.S. financial system should not be exaggerated. It is true that a few affiliates of foreign banks in New York and California have built up an impressive commercial loan business, and [they] now occupy an important place among the medium-size banks in these two states. But none of these institutions seriously challenge the commanding position of the major multinational banks in this country. The Japanese banks' agencies in New York and their subsidiaries and branches in California—by far the most important national group of foreign-owned banking institutions—finance much of the United States-Japanese trade, and some members of this group have become very sizable banking institutions. However, a major part of their loans is refinanced directly or indirectly by domestic banks. The agencies of Canadian banks in New York and several of the New York branches of foreign banks now provide a respectable amount of loans to commercial borrowers. Still, most of their activities, and virtually all transactions of many other agencies and other branches, remain oriented toward money market and foreign exchange operations and attending to the dollar payments traffic of their parent organizations.[6]

The converse picture is true of American banks operating foreign branches. The banks originally opened the branches to follow the overseas spread of U.S. corporations and then expand into overseas money market operations and finally into retail banking. With the exception, perhaps, of Great Britain, they remain as relatively small factors in the retail banking markets of the countries they serve.

PROPOSALS TO REFORM THE FINANCIAL SYSTEM

As we have mentioned, different financial institutions are limited by law to certain types of loans, maximum interest rates payable on deposits, types of deposits they can accept, and so forth. Unfortunately, economic conditions change more often than the regulations do and it frequently happens that the regulations are out of tune with the times. Most of the regulatory structure which affects financial institutions was established during the Depression (this is discussed further in Chapter Four), and many critics feel that the 40-year-old regulations produce aberrant behavior (e.g., in disintermediation) in today's economy. Some of the more common complaints with the U.S. financial system are as follows:

1. The supply of savings is not growing as fast as the projected requirements for capital.
2. Periodic booms and recessions upset people'e plans, and their impact falls unevenly (and unfairly) on small businesses, disadvantaged minorities, and certain other groups.
3. The availability of mortgages dries up during these cycles, collapsing the construction industry and interfering with people's mobility.
4. The consumer faces an unnecessarily complicated array of financial institutions and investment mechanisms, and he must often keep multiple account relationships to meet his needs adequately.

Over the years, a number of proposals have arisen for reform of the financial regulations, and some laws have been passed—e.g., the bank holding company legislation. Still, the fundamental regulations are unchanged, partly because this issue is subject to an unusual amount of lobbying by the interest groups who would be affected and partly because it is difficult to foresee what the ramifications of revised regulations would be. For example, no one can say for certain whether broader powers for thrift institutions would increase or decrease the availability of mortgages.

Between 1958 and 1961, the Commission on Money and Credit, a private group sponsored by the Committee for Economic Development, conducted a wide-ranging study of the U.S. financial structure and recommended that many of the financial regulations be relaxed or eliminated. Few of these recommendations made their way into proposed legislation, and fewer still were passed, partly because of opposition from the interest groups. In 1970, President Nixon appointed the President's Commission on Financial Structure and Regulation (commonly known as The Hunt Commission) to undertake a thorough analysis of the regulation of financial institutions. In general, their recommendations paralleled those of the Commission on Money and Credit and sought to increase competition between commercial banks and thrift institutions by providing them with additional powers and greater operational freedom.

Generally, the Hunt Commission recommendations would allow commercial banks and thrifts to offer a wider range of services to their customers by broadening their deposit, lending, and investment powers. The principle was that all institutions competing in the same markets should do so on an equal basis—for example, as regards reserve requirements, tax treatment, interest rate regulation, and supervisory burdens. The recommendations would abolish specialization which has been imposed by statute or regulation, but institutions that preferred to specialize could do so. Guidelines were provided for an orderly transition to the new system.

Briefly the changes proposed by the commission include the following:

1. Interest rate ceilings on time and savings deposits would be equalized between commercial banks and thrift institutions.[7] Gradually they would be phased out entirely. (The paying of interest on demand deposits would still be prohibited.)
2. Savings and loan associations and mutual savings banks would be given broader and more liberal loan and investment powers. They could offer finance-related services (such as mutual funds), a wider range of time and savings deposits, and third party payment services under conditions of equality with commercial banks.
3. Commercial banks' restrictions on real estate loans would be eliminated. They would have broader investment and lending powers and the authority to engage in nonbank services similar to bank holding companies.
4. Credit unions would be given broader lending and investing powers and a Central Discount Fund would be established to improve their liquidity.
5. Federal charters would be made available to mutual savings banks and mutual commercial banks.
6. Uniform tax treatment and deposit reserve requirements would be provided for all deposit institutions offering third party payment services. Reserve requirements on demand deposits would be lowered, and would be completely eliminated for time and savings deposits.
7. Consumer safeguards would be added regarding deposit insurance and variable rate mortgages. Complicated and costly procedures in mortgage origination and foreclosures would be simplified.
8. State governments were urged to allow statewide branching and to remove usury ceilings on interest rates.
9. The examination and operational supervision of banks would be performed by a new National Bank Administration and a state Bank Administrator; the Federal Reserve System would devote its energies to monetary policy.

In August 1973, on the basis of these recommendations, the Nixon Administration proposed legislation to reform the financial regulations. While some details have been changed, many of the administration proposals reflect those of the Hunt Commission (see Table 3-12 for a detailed comparison). On the other hand, some of the problems addressed by the Hunt Commission (and the remedies recommended) have been omitted from the president's proposals.

Table 3-12. Comparison of Recommendations for Financial Reform—The Hunt Commission Versus President Nixon

The Hunt Commission Recommendations—December 1971	The President's Recommendations—August 1973

A. Regulation of Interest Rate Ceilings on Deposits
  1. Time and Savings Deposits, Certificates of Deposit (CDs)
    • Rate regulations on time and savings deposits (except for deposits of $100,000+) gradually phased out. Board of Governors of FRS have power (for 10 years only) to impose ceilings in emergencies.
    • Maximum on deposits of $100,000+ be removed immediately. Board of Governors have power to lower the $100,000 cut-off amount.
    • Differential between rate ceilings for thrift institutions and commercial banks will not be necessary because of additional powers given the thrifts. Differential would slowly be phased out. Completed in five years.
  2. Demand Deposits
    • Prohibition against paying interest be retained.
B. Regulation of the Functions of Depository Financial Institutions
  1. Savings and Loan Associations (S&Ls) and Mutual Savings Banks (MSBs)
    • Broadened and liberalized loan and investment powers.
    • Wider variety of time and saving deposits and CDs; and third party services to households and nonbusiness entities only, under conditions of equality with commercial banks (or convert their charters to mutual or stock commercial banks).
    • Authority to make equity investments in projects to foster employment and housing for low and middle income persons.
    • Subordinated debt issues be approved as capital by regulatory agencies.
    • Expansion of services (individual and nonbusiness, such as mutual funds and other finance-related services).
	A. Regulation of Interest Rate Ceilings on Deposits
	  1. Time and Savings Deposits, Certificates of Deposit (CDs)
	    • Regulation Q to be phased out over period of five and one-half years (complete elimination of interest ceilings on time and savings accounts). In meantime, parity of ceilings between commercial banks and thrifts to be achieved in four annual steps. NOW accounts subject to ceilings as long as ceilings in existence—such ceilings be uniform for banks and thrifts.
	    • Actual ceiling levels set by FDIC, FHLBB, FRB, and Treasury Department.
	  2. Demand Deposits
	    • Same as Hunt Commission
	B. Regulation of the Functions of Depository Financial Institutions
	  1. Savings and Loan Associations (S&Ls) and Mutual Savings Banks (MSBs)
	    • For federal thrifts, checking accounts, third party payment powers, credit cards, NOW accounts available to all customers, individual and corporate.
	    • Federal S&Ls will have expanded lending and investment powers: consumer loans (on a limited basis); real estate loans not tied to permanent financing; community rehabilitation loans under 3 percent leeway authority; commercial loans only to extent they are closely related to housing.
	    • Limited acquisition of high-grade private debt securities.
	    • FHLBB granted more authority to broaden definition of collateral required for advances to S&Ls.

Table 3-12 continued

The Hunt Commission Recommendations–December 1971	The President's Recommendations–August 1973
2. Commercial Banks • Restrictions on discount eligibility of certain assets be removed. • Abolish restrictions on real estate loans. • Be allowed to value unrated securities (e.g., municipals) at book value, if of investment grade. • Authority to make equity investments in projects to foster employment and housing for low and middle income persons. • "Leeway" investment position recommended, related to equity investments. • Limits on amount of acceptances banks may create be removed; limits be set for particular banks. • Liabilities of any term incurred through sale of assets not be defined as deposits. • Be allowed to issue subordinated debt instruments provided all conditions made clear to purchasers, and differences between them and deposits made clear. • Be permitted to manage and sell mutual funds. • Broadening of the types of securities banks can underwrite. • Be allowed to engage in a variety of financial, fiduciary, or insurance services (like bank holding companies). 3. Credit Unions (CUs) • Establish a lending facility to provide temporary advances to CUs if a liquidity strain develops.	2. Commercial Banks • For national banks, savings accounts and NOW accounts available to all customers, individual and corporate. • Liberalized powers with respect to real estate loans and community rehabilitation loans under a 3 percent leeway authority. • FRB granted more flexible authority to define assets eligible for discount. 3. Credit Unions (CUs) • Establish a Central Discount Fund for insured CUs solely to meet emergency, temporary liquidity problems.

- Wider lending and investment powers permitted CUs.
- Wider variety of accounts offered, eventually with no rate maximums. Offering third party services, but also assume same responsibilities with respect to taxation, reserves, and supervision as other institutions.
- CUs be allowed to convert to other institutional forms. Without conversion, broadened but less than full powers are suggested.

C. Chartering and Branching
  1. S&Ls and MSBs
     - Federal charters be made available
     - State laws should extend power to branch on statewide basis.
     - Chartering authorities develop regulations for converting to stock companies
  2. Commercial Banks
     - State laws should extend power to branch on statewide basis.
     - Federal charters be made available for mututal commercial banks.
  3. CUs
     - Bond of association for chartering be available to groups, and no new charters with bonds based solely on geographic or residential characteristics be issued.
     - Convert charters to MSBs, mutual S&Ls, or mutual commercial banks.

- Some minor liberalization of existing powers, but CUs will retain their tax-exempt status only if they remain within bounds of existing tax law.

C. Chartering and Branching
  1. S&Ls and MSBs
     - Same as Hunt Commission—federal charters be made available.
     - No change in branching law.
  2. Commercial Banks
  3. CUs
     - CUs that want to expand their services and assume burden of full service mutual thrifts can do so, and can exchange charters if they desire.

Table 3-12 continued

The Hunt Commission Recommendations–December 1971	The President's Recommendations–August 1973

D. Deposit Reserve Requirements–All Institutions
• Membership in FRS be mandatory for all state chartered commercial banks and all S&Ls and MSBs that offer third party services.
• Deposit reserves for any banks required to join FRS be set at a low initial rate, with gradual increases for five years to same as all other members.
• With above exception, required reserves for all members be equal; no differences based on classification of city or size of institution.
• Level of required reserves on deposits between 7 and 22 percent with gradual reduction over time.
• Reserves on time and savings accounts, share accounts, and CDs be abolished.
	D. Deposit Reserve Requirements–All Institutions
	• All federal chartered institutions and state chartered institutions which are members of FRS or FHLBS required to maintain reserves for demand deposits and NOW accounts. NOW deposits subject to same range of reserves as demand deposits.
	• Required reserves:
	  demand deposits and NOW accounts 1 to 22 percent
	  savings accounts 1 to 5 percent
	  time accounts 1 to 10 percent
	• State laws will prevail for nonmember banks.

E. Taxation of S&Ls, MSBs, Commercial Banks • Develop and enact a tax system providing uniform tax treatment to institutions offering third party payment services. (Five year transition for new banks offering such services.) • Create single, uniform tax system for all deposit institutions.	E. Taxation of S&Ls, MSBs, Commercial Banks • Modify tax structure of banks and thrift institutions–possibly create an income tax credit available to all lenders which would vary in direct proportion to percentage of invested funds held in housing mortgages.
F. Deposit Insurance • Develop uniform standards for meeting claims arising from failed or failing institutions. Uniformity especially desirable with respect to "deposit assumption" and "deposit payoff", settlement methods and to "right of offset."	F. Deposit Insurance

G. Housing and Mortgage Markets
- Interest rates on FHA and VA mortgages be determined in the market place.
- Authorize variable rate options on FHA and VA mortgages, and establish consumer safeguards for them.
- Congress consider adoption of an insurance program against rate risk.
- Continue to foster and develop secondary market for mortgages.
- Continue to guarantee marketable, mortgage-backed securities.
- States remove interest ceilings on residential mortgages.
- States simplify and modernize the legal work in mortgage origination and foreclosures.
- States abolish barriers to out of state institutions providing mortgages in given states.
- Special tax credit be granted investors in residential mortgages.
- If mortgage financing inadequate to achieve national housing goals, Congress should provide direct subsidies to consumers.

H. Regulation and Supervision of Financial Institutions
- Although the commission's recommendations could be carried out under the existing regulatory framework, some organizational changes were recommended.

I. Life Insurance Companies
- State laws be amended to allow policies containing flexible policy loan interest rates.
- States recognize current heavy tax burden on life insurance companies compared with other financial institutions.

G. Housing and Mortgage Markets
- The FHA and VA interest ceiling will be removed.

H. Regulation and Supervision of Financial Institutions

I. Life Insurance Companies

Table 3-12 continued

The Hunt Commission Recommendations–December 1971	The President's Recommendations–August 1973
• A reasonable balance be maintained between social insurance and private insurance in providing economic security.	J. Trust Departments and Pension Funds 1. Trust Departments
J. Trust Departments and Pension Funds 1. Trust Departments	
• A federal "prudent man rule" should pertain to selection of securities in pension funds.	
• Appropriate regulatory agencies examine and monitor bank and other trust departments.	
• Each corporate fiduciary be required to file an annual report with an appropriate regulatory agency.	
• BHCs be permitted to maintain a single affiliate to carry on trust activities for all banks in the holding company.	
• State laws permit BHCs to operate systemwide common trust funds among all affiliate banks with trust powers.	
2. Pension Funds	2. Pension Funds
• The federal "prudent man investment rule" apply to all pension funds, not only those operated by bank trust departments.	
• Federal Disclosure Act be amended to: require that reports recommended above for bank trust departments apply also. require an annual independent audit of pension funds. strengthen power of secretary of labor to investigate violations and seek injunctions if necessary.	
• Permit employees to supplement their retirement benefits under a qualified pension plan with a limited amount of personal, tax-deductible contributions to such plans.	

Sources: Department of the Treasury, *Recommendations for Change in the U.S. Financial System* (Washington, D.C.: August 3, 1973), *The Report of the President's Commission on Financial Structure and Regulation* (Washington, D.C.: December 1971).

In particular, the president proposed no change in branching laws, reserve requirements on savings and time deposits, and little change in the federal organizations which regulate financial institutions.

The House Committee on Banking and Currency, chaired by Representative Wright Patman, has also made a set of recommendations for reform of the nation's financial system. Traditionally, Patman (and this committee) has favored regulations which protect "the little guy," and has opposed measures which would strengthen big business. Thus, their proposals are more along the lines of strengthening the thrift institutions than of relaxing controls on commercial banks. Also, the committee feels that the Federal Reserve Board has been unresponsive to the wishes of Congress and the people. The committee's recommendations include the following:

1. Savings and loan associations and mutual savings banks would be permitted to convert to commercial banks, and thus offer checking accounts and make business and consumer loans as well as residential loans. Those that did not convert would have more liberal lending powers.
2. Interest ceilings on savings deposits would be eliminated. Interest would be allowed on demand deposits.
3. All financial institutions would be required to invest some minimum percentage of their assets in residential mortgages (and perhaps other priority areas such as small business). Existing restrictions on mortgage lending by commercial banks would be eliminated.
4. The Federal Reserve Board would be reduced to five members and their terms shortened. It would be more subject to congressional control.
5. A new Federal Banking Commission would supervise and regulate all federally chartered banks and some finance companies. Thus, the duties of the Federal Reserve Board would be confined to monetary policy.[8]
6. Trust departments would be separated from commercial banks. A Federal Trust Management Commission would supervise and regulate the management of all pension funds, trusts, and so forth.

The National Commission on Consumer Finance, created by Title IV of the Consumer Credit Protection Act of 1968, has also proposed some changes to increase competition among financial institutions, but their recommendations are directed at increasing competition in one specific market—the consumer credit market. Their recommendations include:

1. Preferential treatment would be given to charter applications of newly forming commercial banks as opposed to branch applications of existing banks. Branching would be allowed only if it promotes competition.
2. Savings and loan associations and mutual savings banks would be allowed to extend secured and unsecured consumer loans up to 10 percent of total assets.

3. As regards finance companies, restrictions on free entry would be abolished.

The commission also proposed the creation of a Bureau of Consumer Credit within the Consumer Protection Agency with regulatory and supervisory authority under the Consumer Credit Protection Act.[9]

SUMMARY AND CONCLUSIONS

Commercial banks act as intermediaries between people (or organizations) who have surplus funds and those who need funds. Their competition comes from other intermediaries, such as thrift institutions and consumer finance companies, and from direct investments such as stocks and bonds.

The competition among intermediaries is a dual one, on the one side to attract funds and on the other to use them. Each type of intermediary specializes to a certain extent in some segment of the market. For example, consumer finance companies specialize in consumer installment loans and obtain their funds from wholesale sources. Non-life insurance companies obtain their funds by offering specialized insurance services and hold most of these funds in government bonds or other secure, liquid investments. Commercial banks, which are by far the largest group of intermediaries, compete in all of these markets by offering a broad array of services.

Although banks do not specialize to the extent that other intermediaries do, their share of the markets in which they compete is strong and in many cases growing. Table 3-13 summarizes some of these markets, who the competitors are, and what the recent trends have been in market share.

At least part of the specialization of financial intermediaries, particularly as between banks and thrift institutions, is imposed by government regulations. Pressures have arisen for reform of the regulations to reduce or eliminate these barriers. Although few laws have yet been passed, future regulations will probably trend in this direction. Whether these changes will strengthen or weaken the competitive position of banks is a moot point. The broadened powers of the thrifts will be offset somewhat by elimination of the interest rate differentials they now enjoy. Also, to the extent that NOW accounts become popular, commercial banks can also offer them, with a consequent reduction in reserve requirements and hence an increase in their supply of loanable funds. In any event, it seem unlikely that the thrifts will gain any new powers that are not also available to commercial banks. Hence, any changes in market shares held by the different types of institutions should be slow in coming. There is always the possibility, of course, that some energetic thrift institutions may greatly expand their markets, but that option is equally available to competing commercial banks.

Regulatory trends in another arena—namely, bank holding company activities—appear to be strengthening the position of banks by allowing them to add

The Competitive Environment of Commercial Banks 105

Table 3-13. Summary of Competitive Position of Commercial Banks in Some Major Markets

		Commercial Banks		Major Competitor	
Market		Present Market Share (percent)	Trend Since 1950	Institution	Present Market Share (percent)	Trend Since 1950
Sources of Funds	Demand Deposits	100	Constant	NOW accounts in MSBs, S&Ls in selected states		
				New EFTS services of thrift institutions		
	Time and Savings Deposits	50	Fairly steady, increasing since 1960	S&Ls	33	Up considerably between 1950 and 1960; down slightly since 1960
				MSBs		Threat of disintermediation when market rates rise
				Direct market instruments	—	
	Mortgage Credit—Total	17	Fairly steady	S&Ls	36	Increasing
				Life insurance companies	14	Decreasing
	Commercial	30	Increasing recently	Life insurance companies	30	Steady
	Single Family Residential	16	Down during 1950s, up slightly since 1960	S&Ls	48	Increasing
				MSBs	12	Fairly constant
Uses of Funds	Multifamily Residential	7	Steady	S&Ls	27	Increasing
				Life insurance companies	22	Up recently
				MSBs	20	Decreasing
	Consumer Credit—Total	45	Increasing	Finance companies and thrifts, especially CUs	34	Up between 1950 and 1960; down slightly since 1960
	Installment	47	Increasing	Finance companies	25	Decreasing since 1960
	Automobile Paper	61	Increasing	Finance companies	23	Decreasing
	Noninstallment	36	Increasing	Retail outlets and other nonfinance companies	53	Decreasing
	Credit Cards, Charge Accounts	37	Increasing	Retail outlets	49	Decreasing
	Business Loans	34	Steady increase (from 25 percent)	Trade credit	49	Fairly stead
				Finance companies	5	Increasing

affiliates in nonbanking activities. Some of these new affiliates are other intermediaries—e.g., leasing companies—that have competed directly with banks in some market segments. Also, the holding company regulations allow entry into nonintermediary services—e.g., investment advice, insurance sales, mortgage banking—which are a fast-growing market.

Economic trends in the past two decades have changed the focus of bank competition from the uses of funds (lending) to the sources of funds (deposits, CDs, and so forth). This naturally has influenced the banks' competitive strategies. Competition in lending meant competition mostly against other commercial banks. Key issues were the evaluation of creditworthiness of borrowers and the building of good relationships with businesses, since they were the principal borrowers. Large banks developed specialized staffs familiar with particular industries. Competition for funds, on the other hand, means competition mostly against other commercial banks, thrift institutions, and direct investments. Key issues are branching, devising new services to attract deposits, and learning how to service consumer accounts, since consumers are the greatest source of funds.

Control of operating costs becomes much more significant in this new environment. Since consumer accounts are characterized by high activity and low dollar volume, handling and processing costs consume a large portion of the earnings banks can make on the use of the funds. The bank which can reduce its operating costs has a significant advantage over its competitors. Thus, some large banks have developed paperwork "factories" in which assembly line production controls are used to minimize costs.

It is not surprising that many of the new bank holding company activities make use of servicing capabilities already possessed by commercial banks. For example, consumer finance companies, one of the more common types of holding company venture, require extensive processing of consumer accounts. Banks already have some expertise in servicing consumer loans at reasonable cost, and their ability to do so should improve as electronic banking technology develops. Mortgage banking affiliates allow banks, in effect, to sell the services of their mortgage departments without necessarily using any of their own funds. Similarly, leasing affiliates allow the holding companies to sell their commercial lending expertise (or one segment of it) without having to tap the banks' own funds. The real source of specialization in financial services is knowledge—of some industry, of some particular type of lending, of how to control operating costs, of consumers' needs, or whatever—and thus the holding company structures give banks a competitive advantage in being able to enter these specialized markets.

NOTES

1. Comptroller of the Currency, *1963 Annual Report,* p. 476.
2. "Number of Institutions Offering N.O.W.'s and N.O.W. Balances as of

July 31, 1974", tabulation by the Research Department, Federal Reserve Bank of Boston (Boston: July 1974).

3. Securities and Exchange Commission, *Institutional Investors Study Report,* Supplementary Volume I, Appendix II, (Washington, D.C.: House Document No. 92-64, Part 6, March 1971).

4. Ben Weberman, "$3 Billion in Disintermediation Threatened by Sales of Treasurys and Variable Notes," *American Banker,* August 6, 1974, p. 1.

5. Government Research Corporation, *National Issues/Outlook* (Washington, D.C.: June 1974), p. 6.

6. Fred H. Klopstock, "Foreign Banks in the United States: Scope and Growth of Operations," *Monthly Review* (New York: Federal Reserve Bank of New York, June 1973), p. 142.

7. Currently, commercial banks can pay up to 5.00 percent on ordinary savings accounts and S&Ls and MSBs can pay up to 5.25 percent.

8. House Committee on Banking and Currency, *Financial Institutions: Reform and the Public Interest,* (Washington, D.C.: Government Printing Office, 1973).

9. Quoted in U.S. Department of Commerce, *U.S. Industrial Outlook 1974, with Projections to 1980,* (Washington, D.C.: Government Printing Office, 1973), p. 356.

Chapter Four

The Regulatory Environment of Commercial Banks

Chapter One mentioned briefly the complex array of laws and regulatory agencies which govern the banking industry. This chapter will discuss the regulatory environment and its effects on banking in more detail. Many people, including two specially appointed presidential commissions, are proposing major changes in the regulation of financial institutions. Others predict that electronics technology will make obsolete most of the present thinking about financial regulation. To evaluate these statements, it is helpful to understand how the present structure came to exist and what the regulators seek to accomplish. That is one purpose of this chapter. The chapter also discusses some of the direct effects of regulation on the structure of banking in different states.[1] Finally, the chapter seeks to convey a sense of the momentum of regulatory change and the steps needed to bring about changes. Several current events will be analyzed in such a context.

The regulation of U.S. commercial banks is based on a "dual" system, with federal and state controls operating jointly. It is the combination of these two regulatory systems, federal and state, which determines the regulatory environment of commercial banks in a particular state. Generally speaking, the federal regulations relate to the kinds of business and some specific activities of banks, while state regulations mostly affect the size and locations of banks or their branches. The material in the next two sections, accordingly, is organized around federal regulations (concerning activities) and state regulations (concerning location) respectively. It is important to keep in mind, however, that some overlap exists; federal agencies do become involved in issues of bank location and some states do limit lending practices, interest rates, or whatever.

FEDERAL BANKING REGULATION

By definition, regulations force an industry to do things it otherwise would not do or to behave in ways it might not under the free play of economic and competitive forces. Some regulations are passed to correct specific abuses, some are precautionary, and others give special aid to certain people or activities, e.g., farming. Opinion surveys repeatedly show that the public believes this control system works. A growing sentiment exists to further regulate private enterprise, especially "big business."[2]

As conditions change, some regulations will need to be revised, or new ones added. The specific impetus for these changes can come from the public, special interest groups, the academic world, other regulatory agencies, or the regulated industry itself. There are certain recognizable patterns to this. Safety regulations (automobile, occupational, etc.) tend to arise from public pressure, while the granting of special privileges (radio frequency allocations, airline routes, etc.) more often result from industry requests or from government efforts to achieve certain social objectives. Although the government efforts presumably serve the public, the connection may be indirect, and the impetus for regulation usually comes from the academic world or some part of the government itself.

Following this pattern, federal regulations affecting banks can be collected into four principal groups according to the interests they serve. The overriding public concern with banking is for safety of the banks. It is not surprising that the most pervasive banking regulations deal with protections for depositors and limits on the risks banks can expose themselves to. The dominant government impact on banks arises from its efforts to stabilize the economy through monetary policy. The Federal Reserve Board employs a variety of tools to directly control the money supply and the amount of bank credit. Another area of government intervention is antitrust enforcement. Fear of concentration of power by banks is one of the oldest traditions in the U.S. Besides the watchdog activities of the Justice Department, there are various rules on disclosure and reporting and specific prohibitions on certain types of activities. Finally, an area of both government and industry concern is special aid to specific sectors of the economy, such as housing and farming. For four decades, the thrift institutions have been given special treatment, as well as some competitive advantages over banks, to assist families to own their own homes.

To some extent, the banking regulatory agencies have come to be the arena in which intra- and interindustry feuds are thrashed out and resolved. There are continuing conflicts between small independent banks and the large ones, between banks and investment bankers, between banks and thrift institutions, between federally chartered and state chartered banks (or thrifts), between banks and insurance companies, and so on. In the heat of debate one side or another may invoke the name of bank safety, or antitrust, or whatever, to support its cause, though the real issue is protection of its own interests. Many regulations have been passed to adjudicate such disputes, and it is not always clear on whose behalf the regulators (or Congress) acted. Regulations applying to electronics funds transfers and to bank holding company activities—two of the frontiers of banking—are being debated and resolved in this manner.

Bank Safety

In the earliest days of the country, bank failures were regarded as a normal risk of life. Many states imposed no reserve requirements, and few had any systematic procedure for examining banks. When the "national" banks were created in 1864, they were required to keep reserves of 25 percent and to submit to periodic examinations by the newly created Comptroller of the Currency. By the standards of the day, this was considered strict supervision, and for many years most new banks opted to open under state charter. Creation of the Federal Reserve Banks in 1913 was largely an effort to improve the safety of banks. By becoming a "lender of last resort," the Federal Reserve could help banks through periods of heavy withdrawals or tight credit. This machinery helped, but it was entirely inadequate for the Depression, when almost half the nation's banks collapsed. More than any other event, the Depression demonstrated that a bank failure could be a disaster for the community as well as for its stockholders. Both the federal government and the states passed restrictive laws which the bankers, in their shock, seemed willing to accept. Limits were tightened on the types of loans banks could make, on the amounts lent to any one customer, on reserves, and so on.

Most of the banks which failed during the Depression were small; 85 percent had less than $1 million in assets. The creation of the Federal Deposit Insurance Corporation in 1933 had a major impact in calming the fears about smaller banks. The FDIC is now regarded as one of the principal reforms arising from the Depression. Virtually all commercial banks and most mutual savings banks are members of the FDIC. In return for its insurance they pay an annual fee of 0.2 percent of the insured deposits and submit to annual examinations. The FDIC also imposes certain restrictions on the bank's asset portfolio, and it insures deposits only up to a set limit, presently $20,000 per account. A parallel structure, the FSLIC, insures deposits in savings and loan associations.

The FDIC tends to make small banks competitively stronger than they otherwise would be. During periods of tight credit people become more cautious about the liquidity of their investments, and rightly or wrongly, small banks seem less trustworthy than large ones. In recent months, large investors have avoided the CD issues of even the medium size banks, buying the CDs of only the largest institutions. For the ordinary (small) depositor, FDIC insurance effectively eliminates any concern over the safety of his account, and he has no incentive to move his funds to another bank.

Concern over bank safety makes itself felt in other ways than insurance, lending limits, or examinations. For one, national banks seeking to open a new branch must first satisfy the Comptroller of the Currency that the new office will not overextend the bank or cause the market to be "overbanked" (implying some risk of failure of the new branch or a competing bank in the market being forced to close). More importantly, the Federal Reserve Board keeps a close watch on the liquidity of banks. It can give specific aid to one bank—e.g., $1 billion in loans to the Franklin National Bank in New York before its failure—or it can adjust reserve requirements and monetary policies to help the banking system as a whole—e.g., lifting interest ceilings on CDs when the commercial paper market faltered in 1970 after the Penn Central collapse. Prevention of bank failures is now regarded as the foremost responsibility of the Federal Reserve System. It is a lesson that was bitterly learned during the Depression, when the Federal Reserve stood by and watched (indeed, hastened, by restrictive policies) the collapse of thousands of banks.

When the Bank Holding Company Act was amended in 1970, supervision of all holding company activities was lodged with the Federal Reserve Board. The rationale for this supervision was bank safety—that is, preventing the holding companies from undertaking ventures that would expose the subsidiary banks to risk of failure. Although the issue has been complicated by antitrust considerations and interindustry disputes, the board still appears to consider bank safety as the overriding concern. In late 1974, the board cautioned holding companies against overextending themselves, and in five weeks rejected four new ventures by leading banks with statements such as, "The bank's capital and liquidity positions have not grown commensurately... and are at present somewhat lower than the Board believes appropriate." On September 11, the board issued a statement that, "The Board believes that these are times when it would be desirable for bank holding companies generally to slow their present rate of expansion and to direct their energies principally toward strong and efficient operations within their present modes, rather than toward expansion into new activities."[3]

Monetary Policy

Chapter Two has already described the relationship between bank credit and the efforts of the Federal Reserve Board to stabilize the economy. With this control system, the amount of banks' basic raw material, money, is determined entirely by the Fed. To expand and earn greater profits, banks must either find ways to earn higher yield on their funds or contrive to somehow beat the reserve requirements. During periods of tight credit especially, banks have incentive to pursue the latter option. That is, rather than turning good customers away, the banks will try to devise ways to extend credit beyond what the reserve regulations would normally allow. One such "loophole" that emerged in the credit crunch of 1969 was for a bank holding company to borrow in the commercial paper market and use the proceeds to buy loans from its subsidiary bank. Since the bank received these funds through the sale of an asset, rather than by a deposit, it was free to lend the new funds in full if it wished. Eventually the Federal Reserve Board stopped the practice, ruling that the proceeds from such a sale would be considered equivalent to a deposit and hence subject to reserve requirements. Other devices for expanding bank credit without additional reserves are Eurodollar borrowings and bankers acceptances. So far, the Federal Reserve has not acted to restrict these devices, although individual members of the board have occasionally spoken of a need for some limitations.

Chapter Two also described the change in banks' deposit mix from demand deposits to time deposits. Because time deposits require reserves only about one-fourth those required of demand deposits, this shift has permitted banks to expand their lending without a proportionate increase in reserves. Since 1960, for example, bank deposits have almost trebled, loans have quadrupled (for members of the Federal Reserve System), while their reserves have increased only about 90 percent. One instrument promoted by the banks to attract new deposits is the large negotiable Certificate of Deposit (CD), a time deposit yielding rates of interest comparable to commercial paper. As part of its monetary policy, the Federal Reserve Board has, from time to time, adjusted the reserve requirements on CDs and the maximum interest rates they can carry.

Antitrust Considerations

Because banking has been such a diffuse industry, with thousands of independent competitors, it is a relative newcomer to antitrust supervision. Prior to the Depression, state laws made entry into the banking business easy. Five men with as little as $10,000 in capital could organize a new bank. The prevailing doctrine was the so-called "spirit of free banking," which sought to prevent bigness by making new entry easy. A few groups of "chain banks" and a few holding companies (including one giant, Transamerica, in the West) emerged during the 1920s but were of relatively small importance.

The Depression, combined with World War II, effectively froze the formation of banks or branches for 15 years. After the war, the urban banks sought to follow their customers into the suburbs. One of their responses was to acquire suburban banks, and the number of consolidations rose to more than 200 per year in the middle 1950s. Something of an impasse developed about the regulation of these mergers. Courts had stood on the position that banking, because it was a regulated industry, was exempt from the antitrust laws. Also, there was a technicality in the interpretation of the Clayton Act which raised doubts about its applicability to banks. Congress sought to resolve the issue with the Bank Merger Act of 1960 (Celler-Kefauver Act) which placed national bank mergers under the administrative control of the comptroller of the Currency, FDIC, or the Federal Reserve Board. Also, in the following year the Justice Department brought suit against the proposed merger of the Philadelphia National Bank and the Girard Trust Corn Exchange Bank, the second and third largest banks in Philadelphia. In a landmark decision in 1963 the Supreme Court blocked the merger, saying:

> The fact that banking is a highly regulated industry critical to the Nation's welfare makes the play of competition not less important but more so. . . . [I] f the businessman is deprived of credit because his banking alternatives

have been eliminated by mergers, the whole edifice of an entrepreneurial system is threatened; if the costs of credit are allowed to become excessive by the absence of competitive pressures, virtually all costs in our credit economy will be affected.[4]

Since that decision, the Justice Department has brought more antitrust suits in the field of banking than in any other field. In the last few years it has vigorously contested (albeit with mixed success) a series of intercity acquisitions of competing banks by bank holding companies.

The Justice Department's antitrust suits do not mean, however, that the department favors unit banking. Quite the contrary, the department has for several years been urging states to allow more widespread branching. The department's position has been that banks should be free to enter markets in other cities, providing they do so by opening a *de novo* branch or by marking a "foothold acquisition" of a small existing bank and expanding its activities. The department has consistently opposed mergers between significant direct competitors in local markets.

We have sought to encourage *de novo* or "foothold" entry by the large, capable banking organizations in a state, as opposed to their entry by acquisition of local leaders. The underlying assumption has been that there were significant competitive gains to be realized if the largest banking organizations in a state are forced to come into local markets as challengers of the stauts quo rather than inheritors of it.[5]

The Justice Department has extended its procompetitive supervision to the areas of competition between banks and thrift institutions, interest rate ceilings, and electronic funds transfer systems. The posture consistently has been one of extending the *Philadelphia* doctrine that competition in financial services is critical to the functioning of our credit economy. Electronic funds transfer technology in particular has elicited policy statements in recent months which strongly favor the unfettered development and trial of new systems.

The Federal Reserve Board has followed similar reasoning in its decisions on bank holding company acquisition. With respect to the acquisition of additional banks, the board has stated and followed the doctrine of foothold or *de novo* entry. With respect to new nonbanking activities, the board has followed an analogous policy. Acquisitions (or new ventures) generally have been allowed if they served a different geographic area than the banks and/or were not among the larger competitors in their own field.

Another antitrust issue which has influenced banking regulation is the doctrine of "separation of banking and commerce." The concern here is to prevent undue concentration of financial power and to prevent potential conflict-of-interest abuses, such as unfair granting of credit. From the earliest history of this country, bank charters have been narrowly written to preclude banks from entering other lines of business, such as, say, manufacturing. In some European countries, banks control all kinds of industries, either directly or through interlocking directorships, and this was seen as antithetical to the American spirit of free enterprise. The potential for favored granting (or denial) of credit is obvious. Thus, a series of laws has evolved which limits the alternate activities of bank directors, banks' ownership of stock in nonbanking corporations (and vice versa), and so on.

The most important legislation concerning the separation of banking and commerce is the Bank Holding Company Act. This law was originally passed in 1956 after a 13 year campaign by the Federal Reserve Board and the Independent Bankers Association of America (which was founded for this purpose) to stop the spread of Transamerica Corporation, a financial conglomerate which controlled 41 banks in five states on the West Coast. Transamerica also operated the Occidental Life Insurance Co., real estate firms, iron foundries, fish processing plants, and others. Although lengthy congressional hearings failed to produce any significant evidence of abuses by holding companies, Congress finally accepted the Fed's argument of potential abuses and placed strict limits on the further acquisition of banks or nonbank subsidiaries by holding companies. The act, over the objections of the Federal Reserve Board, specifically exempted one bank holding companies, most of which were small "country" banks. In the late 1960s, many of the country's largest banks began exploiting this loophole and reorganized themselves as one bank holding companies. Finally, at the end of 1970, Congress passed amendments to the Bank Holding Company Act which brought all holding company activities under supervision of the Federal Reserve Board. The act further stated the holding company activities which the board could approve as being

> of a financial, fiduciary, or insurance nature (and) . . . so closely related to banking or managing or controlling banks as to be a proper incident thereto. In determining whether a particular activity is a proper incident to banking or managing or controlling banks, the Board shall consider whether the performance by an affiliate of a holding company can reasonably be expected to produce benefits to the public, such as greater convenience, increased competition, or gains in efficiency, that outweigh possible adverse effects, such as undue concentration of resources, decreased or unfair competition, conflicts of interest, or unsound banking practices. . . .[6]

The Federal Reserve Board has established a list (the so-called "laundry list") of nonbanking activities that holding companies may or may not enter (see Table 4-1).

This legislation erases the previous distinction between one bank and multibank holding companies. Moreover it creates a strong competitive incentive for the larger existing banks to reorganize themselves as holding companies and

116 Trends Affecting the U.S. Banking System

Table 4-1. Nonbanking Activities Under Section 4(c)(8)

Authorized
Issuing letters of credit and accepting drafts
Making mortgage loans
Consumer finance activities
Operating credit card company
Factoring
Operating an industrial bank
Servicing loans
Providing trust services
Acting as investment and financial adviser as specifically authorized
Furnishing general economic information and advice
Providing portfolio investment advice
Leasing of personal property on a full payout basis
Making investments in community welfare projects
Providing bookkeeping or data processing services
Acting as insurance agent or broker where insurance is connected with an extension of credit
Underwriting of credit life insurance and credit accident and health insurance that is directly related to extensions of credit by the bank holding company system

Denied
Insurance premium funding
Underwriting general life insurance
Real estate brokerage
Land development
Real estate syndication
Property management
Management consulting
Owning savings and loan associations

Under Consideration
Leasing real property
Furnishing armored car and courier services (recently authorized)
Selling mortgage guarantee insurance (recently denied)

Source: Copied from William F. Upshaw, "Bank Affiliates and Their Regulation: Part III," *Monthly Review*, Federal Reserve Bank of Richmond, May 1973, p. 8.

thereby offer a broader range of services. By 1973, 150 of the largest 200 U.S. commercial banks were part of a holding company structure. Finally, the holding company arrangement frequently permits the assembly of a statewide banking structure where state branching laws would otherwise prohibit the possibility. Thus, a law originally designed to prevent concentration of power has probably done more to encourage the concentration of financial resources than any other recent event.[7]

Special Aid to Specific Sectors

Governments in the U.S. have developed a multitude of ways to channel assistance to particular activities or segments of the economy and intervention in the financial markets has been one of the more popular techniques. Thus, the Federal Land Banks, the Farmers Home Administration, the Small Business

Administration, and others channel funds to farms, small business ventures, college students, and so forth. Some, like the Federal Housing Administration, provide a government guarantee (or an insurance against default) on loans made in the private sector. Others, like the Federal Land Banks, sell their own bonds in the open market and lend the proceeds directly to farmers or whatever groups they are trying to assist. Others borrow directly from the Treasury and lend to their special groups. A newer arrangement, used by the Federal National Mortgage Association and the Student Loan Marketing Association (both of which are "semipublic" corporations), is to sell bonds (with a government guarantee) in the open market and use the proceeds to buy loans from banks or other private lenders. By creating a "secondary market" at attractive interest rates, they channel funds to the desired uses through existing lenders and, supposedly, with minimal disruption of the free enterprise system.

At the end of 1972, government-sponsored financing agencies had $42.6 billion in debt outstanding, about 2 percent of the total public and private debt at the time. The bulk of this money is used for mortgages, and at the end of 1972 government agencies accounted for more than a quarter of all farm mortgages and about 7 percent of single family home mortgages (see Table 3-7).

A more significant federal intervention in the financial markets occurs in the special treatment given to thrift institutions for the purpose of channeling funds into home mortgages. In the depths of the Depression, more than one-quarter of the nation's home mortgages were in default. To help to finance mortgages, the government passed a number of reforms, one of which was the creation of the Federal Home Loan Bank System as an analog, for thrift institutions, of the Federal Reserve System. A year later the Federal Savings and Loan Insurance Corporation was added to insure deposits in earnings institutions. Since World War II, the thrift institutions have been given additional support by the Federal Reserve Board's so-called "Regulation Q," which limits commercial banks to paying an interest rate on savings accounts below that allowed to thrift institutions. Also, most thrift institutions have been exempt from income taxes because of their "mutual" form of organization.

The thrift institutions, however, *must* invest their funds in mortgages. They are not free to make business loans, consumer loans (with certain exceptions), and other investments open to banks. This restriction is more than a simple quid pro quo in return for regulatory favors. Many states have usury laws which impose low interest rates on mortgages (e.g., until recently, Pennsylvania limited mortgage rates to 6 percent.) Commercial banks, with better opportunities in business loans, tend to avoid mortgages in these states.

It is difficult to assess the net economic effect of the special treatment of thrift institutions. From World War II to the early 1960s, when thrifts offered substantially higher interest rates on savings than commercial banks could, it is likely that they increased the proportion of savings channeled into housing during this period. (During this period, residential structures accounted for more than a third of gross private domestic investment, about five to ten percentage points higher than in the 1920s or in the past decade.) In effect, small savers have been subsidizing home buyers by accepting a lower yield on their savings than is available in market investments. This has prompted "disintermediation" during periods of tight credit (discussed in Chapter Three) and introduced an exaggerated element of cyclicality into the housing markets. The regulations have also raised the thrift institutions to a large and powerful interest group which must be contended with in any proposals for financial reform.

STATE BANKING REGULATION

As was mentioned at the beginning of this chapter, the most important state regulations are those that deal with branching and bank location. To be sure, some states limit the activities of holding company affiliates, some have usury laws, and so forth. But the greatest impact of state laws has been on the banking structure. As an example, California, the most populous state, has 165 banks, about the same number as North Dakota, with less than one-thirtieth of California's population. California allows statewide branching; North Dakota limits most banks to only a single office. This section will discuss the relationship between state banking regulations and banking structure. A detailed discussion of the New York banking laws and the history of banking in that state is given in the Appendix.

Early History of State Control

Banks were originally chartered by the states. Federal chartering was an issue of some controversy, culminating in Andrew Jackson's veto of the renewal of the charter of the Second Bank of the United States. The Civil War resolved the issue—Congress created the "national" banks, with a common currency, to help finance the war. However, the National Bank Act of 1864 contained a provision that subjected the "national" banks to the locational restrictions of the state laws.

Branching was scarcely an issue before 1900. A few banks operated branches, and others tried and abandoned branches for lack of suitable return. By and large, state laws used singular nouns in referring to a bank's "place of business," but had no explicit prohibitions on branching. Organization of new banks was made easy by state laws (the so-called "spirit of free banking"), often requiring only $10,000 in capital. National banks operated under stricter regulations as to examinations, lending limits, and so forth. For this reason, a great many new banks were organized under state charter. By 1921, there were 29,000 banks in this country, of which about 21,000 were state banks.

The first serious moves toward branching or bank holding companies began after the turn of the century, with the growth of the "streetcar" suburbs. By 1921 there were 1,281 branches maintained by 530 banks, accounting for 15 percent of U.S. bank deposits. By 1930 banks with branches accounted for almost half of all deposits. Since there were only 751 such banks and only 3,522 branches, branching was clearly an activity of the larger banks. A number of states in these early years passed antibranching legislation. Yet from about 1915 onward the overall trend has been toward liberalization of branching laws. The McFadden Act in 1927 opened up branching for national banks, but contained a provision that they must also obey the branching laws of the states.

The Depression brought several moves to strengthen the financial system by allowing more widespread branching of banks. A bill was introduced in Congress to allow statewide branching (and even branching across state lines within 50 miles from the head office) for national banks. Such proposals were defeated by bitter, if minority, opposition from the unit banking lobby. In the states, liberalization was more successful. Nine states passed statewide branching laws (making a total of 18) and eight states allowed limited branching (making a total of 18), during the 1930s.

The postwar period brought a greatly increased interest in branching, as the city banks sought to follow their customers to the suburbs. The number of bank branches reached 10,600 by 1960.

Between 1960 and 1970, there were a few changes in state branching regulations, all of them in the direction of more liberalized provisions:

1. New York, in 1960, allowed branching across district lines between New York City (second New York banking district) and Nassau County (first banking district) or Westchester County (third banking district). Before 1960, branching was allowed only within each of the nine banking districts.
2. The Virginia law was changed in 1962 to permit statewide branching by merger. Branching had formerly been restricted to a limited area around a bank's head office.
3. The New Hampshire law was amended in 1963 to permit branch banking within limited geographic areas (with some limitations). Until that time, branch banks had been prohibited.
4. New Jersey liberalized its law in 1969 to permit branching within each of the three banking districts into which the state had been divided. Until 1969, branching was limited to head office counties and *de novo* branching was prohibited into communities where banking offices were located.

Branching Laws and Banking Structure

On the basis of their branch banking laws, states can be classified into the following three groups: (1) those that allow statewide branching, (2) those that permit branching within limited geographic areas, usually the county in which the bank is headquartered or that county plus contiguous counties, and (3) unit banking states that prohibit branching altogether. Branching laws follow a geographic pattern: statewide branching is widespread on the East Coast and in the Far West; limited branching is prevalent in states between the East Coast and the Mississippi River; and unit banking is dominant throughout the Plains States. The reasons for this pattern are unclear, though the unit banking states seem to contain most of the nation's small medium size farms. It may be that these states have greater proportions of relatively isolated small towns (and small independent banks) than the sparsely populated western states or the more urban, industrialized states. To some extent, the pattern may also be a legacy of "populist" political inclinations.

A state's branching laws have a direct bearing on its number of banks and the concentration of bank deposits (see Table 4-2). Whatever the measure used for concentration, states with more liberal branching laws show greater concentration. Table 4-2 shows that the average share of deposits held by the largest bank in the state is 35.8 percent for states allowing statewide branching, 14.3 percent in limited branching states, and only 3.7 percent in unit banking states. In looking at the five largest banks in each state, a similar pattern appears: they hold, on the average, 75.5 percent of the deposits in statewide branching states, 38.8 percent in limited branching states, and only 30.4 percent in unit banking states.

It is not surprising that the more branching a state allows, the fewer banks it tends to have. Competition pushes the larger banks toward having statewide— or metropolitan-area-wide, or countywide, if that is all that the laws allow— networks of branches. Bank of America, in California, operates more than 1,000 branches, and its major competitors have several hundred each. In such an environment there is clearly less room for small independent banks.[8] Figure 4-1 shows this phenomenon graphically.

An interesting hypothetical question is, how many banks would there be if every state converted to statewide branching? If one were to take a simplistic approach and project strictly on the basis of population, the number would be about 4,900 banks for the whole U.S.[9] This is a surprisingly large number in comparison to the forecasts of some prophets who foresee the U.S. market becoming dominated by half a dozen banks. For that event to occur, the states would clearly need to break down their barriers and allow nationwide branching. Although certain officials (notably the New York Banking Supervisor) have discussed the idea of reciprocal branching agreements, no serious proposal for this has arisen.

State Holding Company Laws

The federal Bank Holding Company Act reserves for the states broad powers to control holding companies:

Table 4-2. Effects of Branching Regulation on Concentration of Commercial Bank Deposits

Concentration of Commercial Bank Deposits in States

	Largest Bank				Five Largest Banks			
Bank Regulation of Branching	Highest Concentration State	%	Average Concentration	Lowest Concentration State	%	Highest Concentration State	%	Average Concentration	Lowest Concentration State	%
Statewide Branching	Nevada	63.1	35.8	Vermont	9.4	Nevada	97.2	75.5	Vermont	35.2
Limited Area Branching	Massachusetts	27.5	14.3	New Jersey	6.3	New York	54.8	38.8	New Jersey	23.5
Unit Banking	Illinois	15.9	9.7	Iowa	4.7	Colorado	47.0	30.4	Iowa	17.4

Source: Calculated from *Frost and Sullivan,* "Banking Information Systems—The Checkless Society," New York, November 1972, Table 3-4, p. 18. (In the Frost and Sullivan table of the Frost and Sullivan report Wisconsin was presented erroneously as a unit banking state. For this table it has been classified a limited branching state.)

122 Trends Affecting the U.S. Banking System

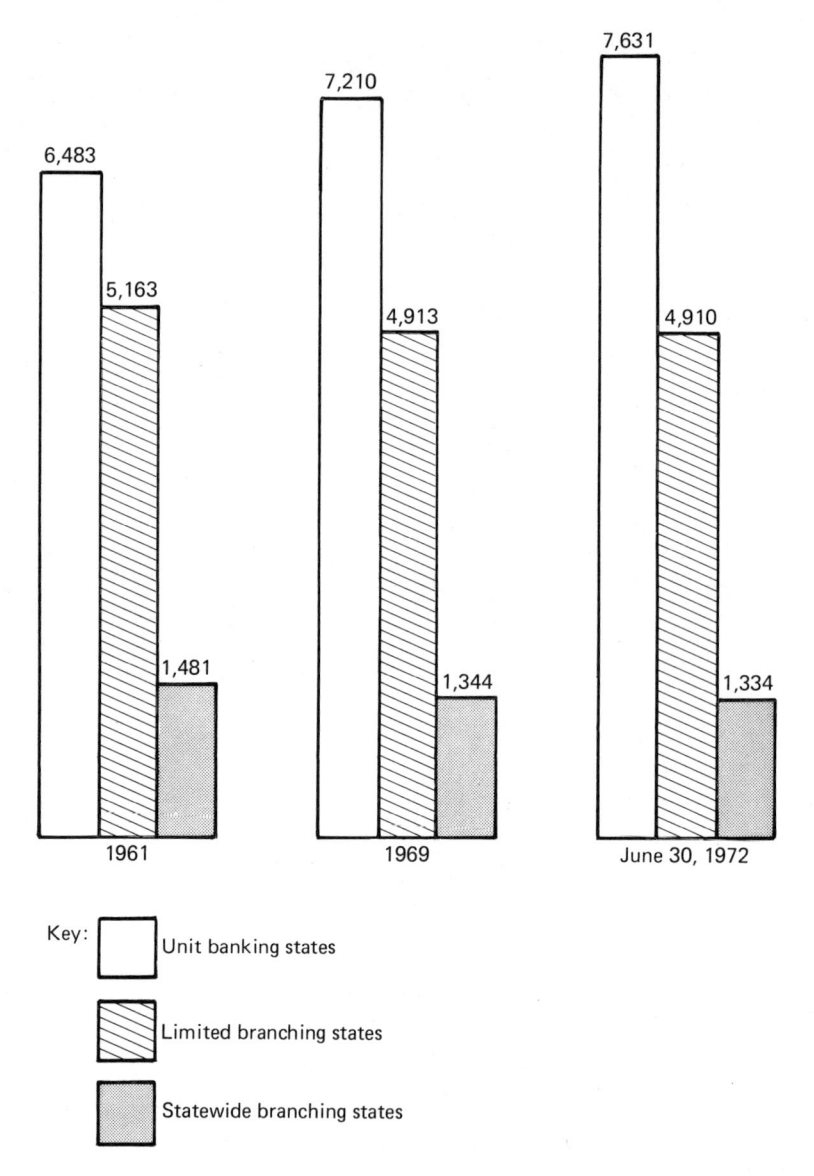

Figure 4-1. Number of Banks by State Branching Law

Sources: Federal Reserve Bulletin, March 1970, p. 210. FDIC, *Summary of Accounts and Deposits in All Commercial Banks–June 30, 1972,* (Washington, D.C.: FDIC), p. 8.

The enactment by the Congess of [this act] shall not be construed as preventing any state from exercising such powers and jurisdiction which it now has or may hereafter have with respect to banks, bank holding companies, and subsidiaries thereof.[10]

Until now, relatively few states have exercised these powers in any significant fashion. Although 35 states have some form of holding company law on their books, only about 15 place severe restraints on the growth of holding companies. Moreover, most of the laws relate to the acquisition of other banks. Relatively few states restrict the nonbanking activities of bank holding companies. Some of the more restrictive laws are as follows:

1. Nine states[11] prevent bank holding companies from owning or controlling more than one bank in the state. Mississippi, West Virginia, and Vermont have ownership or control restrictions which effectively limit holding companies to one bank.
2. Several states, including Iowa, Missouri, and New Jersey, permit a holding company to control no more than some specified percentage (e.g., 20 percent) of the state's bank deposits.
3. Several states require approval by the state banking authorities before a bank can be acquired.

It is the combination of the branching laws and the bank holding company laws which determines the regulatory environment of banks within a state. For example, Florida is a unit banking state, but it has no particular restraints on holding company acquisitions. Thus, over the past decade or so, the major Florida banks have reorganized themselves as holding companies and assembled six or eight statewide banking systems.[12] A similar phenomenon is occurring, at a somewhat slower pace, in Texas, Missouri, and some other states.

The Federal Reserve System recently completed a study of the impact of holding company acquisitions on banking concentration.[13] The study, which examined changes between 1968 and 1973, concluded that holding company acquisitions had almost no impact on concentration in states that already were concentrated (all of these 12 states already allowed statewide branching). The most significant increases occurred in less concentrated states (provided multibank expansion was allowed). Table 4-3 reproduces the statewide concentration increases tabulated by that study.

As of 1972 there were 260 multibank holding companies in the U.S., controlling 1,274 banks, more than half of them in unit banking states (see Table 4-4).[14]

A debate of sorts has arisen as to whether the increase in concentration caused by holding companies is "good" or "bad." Some people argue that the statewide banking structures are impersonal, favoring large corporate customers

Table 4-3. Impact of Holding Company Acquisitions on Concentration in States with Different Levels of Concentration

States	Statewide Concentration (Percentage of Deposits Held by Five Largest Banking Organizations) 1968	Increase in Statewide Concentration Due to Holding Company Acquisitions 1968-1973
Most Concentrated States		
Rhode Island (S)	96.5	–
Nevada (S)	95.6	–
Arizona (S)	95.4	–
Delaware (S)	92.0	–
District of Columbia (S)	91.4	–
Hawaii (S)	91.0	–
Oregon (S)	87.4	–
Idaho (S)	86.5	–
Alaska (S)	84.1	–
California (S)	77.9	–
Washington (S)*	72.9	–
Utah (S)	72.2	0.2
Moderately Concentrated States		
North Carolina (S)	66.5	–
Massachusetts (L)	65.4	1.7
Maryland (S)	62.7	1.9
Minnesota (U)	59.9	1.3
Montana (U)	58.5	0.9
New York (L)	58.5	0.5
Connecticut (S)	56.6	0.2
South Carolina (S)	55.4	–
Georgia (L)*	52.4	–
New Mexico (L)	50.3	11.9
North Dakota (U)*	49.2	–
Maine (S)	48.4	13.2
Michigan (L)	48.4	4.3
Vermont (S)*	47.4	–
Virginia (S)	46.4	5.0
Colorado (U)	45.6	7.7
South Dakota	45.5	1.4
Illinois (U)*	40.6	–
Least Concentrated States		
Tennessee (L)	39.9	3.6
New Hampshire (L)	37.8	–
Pennsylvania (L)*	37.8	–
Nebraska (U)*	37.7	–
Wyoming (U)	37.7	10.6
Oklahoma (U)*	34.5	–
Alabama (L)	33.5	14.6
Kentucky (L)*	33.5	–
Ohio (L)	32.5	4.6
Mississippi (L)*	32.4	–

Table 4-3 continued

States	Statewide Concentration (Percentage of Deposits Held by Five Largest Banking Organizations) 1968	Increase in Statewide Concentration Due to Holding Company Acquisitions 1968-1973
Wisconsin (L)	31.9	3.7
Louisiana (L)*	31.1	–
Missouri (U)	29.4	10.5
Indiana (L)*	28.1	–
Florida (U)	25.2	14.8
Texas (U)	23.5	4.5
New Jersey (L)	22.4	8.8
Arkansas (U)	21.0	1.7
West Virginia (U)	19.3	–
Iowa (U)	17.4	3.1
Kansas (U)*	16.7	–

*States that prohibited multibank expansion between 1968-73.
U = Unit banking state
L = Limited branching state
S = Statewide branching state
Source: Samuel H. Talley, "The Impact of Holding Company Acquisitions on Aggregate Concentration in Banking" (Washington: Board of Governors of the Federal Reserve System), Report No. 80, January 1974.

and neglecting "the little guy." Others, including the Justice Department, argue that statewide banking systems increase competition and eliminate local monopolies of unit banks. Available statistics appear to slightly favor the statewide advocates. Population per banking office is about 10 percent less in limited branching states than in unit banking states, and 10 percent lower still in statewide branching states. This difference would indicate, perhaps, a slightly better availability of banking service to the public.[15] Also, the Federal Reserve study showed that U.S. banking concentration actually declined by two percentage points from 1968 to 1973. (Without the holding company acquisitions, the percentage decline would have been more than twice as great.)

PROSPECTS FOR CHANGES IN FINANCIAL REGULATIONS

In the last six to eight years a number of events have occurred which have put strains on the U.S. financial system and prompted calls for reform of the financial regulations:

Table 4-4. Growth of Multibank Holding Companies

	1960 Holding Companies	1960 Affiliated Banks	1970 Holding Companies	1970 Affiliated Banks	1972 Holding Companies	1972 Affiliated Banks
Statewide Branching States	18	40	34	124	58	181
Limited Branching States	26	129	52	278	89	390
Unit Banking States	28	249	61	489	113	703
U.S. Total	72	418	147	891	260	1,274

Source: Federal Deposit Insurance Corporation, *Summary of Accounts and Deposits in all Commercial Banks* (Washington D.C.: 1970, 1972), Table F (1970), Table G (1972).

1. Periods of tight credit in 1966, 1969-1970, and 1973-1974 have led to disintermediation and a curtailment of mortgages.
2. The same periods of tight credit have prompted banks to push the interpretation of regulations as far as possible in order to increase their lending.
3. Mutual savings banks, after some legal maneuvering, have acquired the powers to offer NOW accounts.
4. Branching has continued to increase rapidly, and bank holding companies have assembled statewide banking systems in states previously thought safe for independent banking.
5. New opportunities for electronic funds transfers have raised all sorts of issues about the definition of branching, concentration of power, and so on.

In 1970, while the amendments to the Bank Holding Company Act were still being deliberated, President Nixon appointed the President's Commission on Financial Structure and Regulation. Commonly known as the Hunt Commission, this group was created to "review and study the structure, operation, and regulation of the private financial institutions in the United States, for the purpose of formulating recommendations that would improve the functioning of the private financial system."

The principal impetus for creation of the Hunt Commission was an official concern over the inadequate flow of savings in our economy. In its 1970 *Report,* the Council of Economic Advisors said: "The demands on our flow of national savings ... will be heavy in the years ahead, and our financial structure must have the flexibility that will permit a sensitive response to changing demands."[16] Thus, the Hunt Commission focused most of its energies on the depository and thrift functions of financial institutions. Questions of consumer credit were left to a separate National Commission on Consumer Finance; questions concerning bank mergers and holding company activities were considered to have been sufficiently debated prior to the Bank Holding Company Act amendments; and the equity markets were left to separate investigations also underway (after the fall of several brokerage firms and the crisis of confidence in the stock market).

Very generally, the Hunt Commission concluded that the financial institutions were overregulated:

> .... The Commission believes that greater flexibility and operational freedom in the financial structure will improve the allocation of resources to the nation's economic and social needs. Within the limits necessary for soundness and safety, the Commission seeks to remove unworkable regulatory restraints as well as provide additional powers and flexibility to the various types of financial institutions.[17]

There followed a series of recommendations that would phase out the limits placed on interest rates payable on savings accounts, allow thrift institutions to offer a wider range of services, eliminate state branching controls, and so on. The commission's intention to erase the regulatory distinctions between competing institutions was clear:

> The recommendations require that after a transitional period, all institutions competing in the same markets do so on an equal basis. It is essential, for example, that all institutions offering third party payment services have the same reserve requirements, tax treatment, interest rate regulations, and supervisory burdens... When financial institutions compete on equal terms, with respect to reserves, taxes, rate regulations, and supervision, there should be no need for *ad hoc* protective policies....[18]

Chapter Three has discussed the commission's recommendations in more detail.

Compared to the realities of state legislatures, congressional committees, and the lobbies of independent bankers, state chartered institutions, and others, the commission's recommendations seem idealistic. There was little to commend them to any interest group except, perhaps, economists and the public at large. However, little public pressure exists for financial reform. Opinion surveys show that people are generally satisfied with the performance of banks and trust bankers more than most other businessmen or public officials. Other studies show that most people regard banking as a minor matter in their lives and are more influenced, in their selection of banks, by convenience than by interest differentials or the other service differences that banks usually advertise.[19] A similar conclusion can be drawn from the relatively small portion of consumer savings accounts (1 to 2 percent) which disintermediate in times of tight credit. Thus, although the small savers and the small borrowers (i.e., the public) would be the chief beneficiaries of financial reform, their actions imply that most of them perceive little need for it.

Contrasted with these beneficiaries, almost every affected group of institutions has reason to oppose the reforms. Both the banks and the thrift institutions are happy with Regulation Q ceilings and have repeatedly opposed efforts to change them. Banks have no desire to strengthen the competitive position of the thrift institutions. State chartered banks do not like the notion of mandatory membership in the Federal Reserve System, and on and on.

The Hunt Commission's reforms included benefits and potential dangers for every interest group involved. What has happened is that each group supports those reforms that operate in its favor and opposes those which would hurt its interests. The commission foresaw this problem and stated:

> The recommendations are interrelated, and the Commission urges that they be considered as a package, even though some of the changes, if enacted separately, would improve the financial system. The Commission believes that piece-meal adoption of the recommendations raises the danger of creating new and greater imbalances.[20]

Despite that warning, the recommendations have become separated and used by interest groups to their own advantage. They have not yet reached the floor of Congress intact. In late 1973, the Nixon administration submitted a diluted version of the recommendations, but that bill became sidetracked in committees. Certain pieces of the reforms—e.g., allowing thrift institutions to reorganize as stock corporations instead of mutual associations—have been attached to other legislation and have had better success.[21]

It is possible that the present economic crisis will arouse sufficient public concern, particularly about mortgages, to overcome the obstacles. However, the Federal Reserve Board has begun to ease its restraint, savings are again flowing into thrift institutions, and no major thrift institutions and no additional banks have been endangered. Thus, it appears that the crisis may pass without significant changes in financial regulation. What seems more likely are some specific measures targeted at the housing industry and other hard-hit groups. These might include additional lending by the Federal Home Loan Banks to thrift institutions, an interest subsidy for the Federal National Mortgage Association, emergency loans to small businesses, and similar temporary actions.

Electronic banking technology probably will become a more powerful force for regulatory reform than the Hunt Commission has been. The Hunt recommendations were introduced "from the top downward" by government agencies, with little public interest and with opposition (or lukewarm support) by the groups directly involved. With EFTS, on the other hand, pressures for change are likely to originate from within the financial industry itself. Competitive balances will be at stake, and the regulators (or Congress) will be more in a position of adjudicating issues in the public interest, rather than of trying to push through new reforms in the (unperceived) public interest.[22]

NOTES

1. The Appendix delves more deeply into the relationship between banking laws and banking structure in a particular state, New York.
2. "Social Issues: America's Growing Antibusiness Mood," *Business Week*, June 17, 1972.
3. Quoted in Joseph D. Hutnyan, "Fed for First Time Denies H.C. Expansion on Grounds Industry Growing Too Fast," *American Banker*, September 12, 1974, p. 1.
4. *United States v. Philadelphia National Bank*, 374 U.S. 321, 372 (1963), quoted in statement by Donald I. Baker, U.S. Department of Justice, before the House Committee on Banking and Currency, September 17, 1973.
5. Donald I. Baker, "Holding Companies After Hunt" (Speech delivered to the Annual Meeding of the American Bar Association, Washington, D.C., August 7, 1973), p. 5.
6. Quoted in Federal Deposit Insurance Corporation, *Annual Report, 1970* (Washington, D.C.: 1971), p. 149.
7. This is not to say that the potential for abuses has necessarily increased. Most observers seem to feel that the expansion of holding companies has increased competition rather than reduced it. See, for example, the recent statements before Congress of the Federal Reserve Board and the Antitrust Division of the Justice Department, *United States v. Philadelphia National Bank*, 374 U.S. 321, 372 (1963), quoted in statement by Donald I. Baker, U.S. Department of Justice, before the House Committee on Banking and Currency, September 17, 1973.
8. This does not imply that they disappear altogether. The California market supports 140 smaller banking organizations, including 47 unit banks. See the Appendix for further details on the structure in California, New York, and Florida.
9. The U.S. population in 1972 was about 3.7 times the population of the 20 states (including D.C.) that permitted statewide branching. These states had 1,310 banks in 1972 which, multiplied by 3.7, makes approximately 4,900 banks for the U.S.
10. Section 7 of the Bank Holding Company Act of 1056, quoted in Peter S. Rose and Donald R. Fraser, "State Regulation of Bank Holding Companies," *Bankers Magazine* (Boston, Summer 1974), p. 45.
11. Arkansas, Georgia, Illinois, Indiana, Kansas, Louisiana, Nebraska, Oklahoma, and Pennsylvania.
12. See Appendix for further discussion of the Florida banking structure.
13. Samuel H. Talley, "The Impact of Holding Company Acquisitions on Aggregate Concentration in Banking" (Washington: Board of Governors of the Federal Reserve System), Report No. 80, January 1974.
14. There were, in addition, about 1,400 holding companies which owned only one bank in 1972. As mentioned in Chapter Three, most holding companies have been formed in order to enter new lines of business, not for the purpose of acquiring additional banks.

15. One reason for Florida's remarkable banking growth is that population growth had raised its population per banking office to more than twice the national average, creating a need for additional banks.

16. President's Commission on Financial Structure and Regulation, *Report*, (Washington, D.C.: Government Printing Office), 1971, p. 7.

17. Ibid., p. 8.

18. Ibid., p. 9.

19. See, for example, Steven J. Weiss, "Commercial Bank Competition: the Case of 'Free' Checking Accounts," *New England Economic Review,* September–October 1969; or Robert J.A. Pratt, "View from the Editor's Chair," *Pittsburgh Business Review,* June 1964, p. 15.

20. President's Commission on Financial Structure and Regulation, *Report,* p. 9.

21. This pattern of response was previewed ten years earlier when a distinguished private group, The Commission on Money and Credit, recommended reforms similar to those suggested by the Hunt Commission. There, too, the commission advised that the reforms be adopted as a package, and there, too, various interest groups subdivided the package and supported only the portions favorable to their narrow interests.

22. Chapter Five discusses some of the regulatory issues that might be raised by EFTS.

Chapter Five

The Technological Environment of Commercial Banks

Banking is not a high technology industry. To be sure, computers have replaced many clerical functions, helping banks to accommodate a rapid growth in business. By and large, however, banking procedures and banking "technology" have changed little in this century. Now, the picture shows signs of changing. On-line computers and cheaper communications have opened new possibilities which may obsolete present procedures. Some observers describe visions of electronic funds transfer systems (EFTS) and the "checkless, no money economy" in which everyone will make his purchases with a plastic card and handle his financial affairs through a touch tone telephone connected to a computer.

These visions have existed for ten years or more, but progress toward them seems slow. About the only EFTS service that seems to have caught on (and that just recently) is an arrangement for direct deposit of payrolls and preauthorized payments of certain bills. Neither of these services necessarily requires electronic technology, and both have been offered in manual form by some institutions for years. Other EFTS experiments have failed for lack of interest or have become bogged down in legal and regulatory actions.

Technological innovations are of interest to us in this report because many people foresee profound changes in the nature and structure of banking arising from them. This chapter attempts to put the technical changes into perspective alongside the competitive, economic, and regulatory forces operating on commercial banks. The first section of the chapter reviews some present methods of performing banking services and suggests a framework for evaluating the impact of technological innovations on banking operations. The next section discusses recent technological changes in banking and the emerging electronic funds transfer systems (EFTS). The third section describes some of the regulatory issues raised by EFTS, and the final section presents some conclusions regarding the relationship between public policy and technological innovation in banking.

132   Trends Affecting the U.S. Banking System

THE DELIVERY OF BANKING SERVICES

When most people think of technology in banking, they are likely to think of checks with strange looking numbers printed along the bottom and the computerized check processing systems installed by banks during the 1960s. Checks constitute the heart of what is called "the payments system" and are by far the largest source of data processing activity for banks.

Checks are estimated to account for more than 90 percent of the dollar volume of transactions in the U.S. Every year almost 25 billion checks are written, worth $5 to 6 trillion. The system through which these checks are recorded, moved from one part of the country to another, and eventually deducted from the checkwriter's account amounts to a $4 billion industry operated by banks and the Federal Reserve System. Figure 5-1 shows some of the transfers that are required when a check "clears" through the banking system. Considering the complexity of the arrangement, it is impressive that checks normally clear within three to five business days. Checks were laboriously sorted and recorded by hand until the 1950s when mechanization was introduced. Now, most of the sorting and processing is handled by computers, through the use of numbers printed

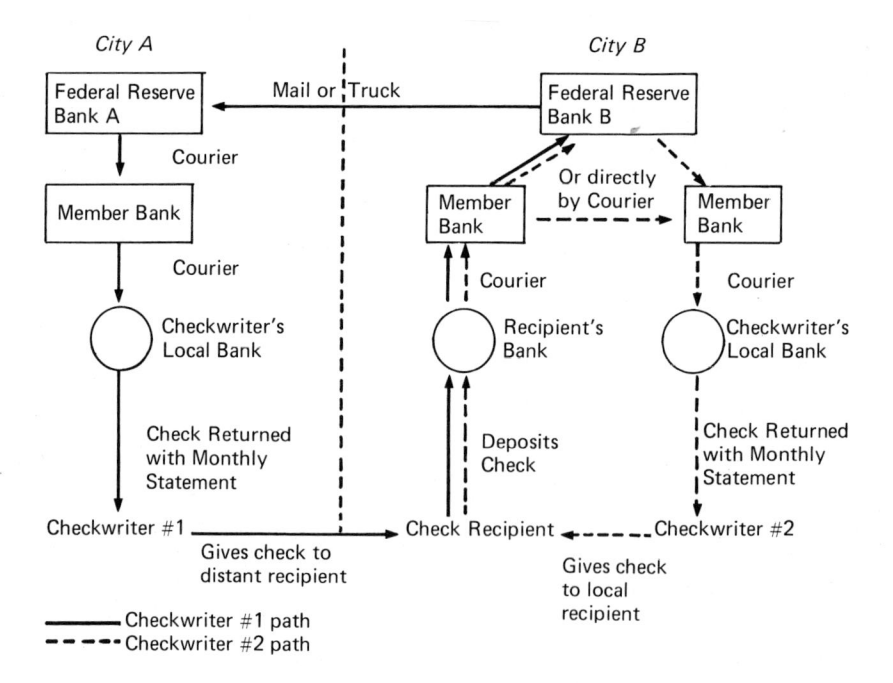

Figure 5-1.   Examples of Check Movements

in magnetic ink along the bottom of the check. Nevertheless, the steps in the process are essentially the same as they were before mechanization.

The annual volume of checks has been growing faster than the economy as a whole—in recent years, about 7 percent per year. This volume of activity carries with it a certain rigid discipline. For example, banks have a limited time to refuse payment on a check, say, if the account has insufficient funds. Also, some checks will be rejected by the automatic machinery, because they have become damaged, and these require special handling. Speed is of the essence, because the sooner a bank can collect the checks due to it, the sooner it can begin earning interest on those funds.

Although the check system creates headaches for bankers, it is well-liked by customers. It allows close control over personal finances, and canceled checks are legal proof of payment. Checks are familiar to almost everyone, and they are much safer than carrying cash. From the customer's viewpoint, perhaps the greatest disadvantage of checks is the reluctance of some merchants to accept them. The merchant bears the responsibility for positive identification of the checkwriter, and he also must cope with bounced checks when they occur.

Bank credit cards, although they currently account for less than 1 percent of the dollar volume of checks, are seen as a forerunner of future transaction systems. In particular, their clearing arrangement has in recent months been moving from a paper-based system, like checks, to an electronic one. Figure 5-2 sketches the two alternative methods of clearing credit card purchases. The original, paper-based system was often called "country club billing" after the practice of country clubs which return the signed chits each month to the member along with his bill. Gasoline credit cards have used a similar system for many years. The "descriptive billing" system now being installed avoids the necessity of shipping credit slips from one place to another. Instead, the information is entered into a computer system when the credit slips are deposited by the merchant. The information is then sorted and transmitted electronically and appears on the card holder's statement simply as an itemized listing of the purchases and amounts.

Corporate customers often wish to transfer funds immediately from one city to another. When large sums are involved, the few days' interest lost while checks are clearing may be substantial. Also, variations in clearing time make control of the corporation's cash position more difficult. Hence, the larger banks offer instantaneous wire transfers for their corporate customers. Banks have two options, as shown in Figure 5-3, for making these transfers. They can use a teletype network established by the Federal Reserve System (the "Fedwire" network), or they can use the private Bank Wire network which connects about 250 banks. To send a transfer via the Federal Reserve network, the bank instructs the Federal Reserve System to reduce its own reserve balances and credit that amount to the other bank for the account of the customer. The process has a disadvantage in the limited amount of information which may be

134 Trends Affecting the U.S. Banking System

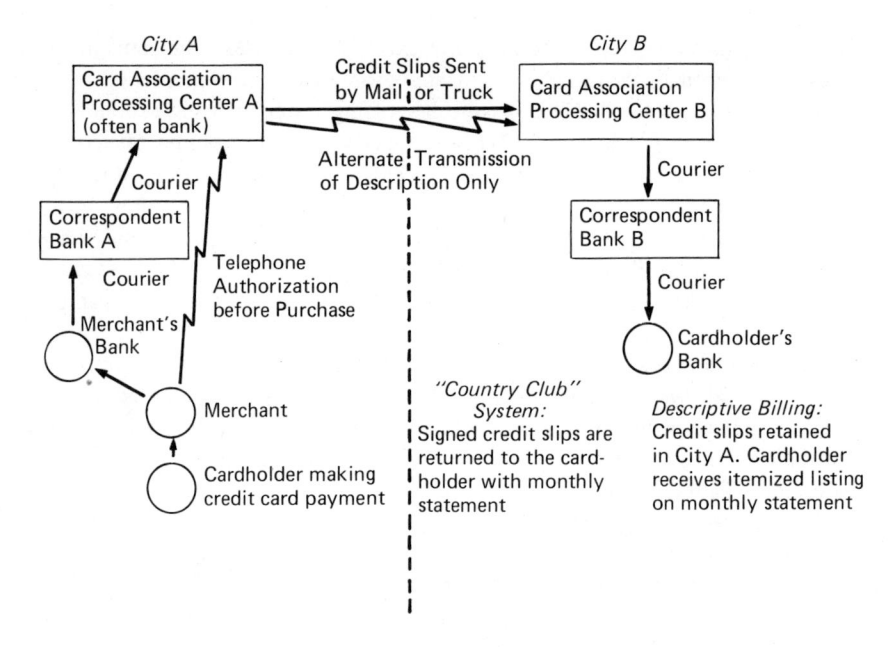

```
          City A                                               City B
  ┌─────────────────┐    Credit Slips Sent       ┌─────────────────┐
  │ Card Association│ ───by Mail or Truck──────▶ │ Card Association│
  │Processing Center A│ ◀──────────────────────── │Processing Center B│
  │  (often a bank) │                             │                 │
  └─────────────────┘    Alternate Transmission  └─────────────────┘
        ▲ │              of Description Only           │ ▲
   Courier│                                      Courier│
        │ ▼                                            ▼ │
  ┌──────────┐       Telephone                    ┌──────────┐
  │Correspondent│    Authorization                │Correspondent│
  │  Bank A  │       before Purchase              │  Bank B  │
  └──────────┘                                    └──────────┘
        ▲                                               │
   Courier                                         Courier
        │                                               ▼
   ○ Merchant's                                    ○ Cardholder's
     Bank                                            Bank
        ▲
        │        "Country Club"          Descriptive Billing:
   ○ Merchant    System:                 Credit slips retained
        ▲        Signed credit slips are in City A. Cardholder
        │        returned to the card-   receives itemized listing
   ○ Cardholder making  holder with monthly on monthly statement
     credit card payment statement
```

Figure 5-2. Clearing Process for Bank Credit Card Purchases

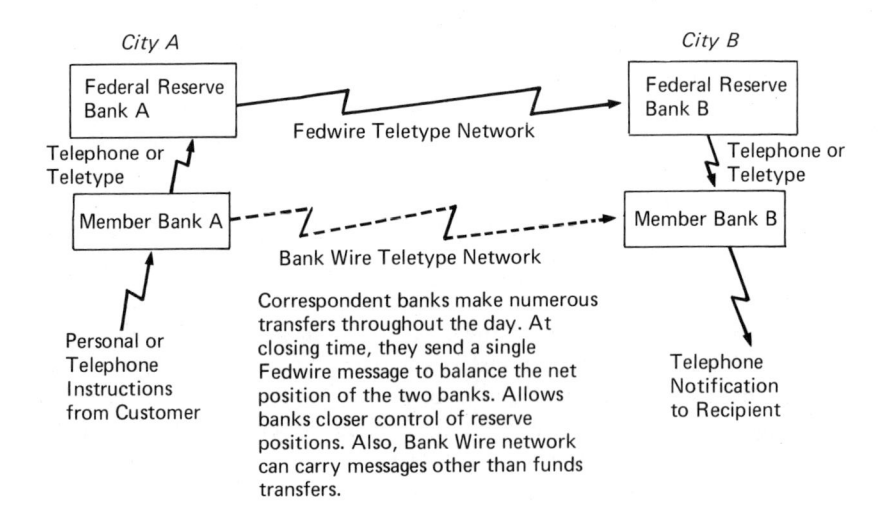

```
          City A                                               City B
  ┌─────────────────┐                             ┌─────────────────┐
  │ Federal Reserve │                             │ Federal Reserve │
  │    Bank A       │ ─────────────────────────▶  │    Bank B       │
  └─────────────────┘  Fedwire Teletype Network   └─────────────────┘
        ▲ │                                             │
 Telephone or                                    Telephone or
 Teletype │                                      Teletype │
          ▼                                             ▼
  ┌─────────────────┐                             ┌─────────────────┐
  │ Member Bank A   │─ ─ ─ ─ ─ ─ ─ ─ ─ ─ ─ ─ ─▶  │ Member Bank B   │
  └─────────────────┘  Bank Wire Teletype Network └─────────────────┘
        ▲                                               │
        │          Correspondent banks make numerous    ▼
 Personal or       transfers throughout the day. At
 Telephone         closing time, they send a single    Telephone
 Instructions      Fedwire message to balance the net  Notification
 from Customer     position of the two banks. Allows   to Recipient
                   banks closer control of reserve
                   positions. Also, Bank Wire network
                   can carry messages other than funds
                   transfers.
```

Figure 5-3. Wire Transfer of Funds Among Banks

transmitted, and it can entail significant fluctuations in the bank's reserve position. The Bank Wire alternative allows banks having correspondent balances to send transfers back and forth throughout the day (bank A instructs bank B to transfer money from its correspondent account to the account of the customer, or vice versa) and, at closing time, to send a single transfer through the Fedwire to balance the net movements from one bank to another.

In contrast to the highly routine, highly mechanized payments system, most other banking services require a more flexible, personalized delivery. Business loans, for example, are normally arranged in face-to-face negotiations and the servicing of such loans often requires a highly personalized approach in the course of which the bank sometimes offers advice or performs special services for the customer. Large business loans also demand a considerable amount of cost analysis by the bank. Consumer loans and mortgages have an intermediate character. They usually involve face-to-face contact, plus some credit analysis at the outset. But later they generate a large number of more or less regular small monthly payments for routine processing. Trust department services require mostly face-to-face (or telephone) communication and negotiation in setting up the trusts and servicing the client. They also, of course, require the bank to analyze and choose investments for their portfolios.

In trying to assess the potential impact of new technologies, it is helpful to classify and compare banking services according to several characteristics such as the importance of face-to-face communication and the amount of paperwork and formal procedure. Table 5-1 illustrates such a scheme. On the basis of this comparison, it appears that video telephones, for example, would have their greatest potential impact on business loan servicing, but would have lesser importance for consumer loans and trust management. Optical scanners, in contrast, would appear most important for the high activity services, such as payments, consumer loans servicing, and so on. No framework of this sort can include all possible characteristics of different kinds of procedures or foretell all possible impacts of all kinds of changes. But the one shown in Table 5-1 illustrates the point that different technological changes will have different impacts and provides a useful analytical tool for thinking about other kinds of services and other possible impacts.

RECENT TECHNOLOGICAL INNOVATIONS IN BANKING

During the 1950s and 1960s banks mechanized a large portion of their operations. A recent survey has shown that more than 50 percent of all commercial banks were automated, mostly for check processing and internal bookkeeping.[1] Virtually all banks with more than $50 million in deposits are now automated. Among those banks not yet automated, more than four-fifths had less than $10 million in deposits.

Table 5-1. Sample Framework for Comparing Characteristics of Banking Services

Banking Services	Activity Level	Dollar Volume	Degree of Analysis	Use of Data Base	Importance of Hours and Access Locations	Importance of Face-to-Face Communication	Degree of Paperwork and Formal Procedure
Business Loans	Low	High	High	High	Relatively Low	High	Relatively Minor
Consumer Loans and Mortgages	High	Mostly Low	Some	Some	Moderate	Moderate	Substantial
Other Consumer Servicing	High	Low	Low	Low	High	Relatively Low	High
Third Party Payments	High	Low	Very Little	Very Little	High	Low	Very High
Trust Management	Moderate	Varies	High	High	Low	Moderate	Some
Bank Management	Moderate	?	High	High	Low	Moderate	Some

Between 1966 and 1972, the trend toward automation had been mostly in forms of off-site rather than on-site computer services (see Figure 5-4). The number of on-site computer installations increased only moderately, but the number of banks using off-site computer services more than tripled in six years. Most of these were smaller banks which contracted for computer services either with a correspondent bank or with a computer service bureau. In the previously cited survey, less than one-sixth of the banks with deposits greater than $100 million made use of off-premise computer services, whereas more than three-fourths of the automated banks with deposits under $100 million did so.

Until recently, automation has affected the internal operations of the banks more than the interface between banks and their customers. People use banking services through essentially the same procedures (over-the-counter deposits, writing checks, etc.) they have used for decades. The technology of banking seems to have reached a practical limit, however, in the extent to which banks' internal operations can profitably be automated. Any major future increases in automation will require changes in the way the customer makes and receives

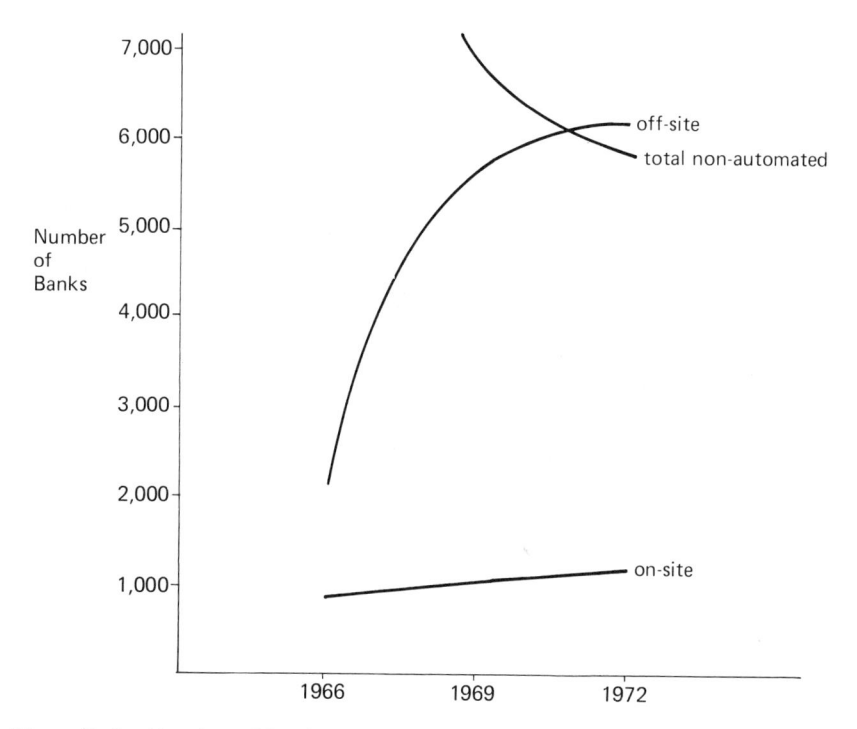

Figure 5-4. Number of Banks by Status of Automation (On-site versus Off-site Facilities)
Source: Copied from Leonard Stier, "Bank Planning Study" (Mahwah, N.J.: Teleprocessing Industries, Inc., 1974 (mimeographed).

payments. Two EFTS changes which affect both demand and savings deposits are most widely mentioned as having such effect:

1. Automatic debits and credits to a depositor's account without his direct involvement. These automatic transfers would be made for routine periodic transactions such as payroll deposits, insurance premiums, utility bills, transfers to or from accounts in other financial institutions, and so forth, subject to prior authorization by the customer. A computerized arrangement for these transfers, the so-called automated clearinghouse (ACH), is now being installed in several large cities. Bankers believe that perhaps one-third of all checks can be replaced by automatic transfers if the ACH system is fully adopted.
2. Instantaneous transfers of funds initiated from remote locations. These transfers would be initiated through electronic terminals at retail stores—the so-called point of sale (POS) device—or at cash dispensing machines or other locations. Instantaneous transfers eliminate the cost of "float" and the merchant's risk of bad checks. A few experimental POS systems have been installed, and bankers foresee eventual nationwide networks. With a fully developed POS system, a depositor would have his funds instantly accessible, wherever he goes, at any time of day.

A further extension of the POS concept is telephone banking. Depositors would use their telephones (or electronic terminals attached to their telephones) to pay bills, transfer funds to savings accounts, inquire about their balances, and so on.

These two changes have fundamental and far-reaching implications for banks; by changing the ways customers interact with banks, they will have an impact upon the very nature of competition in financial services. A good example is the role of branch offices. Since World War II, branching has been a strategic element in the competition among commercial banks and between banks and other financial institutions. Convenient locations, evening hours, sidewalk tellers, drive-up windows, and so forth were expensive but competitively necessary additions to banks' services. In contrast, these two changes should eliminate a large fraction of customers' visits to banks. With payrolls automatically deposited, savings deposits automatically transferred, loan payments and routine bills automatically deducted, and cash readily available at supermarkets or 24 hour cash machines, customers will need to visit their banks only on special occasions. For these special occasions, handy access, drive-in facilities, and the like will probably be less important than other possible aspects of the banks' services, such as personal financial counseling.

EFTS should also increase the importance of price competition in attracting deposits. By making possible simple and instantaneous transfers to (or from) institutions anywhere in the country, EFTS will make it easier for depositors to

Table 5-2. A Possible Scheme for Evaluating the Impact of EFTS

Stage 1

Changes in Banking Mechanics	Automatic interbank debits and credits to to customer's account (ACH)

Stage 2

Changes in Banking Practice	Fewer visits to the bank More "shopping" for best deposit yield Increased short-duration use of savings accounts Changes in liquidity practices of individuals and businesses

Stage 3

Changes in Banking Structure	Banks and thrift institutions more alike* New scope of monetary control More interstate banking and emergence of region "giants" Reduce level of float

*This statement assumes that thrift institutions are granted access to ACH facilities at least to the extent they have been in San Francisco and other early ACHs.

"shop" for the best yield. The result should be a higher turnover of deposits, a higher cost of funds to banks, and a blurring of the distinctions between demand deposits and time deposits.

Other elements of banking which are likely to be affected by EFTS include definition and segmentation of markets, methods of charging for services, methods of saving, degree of concentration of corporate accounts, and so on. It is difficult to foresee all the potential changes arising from EFTS. Our imagination is, in some ways, confined by our familiarity with the mechanics of the present banking system. For example, there are many people who still see EFTS primarily as a means to reduce the "paperwork blizzard" of the present check clearing system. We feel, as suggested above, that the implications of EFTS are more far-reaching than that. Indeed, they reach to the structure of the banking system and its relation to other types of institutions.

Table 5-2 presents one possible scheme for evaluating the impacts of EFTS. The example shown, automated clearinghouse facilities, repeats the ideas presented above about branching and price competition. The changes which occur first (Stage 1) are purely mechanical, but they lead to changes in customers' banking practices (Stage 2), which ultimately can lead to structural changes in the industry (Stage 3). (Table 5-2 is intended to be only suggestive and is not a definitive projection of the impacts of automated clearinghouses.)

Many of the recent technological changes in banking, such as automation of

140 Trends Affecting the U.S. Banking System

check handling operations, have been "transparent" to the customer—that is, they have called for little or no change in his banking practices. In contrast, automatic transfers and point of sale devices by their very nature will change his financial habits. Hence these changes, if adopted, are much more likely to lead to structural changes in the industry.

REGULATORY ISSUES RAISED BY EFTS

Chapter Five mentioned that the development of EFTS is likely to be a major force for changing the nation's financial laws and regulations. There are several reasons to expect significant change. First, new services based on electronic technology will tend to upset competitive balances, and the various interest groups are likely to seek regulatory changes to restore the balance. They may propose either to halt the innovation or to gain equal opportunity to introduce it themselves. This has been a frequent pattern of response to competitive innovations in the past, and it has already manifested itself with respect to some EFTS services—for example, the Transmatic Money Service discussed in Chapter Three.

Second, new EFTS services may upset the "balance" between financial institutions and regulatory agencies, causing a need for new regulations to restore the agencies' ability to control the financial system. Probably the most important problem of this kind is how to maintain the Federal Reserve Board's control of the money supply. EFTS will—again, by their very nature—lead to an increase in the velocity of money. As we stated in Chapter Two, this increase, in itself, tends to inflate prices, because a given amount of money with a capacity to flow or turn over faster can support an increased total value of transactions. Also, to the extent that EFTS services allow time deposits and other liquid assets to function as equivalents of "money," the Fed's monetary control would be further weakened. The Fed would then need countermeasures—e.g., higher reserve requirements for time deposits—to restore its control. Alternatively, the Fed may establish rules which limit the extent to which time deposits may be used for transaction purposes. Conceivably, for example, POS terminals might be restricted to having access only to demand deposit accounts.

If thrift institutions offer instantaneous transaction services on a significant scale, their turnover of deposits presumably will increase. New regulations would then be required to permit thrifts to hold smaller portions of their assets in mortgages and other long term investments. These changes, in turn, might lead to other regulations in order to maintain a continued supply of funds into mortgage financing.

Further, EFTS will create new problems with respect to privacy of information and legal proof of payment. Regulatory safeguards must be developed and implemented to gain public trust in the new methods of payment.

In November 1973, the Federal Reserve Board proposed some amendments to its Regulation J, concerning types of transactions that could be made on its wire transfer network. In calling for responses to the proposal, the board also invited the industry to comment on some of the broader issues raised by EFTS, including who should have access to EFTS, how the system should be financed, and what roles the Federal Reserve and other regulatory bodies should play.[2]

The Fed received more than 240 responses to its invitation, some of them sizable and carefully reasoned documents. The emphasis of the responses was somewhat influenced by the proposal at hand, namely, new uses for the Federal Reserve's wire network. Nevertheless, the respondents raised some of the fundamental questions which must be considered in future regulations regarding EFTS. Table 5-3 presents a sampling of the viewpoints expressed by several interested parties.[3]

A critical issue concerned access to the electronic payments network. If access were open to large banks but not small banks, or to commercial banks but not thrift institutions, or to some other exclusive group, the competitive advantages to the "in" institutions might be enormous. For example, if automatic payroll deposit were possible (through an automated clearinghouse) only in commercial banks, many depositors probably would be diverted away from thrift institutions. This prospect arose when the first experimental ACH was being organized in San Francisco, and a heated debate ensued. Ultimately the Federal Reserve Board resolved the issue by agreeing to assign "pass-through" transit routing numbers for thrift institutions. This arrangement made the access of thrifts to ACH equivalent to their existing access to check clearing systems. Automatic transfers would be made to and from thrift institutions' correspondent accounts in commercial banks, but the ACH computer would treat these accounts as if they were fully participating institutions.

In the Regulation J responses to the Federal Reserve Board, the Justice Department and several of the largest and most prestigious banks took a position favoring equal opportunity of access. The Justice Department stated that for essential facilities (i.e., those for which no comparable alternative exists) terms of access must be reasonable and nondiscriminatory to all competitors. A number of Federal Reserve Board actions, including the development of "pass-through" routing numbers, suggest that it shares these views.

A second fundamental issue concerns the economies of scale in developing and operating electronic funds transfer systems. Most respondents assumed that EFT systems will require high fixed costs but that direct costs per transaction will be very low. This would imply that economically there could be only a few large standardized systems, perhaps only one. A large number of respondents, particularly the smaller and medium-sized banks, felt that it would be appropriate for the Fed to develop and operate a single nationwide network for clearing payments among banks. They argued that the Fed has the resources to undertake such a system, would protect the interests of small banks, and must in any event be part of the settlements process.

Table 5-3. Some Viewpoints of Interested Parties on Questions Raised by EFTS

1. Who should be allowed access to EFTS?

1 Richard D. Hill* American Bankers Association	2 American Express**	3 Bank Wire**
Direct access should be limited to demand depository member banks, with adequate provisions for nonmember banks and other financial institutions to participate in the system on a basis equivalent to that of today's paper-based procedure. (So-called "pass-through system".)	- - - - -	Thrift institutions should not be allowed access to EFTS, otherwise convert time deposits into "money." Institutions without demand deposits should have access only through commercial banks.
4 John F. Fisher* City National Bank and Trust Co. (medium-size bank)	5 George W. Mitchell* Federal Reserve Board	6 First National City Bank**
- - - - -	- - - - -	Some arguments can be advanced to restrict participation in the payments mechanism to commercial banks; in the long run, it is too narrow a restriction. Difficult to continue to separate consumer demand deposits, savings accounts, and revolving credit in EFTS.
7 John Reynolds* Interbank Card Association	8 Justice Department**	9 D.W. Hock* National BankAmericard, Inc.
- - - - -	Competition will set the terms and conditions of access. For *essential* facilities, antitrust law requires access on reasonable and nondiscriminatory terms to all competitors. Department considers thrifts as competitors for deposits.	- - - - -
10 Norman Strunck* U.S. League of Savings Associations		

The Technological Environment of Commercial Banks 143

Delighted to see that thrift institutions can get transit routing numbers, without having to trail on to the commercial bank number.

Pass-through system has problems: Where does data go; first to correspondent bank and then institution (accounting is done outside): Would be more effective to go directly to these accounting centers. Problem is resolved through transit system of FRB.

2. How should EFTS be paid for?

1 Richard D. Hill*
American Bankers Association

The cost of using the system should be paid by the user; full charges should be made to both members and nonmembers with analysis-credit provisions allowed for members' reserve balances. It gives a tangible recognition of the value of reserve balances and serves as a motivating factor for maintaining Federal reserve membership.

4 John F. Fisher*
City National Bank and Trust Co.
(medium-size bank)

2 American Express**

- - - - - -

5 George W. Mitchell*
Federal Reserve Board

3 Bank Wire**

FRB should charge for use of EFTS.
Interest should be paid for reserves in member banks.

6 First National City Bank**

---

*Refers to views expressed in a roundtable discussion on EFTS convened by the American Bankers Association and reprinted in the May 1974 issue of *Banking*. Opinions expressed by individuals do not necessarily represent the views of the organizations with which they are identified.
**Viewpoints expressed in letters to the Federal Reserve Board concerning proposed amendments to Regulation J and other matters.
- - - - - - Indicates subject not discussed by source cited.

Table 5-3 continued

Cost and service input of competitive services should be developed together (Fed and other regional systems).

Pay service through proceeds paid by Fed for interest on the reserve balances is against theology of FRB on the surface.

Congress could be quickly included in matter.

Seems that each service should be paid separately to eliminate those which are too expensive.

A possibility: all services are provided by outsiders of the banking industry. Banks take care of transferring net balances.

Services should be paid by users.

Costs could be paid by interests on reserves or some other mechanism.

Costs should be made explicit and available for public scrutiny.

7 John Reynolds*
Interbank Card Association
- - - - - -

8 Justice Department**

Costs of any FRB system should be identified and charged to user (to enhance competition).

9 D.W. Hock*
National BankAmericard, Inc.
- - - - - -

10 Norman Strunck*
U.S. League of Savings Associations
- - - - -

3. What role should the FRB play?

1 Richard D. Hill*
American Bankers Association

Technological advances should not alter the scope and extent of FRB in the nation's check clearing systems.

FRB should not be involved in contact with a customer. When the customer moves to the merchant, the merchant then moves into

2 American Express**

FRB's role in EFTS should be similar to its present role in check clearing. Role is limited by questions of authority (can FRB reach nonbanking institutions?) and by political determination of FRB role in their part.

3 Bank Wire**

Should be involved in settlement and clearing process. Should not have dominant position.

The Technological Environment of Commercial Banks 145

whatever device his bank of deposit has (e.g. concentrator).

Only role of FRB in switch would be between banks.

4 John F. Fisher*
City National Bank and Trust Co.
(medium-size bank)

FRB should operate EFTS mechanisms, mainly ACH.

Ground rules for ACH will be the same for POS (thus pass-through concept can work in both cases).

FRB should operate switching and processing. Banks would retain right to serve customer.

Foregoing is based on experience with credit card and experimentation with automatic banking machine and POS. Showed need for *national* system.

Should allow the marketplace to provide a framework of choice among competence technologies.

5 George W. Mitchell*
Federal Reserve Board

Now interface among the 14,000 banking institutions in the check clearing mechanism. (a) Sorting checks: where volume between one bank and another is large, FRB requires that items be machinable and in some cases fine-sorted and packaged. Otherwise FRB does it. (b) Delivery of items: present items for collection to payor bank (RCPC).

6 First National City Bank**

FRB should withdraw from operational role in payment mechanisms as much as possible.

Activities that are "joint and cooperative" in payment mechanism should be open to all financial institutions.

Any FRB involvement in switching and processing centers (such as Atlanta) should be prohibited.

FRB should look at equity as regards various institutional roles (through regulation).

7 John Reynolds*
Interbank Card Association

Let FRB be a depository with net settlements to their accounts.

Fed is clearing checks for "free." What is free? Means we don't know what it costs.

ABA does not represent all banks. Some large banks believe Fed should not be involved.

FRB should not be involved in link between POS and computer such as Atlanta project. Danger that pilot test such as Atlanta might eliminate competition.

8 Justice Department**

FRB should encourage competitive development of electronic clearing.

FRB might set up standards for interfacing.

FRB should announce a general policy of competitive private development of EFT (does not necessarily lead to national or local monopolies), particularly for POS.

After announcing its general policy, the board should allow two years before mak-

9 D.W. Hock*
National BankAmericard, Inc.

Cannot be limited to traditional role as interface between banks: see Atlantic ACH project and Cleveland project which indicate that Fed will also be involved in development of the software, communication lines and techniques, the data techniques that relate to terminal devices. Seems to indicate all competitors will work together. How?

Table 5-3 continued

10 Norman Strunck*
U.S. League of Savings Associations

Suggest that FRB own and operate the ACH 31a: (1) FRB is in business already; (2) Atlanta ACH shows FRB would be cheaper; (3) it is so vital it should not be dominated by private interest; (4) it would provide protection of thrift institution; (5) it would provide security; (6) it would provide better standardization if one system rather than an aggregation of many regional systems.

1 Richard D. Hill*
American Bankers Association
Possible alternatives:
Supply a substitute for checks without fundamentally reordering existing institutional structure for transfer or settlement.
Change relationship between institutions: position of thrift institution.
increase or decrease participation of FRB in EFTS.
new opportunities for banks or credit and organizations.

4 John F. Fisher*
City National Bank and Trust Co.
(medium-size bank)

- - - - - - -

ing final decision on its EFTS services. If private services are not offered, then FRB would provide EFTS. (Two interchange organizations seem to be moving in: National BankAmericard and Interbank/Mastercharge.)

4. *What should be the functions of EFTS?*

2 American Express**

EFTS system must serve and take into account totality of users' needs, including those which are not directly computer- or communication-related.

3 Bank Wire**

Fedwire system should continue to serve only FRB member banks, government institutions and other Regulation K institutions.

5 George W. Mitchell*
Federal Reserve Board

6 First National City Bank**

Healthy expanded role of government—similar to GIRO: credit transfers rather than debit transfers—would be major policy reversal.

6 John Reynolds*
Interbank Card Association

Need for two separate systems. Can be coordinated if deposits are left to FRB. Let FRB be depository.

Interbank has developed funds transfer system which works very efficiently and economically: either credit or debit transaction. Receipts could also be transmitted over system. Technology is there.

10 Norman Strunck*
U.S. League of Savings Associations

- - - - - -

1 Richard D. Hill*
American Bankers Association

Growing competition between different types of depository institutions.

Evolving effects of the Hunt Commission studies.

Rapid growth of technology in funds transfer, banking services, and retail and credit card percent of sales devices.

Services will result from design of technology and from competition: either homogenized (if one system), or differentiated (if several).

ACHs will probably be linked to enhance functions of each of them.

Technology will change functions of clearing mechanisms by providing them with direct competitive consequences on institutions and customs.

9 D.W. Hock*
National BankAmericard, Inc.

More automating than what they are doing today (see NDC, ITT and others.) Pacing item is not technology: it is fragmented structure of handling which limits nationwide services.

Customer is key. Not satisfied with service from authorization.

Capturing value data is only small part of service: purpose is also to electronically price merchandise, control inventory, and obtain complete marketing statistics. This means that more than value data will go through system.

5. *What are the factors affecting development of EFTS?*

2 American Express**

EFTS should be shaped by demand in marketplace, regulation, state legislature, Congress.

Should be shaped by needs and decisions of users of EFTS, not FRB.

Need for competition.

Future might be affected by premature FRB involvement.

EFTS systems must take into account all of *users' needs*, including retailers (not only

3 Bank Wire**

Development of EFTS should occur within competitive framework. Some functions can be developed on joint basis: nationwide settlement.

Development of regional automated clearing houses which tend to become linked: in the case of preauthorized debits and credits, this may narrow markets and affect small banks.

Switching and processing center design will determine the nature of these product offerings (homogenizing effect).

Table 5-3 continued

communication and computers, but also accounting, inventory control, credit authorization, or marketing).
Individual right to privacy.
Antitrust policies.
Emerging technologies.

5 George W. Mitchell*
Federal Reserve Board

- - - - - -

6 First National City Bank**

Development of EFTS should occur within competitive framework.

One should not try to predetermine a specific configuration for EFTS.

Competitive EFTS developments will shape the role of the entities involved.

8 Justice Department**

The existing paper-based system does not provide an appropriate model for EFT development: cost and configuration differ.

9 D.W. Hock*
National BankAmericard, Inc.

- - - - - -

4 John F. Fisher*
City National Bank and Trust Co.
(medium-size bank)

How will Fed system develop together with other regional systems?

Important to let competition shape the final system.

7 John Reynolds*
Interbank Card Association

Interbank system is developed on democratic basis with cooperation of 6000 member banks. Minimal standards are set but banks are free to do what they want.

Not sure whether ACH emerging (with Fed role) is consistent with separate independent credit card system.

10 Norman Strunck*
U.S. League of Savings Associations

- - - - - -

The Technological Environment of Commercial Banks   149

6. Should there be competing EFT systems?

1 Richard D. Hill*
American Bankers Association

------

2 American Express**

------

3 Bank Wire**

There should be alternatives to FRB system in order to maximize long-term efficiency and minimize costs.

Envisions a number of independent EFTS.

4 John F. Fisher*
City National Bank and Trust Co. (medium-size bank)

ABA position does not represent threat to small banks and medium-size banks. It would be less acceptable to large banks because it would eliminate their competitive advantages in developing separate systems.

5 George W. Mitchell*
Federal Reserve Board

Parallel courier routes in the check system appear questionable, as duplicate costs can be incurred that really do not make sense.

Criterion for evaluating usefulness of alternate system: how much duplication of these courier routes is feasible and cost-justified (including duplication of funds).

Up to now, there have been alternative clearing and courier arrangements.

Member banks have $30 billion in balances with FRB. Cannot afford to duplicate them.

6 First National City Bank**

Importance of competition, especially with regard to technical and product development of EFTS.

Feasibility of privately owned EFTS seems apparent (failure was justification of role of FRB in the past).

No reason to believe FRB would be particularly innovative or cost-efficient in EFTS.

Resistance of banking industry to private competition results from complexities of EFTS and investment risks associated with such risks.

7 John Reynolds*
Interbank Card Association

Only desire is to create a service which facilitates roughly 6000 banks to compete, one with the other.

Competition among member banks in Interbank card system.

Since 10,000 banks are affiliated to credit card system, it means that they don't expect FRB to provide that system.

8 Justice Department**

Competition exists in underlying financial intermediary system (may increase with NOW account).

Competition exists at the clearing level.

Competition in development of both hardware and software for EFTS.

Competition is important in banking.

Competitive EFT development will provide public benefits (innovation and efficiency), particularly in this early stage.

9 D.W. Hock*
National BankAmericard, Inc.

Need for competition in American society? Competition always has wasteful aspect as someone fails. But cost-effective through competition.

Example of bank cards: what would have happened if banks had had to wait for FRB to work out mechanics of a single system to clear bank card drafts, develop plastic identity devices and software, create marketing material and other innovators.

150 Trends Affecting the U.S. Banking System

Table 5-3 continued

7. Problems

10 Norman Strunck*
U.S. League of Savings Associations

- - - - - -

1 Richard D. Hill*
American Bankers Association

- - - - - -

4 John F. Fisher*
City National Bank and Trust Co.
(medium-size bank)

- - - - - -

7 John Reynolds*
Interbank Card Association

- - - - - -

2 American Express**

- - - - - -

5 George W. Mitchell*
Federal Reserve Board

- - - - - -

8 Justice Department**

- - - - - -

3 Bank Wire**

- - - - - -

6 First National City Bank**

Roles of various participants in the development of the switching and processing center as a component of POS systems are a central question. SPC links retail transactions to financial institutions. To preserve competition, switch services should be competitive and FRB should not participate in such activities, either on a *test* or operating basis.

9 D.W. Hock*
National BankAmericard, Inc.

If FRB gets involved in pivotal role in outlining links in EFTS or developing software of technology involved, then those services which you can provide are to a degree contingent on what FRB, in concord with banks, will agree to do. This would mean a monopoly.

There *are* already cost-effective, parallel bank card clearing systems, authorization systems. NBI is building effective electronic clearing system.

Competition (see antitrust law) means separate system.

10 Norman Strunck*
U.S. League of Savings Associations
No problem on debit side: large amount of preauthorized checks (traumatic for loan payment) can be turned into system.

Problem on credit side: payroll credit, social security credits.

1 Richard D. Hill*
American Bankers Association
Mentioned the position of the Independent Bankers Association of America which considers that Fed should not be involved in EFT, but rather that it should be under control of an approximately public organization, like Amtrak.

4 John F. Fisher*
City National Bank and Trust Co.
(medium-size bank)
------

8. Other issues raised by EFTS

2 American Express**
FRB should not develop on-line POS system because it
is very expensive service.
would prejudice the operation of the marketplace.
will affect the modes of competition among banks and force some banks to use EFTS services that they may not desire.

5 George W. Mitchell*
Federal Reserve Board
------

3 Bank Wire**
------

6 First National City Bank**

Competition is most keen in the POS area.
Competition has prompted many institutions of varying size to undertake EFTS experiments.
POS
National Card Program: Both Interbank and NBI are developing nationwide networks for charge card authorization and eventual funds transfers. Computer interface will be offered by NBI with BASE system. Interbank will be linked with other systems.
Regional "Debit Card" Programs: Hempstead Bank project, FNCB and Chase, and City National POST project in Columbus. Emergence of "debit cards."

Table 5-3 continued

		Automated Clearing House
		House EFTS
		Thrift Industry Activities
		Hardware Supplier Activities
7 John Reynolds*	8 Justice Department**	9 D.W. Hock*
Interbank Card Association		National BankAmericard, Inc.
- - - - - -	If NBI the smallest system in the U.S. with only 250 class A members, can build these systems on a cost-justifiable basis, why can't savings and loan industry do it, with far more membership.	- - - - - -
	Competition might decide when and if and how it is in their best competitive interest to switch messages between systems.	
10 Norman Strunck*		
U.S. League of Savings Associations		
- - - - - -		

The Justice Department, along with the credit card associations, some of the largest banks, and others, argued that such a view assumed a relatively static world:

> There is always a danger that existing systems and technology will unduly limit the perception of policy makers as to what is feasible in the future.... The configuration of an efficient electronic clearing system may well differ greatly from that of the paper-based system....
>
> One of the original purposes of the Federal Reserve System was to replace the rudimentary interbank clearing system that existed in the first decade of this century with a central system that would be faster and more efficient.... Conditions prevailing today with regard to electronic clearing differ markedly from those that prevailed sixty years ago with regard to clearing paper. Accordingly there may well be no pressing need for the Federal Reserve to build and operate a comprehensive EFT system.[4]

The concern of the Justice Department and others was to allow sufficient time for experimentation with alternative EFT systems. To build a single government system now would stifle competition and "lock in" people's present conception of the payments system. The department recommended that the Federal Reserve Board announce a general policy of maximum reliance on competition and private enterprise to meet EFT needs.

First National City Bank, perhaps most clearly of all respondents, set forth the reasons for avoiding a single EFTS system. As an example, the bank cited the competitive role of the switching and processing centers (SPCs) which will link point of sale terminals with banks:

> To an extent not yet fully realized, SPC's will determine the nature of [banks'] product offerings.... Unfortunately, an SPC has the effect of eliminating any important product differentiation—hence competition *between those [institutions] linked through the switch.* A single SPC embracing all important entities within a single market will create a monopoly. In short, SPC's are an homogenizing influence....
>
> We feel that a number of SPC's can and should come into being within a given geographic marketplace. Even at this time organizations such as NBI [National BankAmericard, Inc.], NDC [National Data Corporation], TRW [TRW, Incorporated] and even individual banks such as the First National City Bank are prepared to establish competing service offerings within a given marketplace, and each such offering would incorporate an SPC.[5]

It appears that the Federal Reserve Board may move in the direction recommended by the Justice Department. In a recent decision it denied a request by several Atlanta banks that the Fed build and operate an experimental SPC.

In many respects, the debate about EFTS is just beginning to crystalize. Also, sizable pilot projects in electronic transfers have only begun in recent months. Thus, the next two years' experience, in combination with the deliverations of the new National Commission on EFTS,[6] probably will determine a great many aspects of the new systems that eventually will be adopted.

CONCLUSIONS

One thing can be said with some certainty: Technological considerations are no longer the limiting factor in the adoption of EFTS. The technology for achieving a checkless, cashless economy already exists. Improving the speed of computers or reducing the cost of communications will not, at present, greatly accelerate the adoption of EFTS. The critical issues are now centered on customer acceptance, the competitive balance among institutions, states' control over their banking systems, and the scope of the federal government's control of the monetary system, commercial banking, and the financial industry.

The factors which make EFTS profound in its implications for the financial industry also create resistance to its adoption. Individuals are reluctant to change their habits; institutions are anxious to protect their competitive positions; and regulatory agencies are hesitant to take steps which may upset the present balances. Almost everyone perceives EFTS as involving mixed benefits. Individuals can gain some convenience at the expense of a change in their habits and some risk to their financial privacy. Financial institutions can create some new markets, but almost certainly will face more intense competition (not to mention the operational problems of transition). Government officials foresee a more perfect financial system, but there will be some loss of power by the states, and a large fraction of the existing financial laws and regulations will have to be reconsidered.

In all of these concerns there appears to be a considerable fear of the unknown and an evident lack of confidence in people's ability (or willingness) to solve the problems that will arise. Perhaps this attitude reflects a national mood, in the aftermath of Vietnam and Watergate. Whatever the cause, there has been until recently little leadership by any group in trying to implement EFTS. Now the pace of events seems to be quickening, and the impetus appears to be coming from the government sector. The creation of a National Commission on Electronic Funds Transfers, the call for industry discussion by the Fed, proposed regulations by the Comptroller of the Currency and the Federal Home Loan Bank Board, the organization of ACH facilities operated by the Fed, and the planned conversion of Social Security checks to automatic deposits all suggest a government "push" to start the transition to EFTS.

Assuming that the financial industry does convert to automated clearinghouses and point of sale terminals in the next eight to ten years, it is interesting to look beyond at what further changes might be in prospect. It seems likely that better computers (and especially improvements in computer software) will increase the flexibility of financial institutions to offer new services and to adapt services to individual needs. This flexibility should further blur the distinctions between banks and other financial institutions and between financial intermediaries and nonintermediary service corporations—e.g., mortgage bankers, brokerage firms, and so forth). This phenomenon, in turn, might bring about a new set of regulatory changes leading toward very broad, performance-oriented regulations and perhaps some consolidation of regulatory functions. The range of speculation is fascinating, but a large part of what happens in the 1980s will be determined by regulatory actions, and the industry's response, in the next two to three years.

Viewed in historical perspective, the coming of automated financial transactions and interstate (soon to be international) electronic payments networks are only the latest episodes in the evolving history of banking. The foundations of the industry were laid in earlier times, when commercial and financial activities were largely local in scope. Local laws and local institutions were well suited to the restricted arenas of economic life. Over decades, new methods of transportation and communications have expanded the spheres of economic activity; and, as they did, local boundaries tended to lose much of their significance. New financial institutions were brought forth in response to new needs and new opportunities: the National Banks, the Federal Reserve System, the Federal Home Loan Bank Board, and bank holding companies, for instance.

Now, technological innovations are setting in motion forces that tend further to erase old boundaries; they exert pressures—already visible—that operate to blur or erase distinctions among different kinds of financial institutions. But, in banking as in other fields, the structures and traditions of the past often linger on, long beyond their relevance, because of established interests, ingrained habits of mind and behavior, and widespread inherent conservatism when it comes to modifying political structures and their jurisdictions. These are sources of resistance.

The nature of future impacts of the new technologies and the rapidity with which they come will depend on the outcomes of the long-continuing "tug of war" between the forces of localism, tradition, and specialization on the one hand and the forces of nationalism, modernism, and integration on the other. If history is a guide to the future, one must suppose that the forces of change, nationalism, and integration will eventually prevail. But the questions of how, where, when, and how fast cannot yet be answered.

NOTES

1. American Bankers Association, *Results of the 1972 National Automation Survey* (Washington, D.C.: 1972).

2. Fed Invitation for Comments on, and Text of Proposed EFTS Rules," *American Banker,* November 21, 1973.

3. Several of the summaries in Table 5-3 were extracted from similar, but briefer, statements by the same parties at a discussion session convened by the American Bankers Association.

4. "Comments of the United States Department of Justice," submitted to the Federal Reserve Board, May 14, 1974.

5. Letter from Walter B. Wriston, Chairman, First National City Bank, to the Federal Reserve Board, April 3, 1974, p. 8.

6. A bill was recently passed, virtually without opposition, to establish a National Commission on Electronic Funds Transfers. This commission will have a budget of $2 million and at the end of two years is expected to make recommendations for legislation.

Chapter Six

Conclusions

We have looked, in turn, at the economic environment of banks, the competitive environment, the regulatory environment, and the technological environment. The job remains for this chapter to draw together what has been set forth in the earlier chapters into an integrated picture of banking as it stands today. This chapter will produce no stunning new discoveries or great pronouncements about the future of banking. The purpose of this report has been to build an understanding of the banking industry and the forces that act upon it. Thus, a fitting way to conclude the report is to review what we believe are the salient characteristics of the industry which will influence or explain many of the changes that will occur in the next decade or so.

BANKS' POSITION IN THE FINANCIAL SYSTEM

Commercial banks are only one element in our complex financial system. They hold the cash balances and savings of individuals and businesses, in the form of deposits, and make them available to those who need funds. In this intermediary function they compete with other, more specialized intermediaries such as thrift institutions, consumer finance companies, life insurance companies, and others. They also compete with direct credit investments, such as commercial paper or corporate bonds, by means of which the funds flow directly from lender to borrower.

In their intermediary position, banks face two kinds of competition, namely, competition for sources of funds and competition in the lending of funds (refer again to Figure 3-1). Competition for funds takes place most directly against thrift institutions and direct investments. Competition in lending funds occurs most directly against thrift institutions (for mortgages), life insurance companies (for mortgages), consumer finance companies, direct credit instruments such as commercial paper, and trade credit extended by businesses to their customers.

157

The nature and style of competition against each of these other institutions differs, but as a general statement, commercial banks in the last 15 years have held or increased their share of every major market they serve. These include demand deposits, time deposits, mortgages, business loans, and consumer credit. Banks currently hold 38 percent of the assets of all financial intermediaries, a much greater share than any other type of institution.

Their intermediary role defines many of the basic aspects of commercial banks' business:

1. Banks' profits arise from the spread between the interest rates borrowers pay on loans or yields on investments and the rates banks pay to depositors. In recent years, for a variety of reasons, these spreads have been declining. Between 1955 and 1972 these spreads or margins fell by more than half.

2. Banks expose themselves to two kinds of risk when they make loans. The most obvious risk is that the loans may default. For this reason banks are more exposed in an economic downturn than many other types of businesses. Indeed, they are more exposed than most other intermediaries.

The second risk is unexpected withdrawal of deposits. When banks decide the length of term they can offer on loans, they in effect assume a statistical regularity of deposit inflows and outflows. Any event which upsets that regularity and causes premature withdrawals (or reduction in deposit growth) can leave banks subject to a liquidity crisis.

In the years since World War II, banks have become more exposed to both types of risk. On the one side, loans have become a larger percentage of banks' asset portfolios, replacing government securities. On the other side, bank deposits have become subject to higher turnover rates at the same time that terms of loans have been lengthening. Also, the increasing use of "bought" money such as Federal Funds and large certificates of deposit makes some banks more subject to a rapid runoff of funds.

3. The risks banks take are not merely their own. The money they risk belongs to their depositors. Also, if a bank's supply of loanable funds runs short, the activities of its borrowers can be disrupted just as much as the banks' own affairs. Hence, there is a strong public interest in protecting both the safety and the liquidity of banks. A later section of this chapter will discuss this subject in more detail.

4. The aggregate growth of commercial bank assets and liabilities is determined mainly by Federal Reserve Board decisions. The Federal Reserve Banks are the primary source of bank reserves, and the Fed also establishes the required percentages of reserves to be kept behind various classes of deposits. Thus, the Fed has effective control over the amount of total deposits. The mix between demand deposits, time deposits, and CDs, however, reflects the competition for funds between commercial banks and other financial institutions. The major concern of the Fed is the level of demand deposits which constitute the bulk of the U.S. money supply. The Fed has allowed demand deposits to expand only at a slower rate than GNP, initially to restore a more normal

Conclusions 159

relationship between money supply and GNP following World War II and more recently (after about 1965) in an effort to curb inflation. Time deposits and CDs have grown faster than GNP and they now comprise more than half of total commercial bank deposits.

5. Banks (and other intermediaries) tend to serve those depositors who are too small economically to make their own direct investments or loans. As interest rates increase, and as improvements are made in the mechanisms of direct investment—(e.g., a broader commercial paper market)—more bank customers, especially large individual depositors and businesses, will choose to disintermediate. That is, they will begin making direct investments or loans without the use of a financial intermediary.

6. Factors other than price are important in banking competition, particularly at the household level. People seem to consider convenience, liquidity, image, or tradition more important than interest yields on deposits. Habits change slowly, even in the face of clear financial advantages to searching for higher yields. For example, the price-sensitive depositors who chose to "disintermediate" during the recent period of high money market rates accounted for only 1 to 2 percent of the nation's saving deposits. Thus, in the competition among different types of financial intermediaries, market share percentages tend to shift rather slowly.

THE SHORTAGE OF FUNDS

As we have discussed in Chapter Two, the U.S. money supply was expanded greatly to help finance World War II, and then expanded at a slower pace than GNP for about 15 years until economic activity "caught up" to traditional levels in relation to money supply. Since 1965 the continued growth of GNP combined with Federal Reserve efforts to control inflation by restricting the growth of the money supply have contributed to a sharp rise in interest rates.

It requires no great insight to see that inflation is likely to continue in this country. Public sentiment seems unwilling to tolerate the drastic measures necessary to curb inflation. The postwar average rate of price increases has been slightly more than 3 percent per year; from 1968 through 1973 the increase averaged 4.7 percent per year. The rate in the foreseeable future seems likely to be somewhat higher, though probably not as great as in 1974.

Persistent inflation will mean continued high interest rates and a continued shortage of funds. Also, economic forecasts for the next five to ten years suggest that business investment levels in the U.S. are likely to be substantially higher than they have been for the last decade or so, and this trend will put further strain on the available supply of funds.

As we detailed in Chapter Two, the shortage of funds has already caused significant changes in the banking industry. The continuation of this shortage will reinforce and accelerate these movements:

1. *Bank customers, particularly business customers, will try to keep cash*

balances at a minimum. They will search for ways to put their short-term liquid funds to work earning interest. This phenomenon creates both a threat and an opportunity for banks. On the negative side, it means that the turnover of demand deposits will rise, resulting in higher operating costs. On the positive side, it means an increased demand for specialized fast transfer services, such as lockbox facilities.

The efforts of corporate treasurers to reduce their cash balances and low yield reserves results in a net reduction of liquidity (by traditional measures) of businesses. Whatever its ultimate ramifications may be for the economy, this reduction has one immediate implication for banks, namely, that *businesses will increasingly* seek *to rely on short-term borrowing as their "reserve" to meet unusual cash needs.* It seems likely, also, that this practice will gradually extend to small businesses and consumers. This borrowing may take the form of overdraft checking accounts such as already exist in British banks.

2. *Banks will continue to emphasize "liability management" in the search for new sources of funds.* This will lead to increased use of CDs, repurchase agreements, and perhaps some new, even more flexible, instruments. It will probably lead also to an intensified competition with the thrift institutions for savings deposits. The competition for the savings of households may well become one of the major areas of innovation, because of the relatively wide discrepancy between money market interest rates and the allowable rates on savings deposits. The money market mutual funds and the floating rate bonds of bank holding companies are two recent innovations in this competition.

3. *There will be increased efforts to tap underutilized funds in small and "country" banks.* Traditionally, smaller banks have adopted a more liquid, more conservative posture than the larger big city banks. They frequently hold reserves in excess of regulatory requirements. Increasingly over the past ten to 15 years the larger banks have been borrowing the excess reserves of smaller banks through the Federal Funds market. This has been a costly arrangement for the large banks, however, and it also carries the risk of a runoff of funds. Hence, there is a strong incentive for the larger banks to buy the smaller banks or to branch into their territory to capture the deposits directly. State branching laws and antitrust considerations have been the principal restraints against this appetite of the larger banks. To the extent that state laws are liberalized, there is likely to be a further consolidation of the banking structure toward the patterns exhibited in California (branching) and Florida (holding company acquisition).

4. *There will be continued pressure on bank profit margins.* Many factors are acting to increase banks' costs: the use of high cost sources of funds, the growth of time deposits as a percentage of liabilities, and the increasing turnover rates of demand deposits. At the same time banks' interest rates on loans have been held back by usury laws, consumer price resistance, and increased competition from commercial paper, thrift institutions, and other sources of competition. Banks'

gross profit margins have dropped by half in 17 years, from 37 percent in 1955 to 18 percent in 1972.

The reduced profit margins have several important consequences for banks. First, they mean that *control of operating costs will be more important.* This means not only some efficiency measures, but also, quite likely, a search for economies of scale in the processing of routine transactions. These economies may come from increased automation, or consolidation of operations, or from new technology. Economies of scale also exist in advertising, market research, and other specialized management services. Smaller banks have traditionally relied on correspondents for such services, but as the correspondents increasingly charge fees for services previously rendered free, the smaller banks may find it more advantageous to merge or enter into cooperative arrangements for sharing some facilities in order to obtain economies of scale they could not obtain on their own.

A second impact of the squeeze on bank profit margins will be an *increased search for higher yields.* Banks have already increased their proportions of longer term, higher yield loans. Also, bank holding companies have the flexibility to enter into a variety of non-funds-using services which may offer better profitability.

Finally, reduced margins make it more difficult for banks to raise equity capital, at a time when the regulatory agencies have expressed concern over the adequacy of bank capital.

THE REGULATION OF BANKS

In the earlier chapters we have discussed how laws and regulations pervade almost every aspect of the banking business. Indeed, the very structure of the industry—thousands of institutions with limited geographic scope, multiple types of banks, various types of holding companies, and so forth—is largely determined by legislation and regulations. Financial institutions have at times developed new markets, or even redefined their basic strategies, on the basis of loopholes or technicalities in the laws (for example, NOW accounts and the growth of one bank holding companies in the 1960s).

The most fundamental purpose of statutory and administrative regulation is to prevent banks, in the heat of competition, from taking undue risks with their depositors' funds. Banking safety regulations include examinations, deposit insurance, limits on the types and sizes of loans, and limits on the interest rates banks may offer on deposits. A second major concern is to maintain government control of the money supply as a means of stabilizing the economy. The Federal Reserve System sets reserve requirements and, through various mechanisms, controls the total amount of credit the banking system extends at any time. A third major source of constraints upon banks and banking is public concern over concentration of economic power. Besides some conflict-of-interest rules, there are restrictions which specifically exclude banks (or bank holding companies) from certain lines of business. Also, banking has been a frequent target of Justice Department antitrust actions, and the Federal Reserve Board has adopted a similar policy with regard to mergers and acquisitions. States' rights remains an issue in banking, with dual chartering and supervision of banks by both the states and the federal government. This issue manifests itself most visibly in the state branching laws, which permit the survival (in some states) of far more small independent banks than would exist under free branching. Finally, the federal government has sought to give special support to the housing market through a variety of measures which give competitive advantages to thrift institutions.

Many people feel that the banking regulations are out of date and pay too much attention to procedural minutiae rather than to the overall performance of the financial system. Most of the financial regulatory structure was erected during the Depression, when the financial industry was under duress. A private Commission on Money and Credit in the early 1960s, and more recently the President's Commission on Financial Structure and Regulation (the so-called Hunt Commission) have recommended a series of steps to modernize the nation's controls on the financial industry and to eliminate many of the artificial distinctions among kinds of institutions. So far, intensive lobbying by industry groups to protect their respective interests has resulted in slow progress for the recommended reforms.

It appears likely that future regulatory changes will arise largely from changes in the relative competitive positions of banks and thrift institutions and from developments in two frontier areas of banking: holding company expansion and electronic funds transfer systems. Innovations tend to upset the existing competitive balance, and this, in turn, leads competing institutions to propose regulations to stop (or nullify) innovations which might hurt their position or to gain for themselves equal access to the same opportunities. It is, of course, impossible to forecast with confidence how these issues will be resolved, because the various segments of the financial industry are so incredibly interdependent and interrelated. However, it might be useful to restate some of the overriding considerations which are almost certain to constrain the future development of controls on banks and banking:

1. *There will be no changes that will seriously weaken the Federal Reserve System's monetary control.* Some present trends, such as the development of NOW accounts, tend to make monetary control more difficult. If these trends become large enough to threaten the effectiveness of monetary policies, then new controls almost certainly would be applied to maintain the Federal Reserve's control—e.g., greater reserve requirements for such deposits.

2. *There will be no changes to undermine the mortgage market.* Even though thrifts may gain added powers, there will remain some controls (or, more likely, incentives) to ensure an adequate supply of funds to residential mortgages. It is, of course, conceivable that the nation might decide to allocate a substantially

smaller proportion of its resources to housing. But this would require major changes in social values or a breakthrough in the cost of housing, neither of which is likely to happen quickly.

It is possible, however, that there might be *institutional* changes in the financing of mortgages. One possibility for instance, might be government subsidies to the secondary market institutions such as the Federal National Mortgage Association (FNMA) or the Federal Home Loan Mortgage Corporation (FHLMC). Another might be some form of tax shelter for investments in mortgages.

3. *Concentration of economic power and antitrust considerations will continue to be closely controlled.* The Federal Reserve Board has already imposed restraints on bank holding company activities, and these or similar limits are likely to remain. Also, the principle of encouraging *de novo* or foothold entry into new territories or new lines of business rather than acquisitions of substantial competitors will almost certainly remain.

4. *The safety of the banking system will not be compromised.* It is likely, in fact, that examination procedures will be strengthened and made considerably more sophisticated to cope with the new sources of funds and the new activities of banks. Efforts are already underway to standardize and consolidate the examination of banks. A major concern in any new electronics funds transfer systems must be the regulator's ability to monitor and control the banking system. The Federal Reserve Board has already denied several holding company expansion proposals on the grounds of inadequate capital. Also, if banks begin paying interest on demand deposits or if Regulation Q ceilings on time deposit interest rates are lifted, it is likely that the Federal Reserve Board will retain standby authority to reimpose the controls if it perceives a danger of overcompetition which compromises bank safety.

In sum, it appears that new competitive pressures, along with bank holding company expansion and electronic funds transfers, may force some revision of banking laws and regulations along the lines suggested by the Hunt Commission. Regulations may become concerned less with procedural details and more with performance. Indeed, some regulations may be removed altogether, subject to standby controls. But the basic reasons for regulation remain, as they always have been, grounded in very strong public sentiments, and these fundamentals will define the framework of new regulation. In general, it is surely safe to say that the trend is toward more, not less, government supervision of the financial industry.

Appendix

Potential Effects on the 1971 Statewide Branching Law on New York State's Banking Industry

In 1971 the New York State legislature passed a law that would allow statewide branching beginning in 1976. This law has raised speculations about massive upstate branching by New York City banks to form a few monolithic banking systems that would dominate financial markets. Also, because other states are expected to allow statewide branching in coming years, New York is seen as a prototype of changes likely to take place in these other states in response to statewide branching laws.

This appendix attempts to formulate possible patterns of reaction to the changes that are likely to occur in New York banking after 1976, first by examining the history of New York banking and relating it to characteristics of the state, then by comparing New York with California, which has allowed statewide branching for over 60 years, and Florida, a unit banking state which has recently seen the growth of statewide banking systems through the holding company form of organization. Finally, the appendix reviews the opinions of some key persons or interest groups regarding statewide branching.

HISTORY OF NEW YORK STATE'S BANKING INDUSTRY

This section provides a historical picture of changes in regulation of banking in New York State and the effects these changes had on the structure and characteristics of the industry. The objective in providing this picture is to show the events which led up to the enactment of the 1971 Statewide Branching Law and to help identify the direction of changes in banking which can be expected from the new law.

1898-1927

State chartered banks in New York City have been permitted to establish branches throughout the city since 1898. A 1919 state law extended the authority of banks to branch by allowing all state chartered banks in communities with a population of more than 50,000 to establish branches in their home office communities. And in 1927 the McFadden-Pepper Act authorized national banks to branch in their home office communities if state law permitted state chartered banks to do so. Thus, as of 1927, banks headquartered in large (over 50,000 population) cities were allowed to serve their customers more conveniently by establishing branches within their home office cities.

1934: The Stephens Act

During and immediately following the Depression years, several states attempted to strengthen the banking system by liberalizing the expansion powers of their banks. Thus, in 1934, the New York State legislature passed the Stephens Act. This legislation divided the state into nine districts within which commercial banks could branch and merge. It did, however, have one important restriction—banks were prohibited from establishing *de novo* branches in any "home office protected" community within their banking district.[1] Thus, the only way a bank could enter a home office community was through merger. Furthermore, this act effectively provided no additional branching powers to New York City banks over those granted them in 1898, because one of the nine districts established by the law was New York City itself. Thus, New York City banks continued to be restricted to in-city branches only, while upstate banks were granted considerable freedom to expand over broad multicounty areas.

Few banks acted to take advantage of the liberties granted them under the 1934 act until after World War II. In fact, intercounty branching was rare as late as 1950, and banks generally confined their branching activities to the local area surrounding their home office. In that year only one-eighth of the upstate banks operated branches, and all but 31 of these branches were located on the same county as their banks' home offices.[2] During the suburban growth of the 1950s, banks began to take advantage of the 1934 law by branching over wider geographic areas and by merging with other banks. Between 1950 and 1960 the number of upstate banks declined from 567 to 353. The buildup of metropolitan-area-wide banks, either through merger or branching (or both) led to an increase of deposit concentration in the upstate metropolitan areas. Table A-1 shows this increase for each metropolitan area.

1956: The Federal Bank Holding Company Act

Although this legislation was intended to limit the growth of bank holding companies, it opened an opportunity for New York City banks to expand beyond the city limits. At that time, there was no state law regulating bank holding companies. By 1957 it had become evident that banks within the city would try to extend their geographic bounds by forming holding companies. The state legislature began to pass annual "freeze" laws to prohibit further creation of

Table A-1. Percentage of Deposits Held by the Three Largest Banks in Metropolitan Areas of New York State—1950 and 1960

SMSA[a]	June 30, 1950 (percent)	December 31, 1960 (percent)
New York City	42	46
Buffalo	75	92
Rochester	70	84
Syracuse	68	77
Albany-Schenectady-Troy	64	72
Binghamton	53	90
Utica-Rome	52	81

[a]Standard Metropolitan Statistical Areas as defined by the U.S. Bureau of the Census.
Source: Karen Kidder, "Bank Expansion in New York State: The 1971 Statewide Branching Law," Federal Reserve Bank of New York, *Monthly Review*, November 1971, p. 269.

holding companies in the state until permanent legislation could be passed. Such permanent legislation was finally enacted in 1960.

1960: The Omnibus Banking Act

The Omnibus Banking Act of 1960 terminated the freeze and provided machinery for state regulation of bank holding companies. Holding companies were required to seek approval from the state banking commissioner for acquisitions and certain other transactions. New York City banks were permitted to branch and merge beyond district boundaries (established in 1934) into neighboring Nassau and Westchester Counties. Savings banks in the major upstate cities and in Nassau and Westchester Counties were given broader authority to branch, and additional branches were authorized for state chartered savings and loan associations.

Banks, especially those based in New York City, almost immediately began to expand under the provisions of the Omnibus Banking Law. Between July 1, 1960 and year end 1964, 41 new branches were opened by New York City banks in Nassau County and 31 were opened in Westchester County (including a few savings bank branches). By 1968 New York City banks accounted for 22 percent of all commercial bank offices in Nassau County and 28 percent of those in Westchester County. First National City Bank had established 19 offices in these two counties; Chemical Bank had 20 offices; and Bankers Trust Company and Chase Manhattan Bank each had established 16 such branches. Table A-2 shows the changing pattern of commercial bank offices in these two counties.

For the state as a whole, the total number of banks declined between 1960 and 1970, from 403 to 296, mostly through mergers. With the liberalized branching powers granted banks under the 1960 law, the number of banking offices (home offices plus branches) increased by more than 100 per year, from

Table A-2. Number of Commercial Bank Offices in Nassau and Westchester Counties, New York—1959 Versus 1968

Nassau County

Bank	Number of Offices in Nassau County December 31, 1959	December 31, 1968	Percentage of Total Offices December 31 1959	December 31, 1968
Nassau-based banks				
National Bank of North America	39	48	32.5	20.8
Franklin National Bank	27	42	22.5	18.2
Hempstead Bank	13	18	10.8	7.8
Long Island Trust Co.	8	15	6.7	6.5
All other banks	33	57	27.5	24.7
Subtotal	120	180	100.0	77.9
New York City–based banks				
First National City Bank	0	19	0	8.2
Chemical Bank	0	11	0	4.8
Bankers Trust Co.	0	8	0	3.5
Chase Manhattan Bank	0	8	0	3.5
Manufacturers Hanover Trust Co.	0	3	0	1.3
Marine Midland Grace Trust Co.	0	1	0	.4
Trade Bank and Trust Co.	0	1	0	.4
Subtotal	0	51	0	22.1
Total	120	231	100.0	100.0

Westchester County

Bank	Number of Offices in Westchester County December 31, 1959	December 31, 1968	Percentage of Total Offices December 31, 1959	December 31, 1968
Westchester-based banks				
County Trust Co.	39	50	41.1	30.9
National Bank of Westchester	19	32	20.0	19.8
FNB of Yonkers	10	11	10.5	6.8
First Westchester National Bank	9	17	9.5	10.5
All other banks	17	6	17.9	3.7
Subtotal	94	116	98.9	71.6

Table A-2. continued

	Westchester County			
	Number of Offices in Westchester County		Percentage of Total Offices	
Bank	December 31, 1959	December 31, 1968	December 31, 1959	December 31, 1968
New York City-based banks				
First National City Bank	0	19	0	11.7
Chemical Bank	0	9	0	5.6
Chase Manhattan Bank	0	8	0	4.9
Bankers Trust Co.	0	8	0	4.9
Manufacturers Hanover Trust Co.	0	1	0	.6
Bank of Commerce	1	1	1.1	.6
Subtotal	1	46	1.1	28.4
Total	95	162	100.0	100.0

Source: Ernest Kohn and Carmen J. Carlo, *Potential Competition: Unfounded Faith or Pragmatic Foresight?* (New York: New York State Banking Department, 1970), pp. 11-12.

2,066 in 1960 to 3,215 in 1970. State authorities felt that public convenience had been enhanced because of the wider choice available among financial institutions.

During the late 1960s many of the nations' larger banks, led by the large New York City banks, converted to a one bank holding company structure, largely for the purpose of expanding into new lines of business. At that time, federal law permitted one bank holding companies certain powers that were prohibited to banks or multibank holding companies. Thus, these holding companies were caught in a dilemma. If they wished to expand by buying additional banks, as allowed by New York's 1960 law, they would lose their exemption from the federal limitations on nonbank activities. Most of them opted to remain as one bank holding companies and pursue new ventures in leasing, mortgage banking, and so forth. When one considers that most were already giant banks, the choice seems logical. Upstate expansion, besides being a slow process, would have increased their size by a relatively small proportion.

In December 1970 the federal law was amended to eliminate the distinction between one bank and multibank holding companies, and to ease the restrictions on their activities. Within a few months, the big New York City banks announced plans to acquire upstate banks or establish new ones. This movement effectively nullified the concept of district banking in New York. By June 1971 the legislature had passed the statewide branching law; and the 1970 federal law has been credited as a major force in bringing it about.[3] Table A-3 shows the conversion of banks to one bank holding companies during the late 1960s, followed by their becoming multibank holding companies through acquisition (and newly established banks) in the early 1970s.

New York's Banking Industry Today

New York, with its big business and financial center in New York City, is the largest bank state in the country. Its 267 commercial banks,[4] with deposits of nearly $114 billion (year end 1973), account for close to one-fifth of all bank deposits in the United States.

Commercial banking in New York is dominated by eight large holding companies which hold some $89 billion in deposits (78 percent of the state's total, see Figure A-1). Not surprisingly, these are built around the eight largest Manhattan banks. One, Morgan Guaranty, is a one bank holding company; the others each consist of the Manhattan bank plus a collection of six to ten relatively small upstate banks.[5] A tpyical example is First National City Corporation. Its "anchor" bank, First National City Bank, has $18.3 in (domestic) deposits, and its remaining six banks have a combined total of $116 million in deposits. The eight Manhattan banks alone held 72 percent of the state's deposits.

The size of these giant banks is, of course, far out of proportion to the population of New York City. If the residents of the city kept the same per capita deposits as the national average (about $3,400 per person), the city's banks would hold something on the order of $27 billion in deposits. Instead, these eight large banks alone held $82 billion in domestic deposits at the end of 1973. Furthermore, the largest ones held foreign deposits nearly equal to their domestic funds.

1971: Statewide Branching Law

As we have said, the 1970 amendments to the federal Bank Holding Company Act effectively eliminated New York State's district boundaries and played an important role in bringing statewide branching to the state. The New York law, enacted in June 1971, establishes a single banking district in New York State as of January 1, 1976. Beginning then, commercial banks, savings banks, and savings and loan associations will be permitted to establish branches throughout the state. A four and one half year transition period was included to allow upstate banks to prepare for the new competitive environment. During this transition period, the following limitations apply to branching and to holding company expansion:

1. Bank holding companies may not charter a new bank or acquire a bank which has been chartered less than five years in a home office protected community. (This limitation will remain in force after 1976.)

Potential Effects on the 1971 Statewide Branching Law 171

Figure A-1. Holders of Commercial Bank Deposits in New York State—December 31, 1973

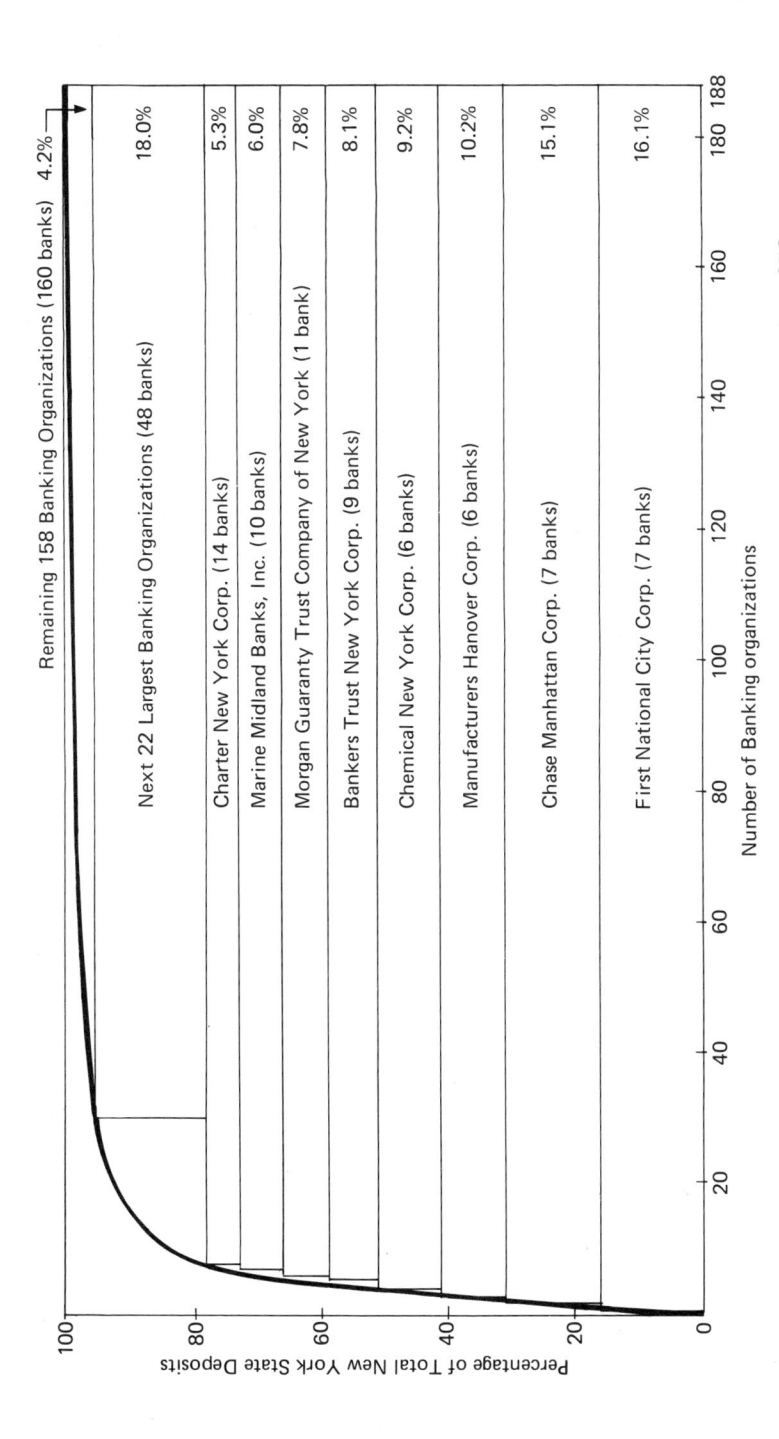

Source: New York State Bankers Association. *Profile: Commercial Banks, New York State, at Year End 1973* (New York: 1974), pp. 76-77, 82-86.

Table A-3. Proportion of Commercial Bank Deposits in New York Held by Bank Holding Companies—1965, 1970, 1971 (percent)

Type of Banking Organization	December 31, 1965	December 31, 1970	Planned June 30, 1971	Actual December 31, 1973
One Bank Holding Companies	Less than 1	56 (34 banks)	14	13 (10 banks)
Multibank Holding Companies	6	34 (62 banks)	78	79 (95 banks)
Independent Banks	94	10 (200 banks)	8	8 (162 banks)
Total	100	100 (296 banks)	100	100 (267 banks)

Source: Karen Kidder, "Bank Expansion in New York State: The 1971 Statewide Branching Law," Federal Reserve Bank of New York, *Monthly Review*, November 1971, p. 272, and New York State Bankers Association, *Profile: Commercial Banks, New York State at Year End, 1973* (New York: 1974), Tables 40 and 44.

2. Bank holding companies are limited to establishing one *de novo* bank per banking district.
3. A newly chartered bank may not branch until it has been in operation for one year, and thereafter it may establish two branches per year until it has been chartered for five years.

The new law also provides for a reduction in the population ceiling established for home office protected communities. In 1972, the ceiling was lowered from 1,000,000 to 75,000 thus opening a number of cities to *de novo* branching by banks not headquartered here.[6] Under the old limit, New York City was the only community exempted from home office protection. The ceiling will again be lowered in 1976—to 50,000—but, based on present population projections, few additional cities will be affected.

How will banks, especially New York City-based banks, react to the provisions of this new law, and how will the structure and characteristics of New York State's banking industry be affected? The following section provides a framework for analyzing possible patterns of reaction.

ANALYSIS OF POSSIBLE EFFECTS OF STATEWIDE BRANCHING IN 1976 ON THE STRUCTURE AND CHARACTERISTICS OF NEW YORK'S BANKING INDUSTRY

To assess the likely effects of the 1971 law on New York's banking industry, three approaches have been selected:

1. A comparison of New York with California, a more liberal state which has

permitted statewide branching since 1909, and Florida, a unit banking state which has recently seen the growth of statewide banking systems through the holding company form of organization.
2. An analysis of the patterns of reaction within New York State itself to previous laws which liberalized the expansion powers of commercial banks.
3. A review of the opinions of key persons or interest groups in New York regarding statewide branching.

Comparison of New York with California and Florida

California is a relatively young state with a high percentage of young people. It is the most urbanized state in the country and until very recently it has been growing at a faster rate than the country as a whole. It also has a higher than average educational level and per capita income. California's banking laws are quite liberal; the state has allowed statewide branching since 1909. Aside from normal safety regulations, there are few restrictions on banks or bank holding companies. Unlike New York and Florida, California does not require state approval for holding company formations (this is left completely to the federal regulatory authorities) and does not regulate nonbanking activities of holding companies.

The banking industry in California reflects these environmental characteristics. One bank operates more than a thousand branches, and several others blanket the state with offices in every significant market. The population per banking office is 6,100, slightly lower than New York's 6,300 but still higher than the national average of about 5,500 persons per office. In California there are an average of 20 branches for each bank; in New York, there are only seven. Because California banks can branch freely within the state there is little reason to organize as multibank holding companies. There are two small ones (with a total of nine banks) and one large one, Western Bancorporation, with one large bank in California and 22 others in nearby states.

Like most other statewide branching states, California's banking industry is relatively concentrated. The largest bank, Bank of America, accounts for 37 percent of total commercial bank deposits and the five largest banks hold 77 percent of deposits. And, 90 percent of total deposits are held by only 12 of the 158 banks or holding companies in the state (see Figure A-2).

The large California banks have enjoyed above average growth over the past two decades. Partly this is due to California's population and economic growth, and partly it results from a build-up of international trade through Los Angeles and San Francisco.

Florida is a much smaller state than either New York or California in terms of total population, employment, or personal income (refer again to Table A-4). The state has a large retirement community (16 percent of the population is 65 years or older, compared with 11 percent in New York and 9 percent in California) and a relatively low per capita income. Until recently, Florida was less urbanized than the others. Since World War II, Florida has been one of

Table A-4. Comparison of Demographic, Economic, and Regulatory Environments of the Banking Industries in California, New York and Florida

Characteristic	California	New York	Florida
1. Demographic and Economic Environment			
a. *Population*			
Total, 1972 (millions)	20.5	18.4	7.3
Density, 1972 (total population per square mile)	131.0	384.0	134.0
Growth of population (average annual percent change)			
1950–60	4.8	1.3	7.9
1960–70	2.7	0.9	3.7
1970–72	1.1	0.3	3.0
Urbanization of population Percent of 1970 population in urban areas	90.9	85.6	80.5
Growth of population in urban areas (1960–70 average annual percent change	3.4	0.9	4.9
Age of population Percent of 1971 population 65 years and over	9.2	10.8	15.5
b. *Employment and Income*			
Employment (in nonagricultural establishments) 1972 (in thousands)	7,229	7,022	2,408
1960–72 percent change	47.7	13.6	82.3
Unemployment rate, 1972 (percent)	5.8	5.8	3.2
Personal income			
Total, 1972 (billions)	$102.1	$96.3	$31.8
Per capita, 1972	$5,002	$5,319	$4,188

Potential Effects on the 1971 Statewide Branching Law

Percent change in per capita income, 1960–72	85.0	94.0	115.2
Index of per capita income (U.S. = 100)			
1950	123.8	125.2	85.6
1960	122.0	123.7	87.8
1970	113.0	120.3	93.2
1972	111.7	118.8	93.5
2. Regulatory Environment			
a. *Branching*	Statewide branching (since 1909).	Limited branching (law has been progressively liberalized since 1898). Statewide branching in 1976.	Unit banking (since 1913).
b. *Bank Holding Companies*	A few miscellaneous regulations (regarding loans to directors and officers).	State approval required. Some restrictions on nonbanking activities.	State approval required. Regulation of nonbanking activities.
3. Banking Industry			
a. *Concentration*			
Percent of deposits held by five largest bank organizations			
1957	76.5	53.2	21.0
1961	81.9	54.9	21.7
1968	77.9	58.5	25.2
1973 (national average = 5 largest = 51 percent)	75.6	55.4	31.7

	1960	1972	1960	1972	1960	1972
b. *Multibank Holding Companies*						
Number	4	17	8	16	2	24
Number of affiliated banks	5	22	22	66	12	255

Table A-4 continued

c. *Banking Offices* (number)

	Banks	Branches	Total Offices	Banks	Branches	Total Offices	Banks	Branches	Total Offices
1955	149	1,212	1,361	638	1,163	1,801	238	12	250
1960	117	1,676	1,793	529	1,537	2,066	309	14	323
1965	199	2,424	2,623	470	2,163	2,633	443	18	461
1970	152	3,033	3,185	432	2,783	3,215	500	33	533
1972	165	3,259	3,424	426	3,146	3,572	581	60	641
Population per banking office, 1972		6,066			6,281			11,880	

Sources: U.S. Bureau of the Census, *Statistical Abstract of the United States: 1973* (Washington, D.C.: 1973); U.S. Bureau of Economic Analysis, *Survey of Current Business* (August 1973) vol. 53, no. 8, pp. 44-48, Federal Deposit Insurance Company, *Annual Report* (various years); Samuel H. Talley, "The Impact of Holding Company Acquisitions on Aggregate Concentration in Banking," Board of Governors of the Federal Reserve System, Report No. 80, (Washington, D.C.: 1974).

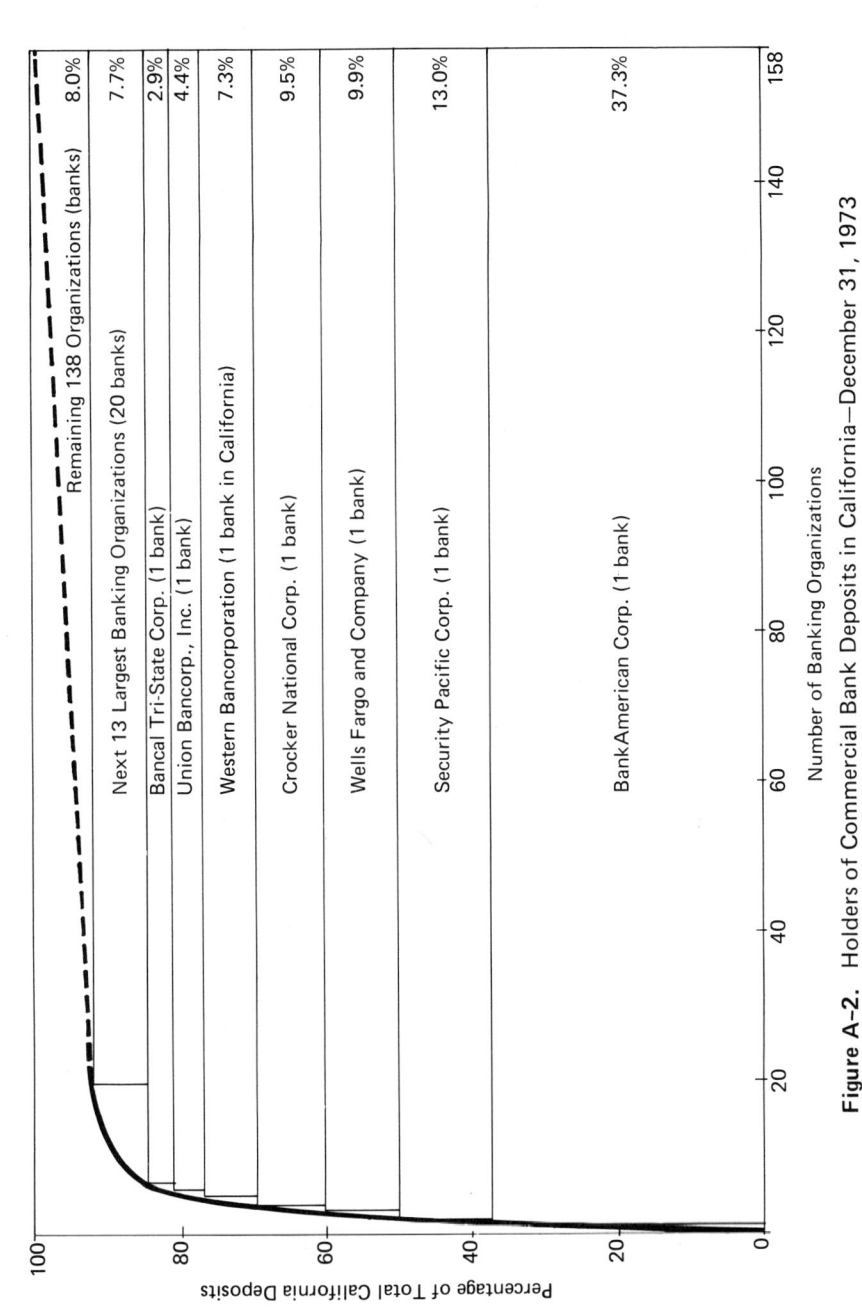

Potential Effects on the 1971 Statewide Branching Law 177

Figure A-2. Holders of Commercial Bank Deposits in California—December 31, 1973

Source: American Banker (New York, N.Y.), August 26, 1971, pp. 8-9 and July 31, 1974, pp. 146, 148, 150; California State Banking Department, Research Division.

the fastest growing states in the U.S. Its population growth rate (4 percent per year in the 1950s, 2 percent in the 1960s) has been almost four times the national rate. The state has become urbanized, and its income levels are coming closer to the national average. It continues to be the fastest growing state in the country.

Florida's banking laws are the most restrictive of the three states. It is a unit banking state, and the few branches which exist today were established under special charter agreements or prior to the 1913 law which prohibited branching. Bank holding companies in Florida must acquire state approval of any new banks or acquisitions and their nonbanking activities are also regulated by state authorities. Despite the limitations, holding companies have played a prominent role in Florida banking for 50 years or more. During the 1920s, especially after the collapse of the Florida land boom, three holding companies based in Jacksonville began acquiring banks across the state. By 1959, these three companies controlled about 19 percent of Florida's commercial bank deposits. Also, since the 1930s Florida has had numerous groups of "chain banks" (independent banks owned by common stockholders). In 1959 these various groups were estimated to control almost 16 percent of the state's deposits.[7]

Florida's growth and urbanization have provided strong incentives for banks to add new offices. Since they cannot branch, they have turned increasingly to the holding company arrangement and the federal Bank Holding Company Act has assisted this movement. Today there are 32 multibank holding companies in Florida operating 390 affiliated banks. (The state has 643 commercial banks altogether.) Despite this growth of holding companies, Florida is underbanked in comparison to other states. Its population per banking office, 11,900, is the highest in the U.S., more than twice the national average.

As might be expected, the growth of holding companies in Florida has resulted in an increase in concentration of the industry. The five largest holding companies controlled 22 percent of commercial bank deposits in 1961; by 1973 this proportion had increased to 32 percent. Figures A-3 and A-4 compare the distribution of Florida deposits in 1969 and 1973, showing the increase in concentration which followed the 1970 amendments to the Bank Holding Company Act.

The Past Experience in New York State

When New York is compared with California and Florida, three conclusions become apparent. First, as states become more populous and more metropolitan, the banking structure tends to coalesce toward a half dozen or so major banks or holding companies which have strong competitive incentives to expand statewide, surrounded by a few hundred independent banks which share a relatively small portion of the market. This process can be retarded by restrictive laws, but to the extent that the restrictions are relaxed, the process continues.

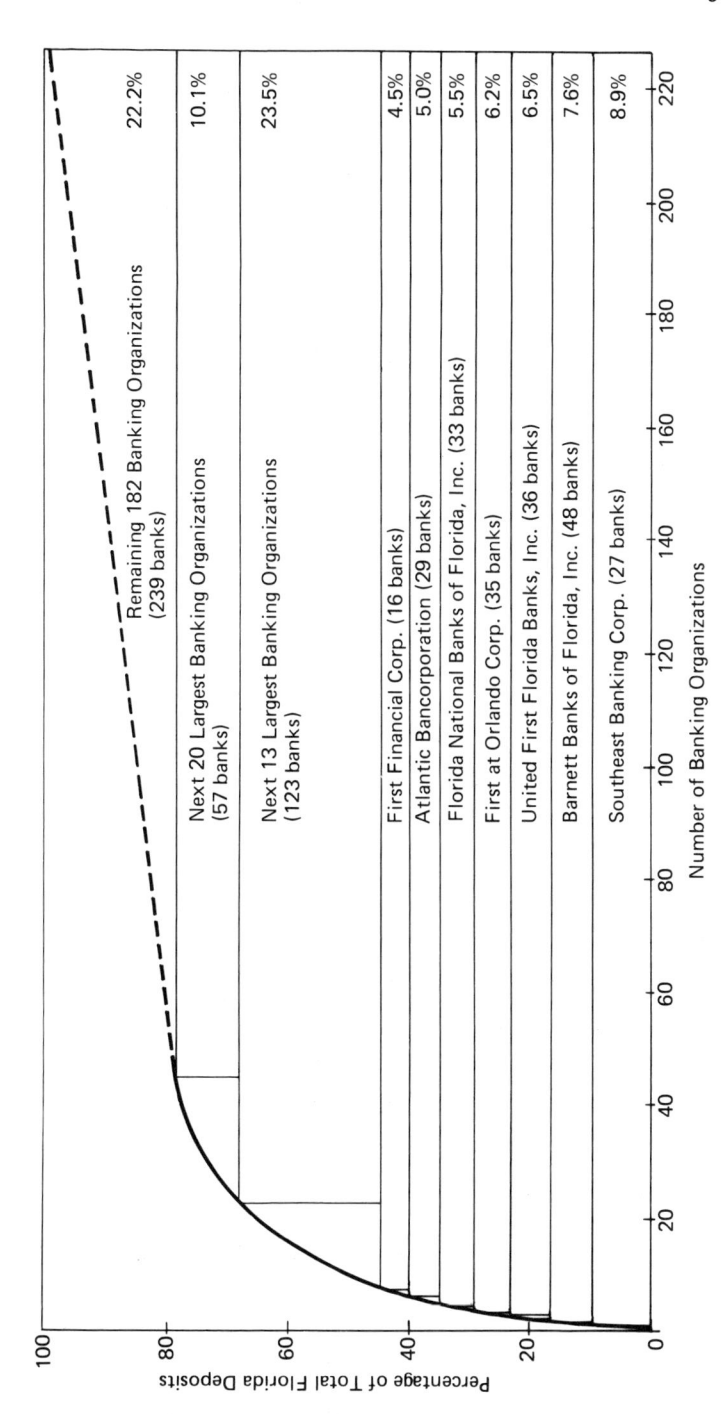

Potential Effects on the 1971 Statewide Branching Law 179

Figure A-3. Holders of Commercial Bank Deposits in Florida—December 31, 1973

Source: Florida Bankers Association, *Florida Banking Structure* (Orlando, Florida: 1974), p. 2.

180 Appendix

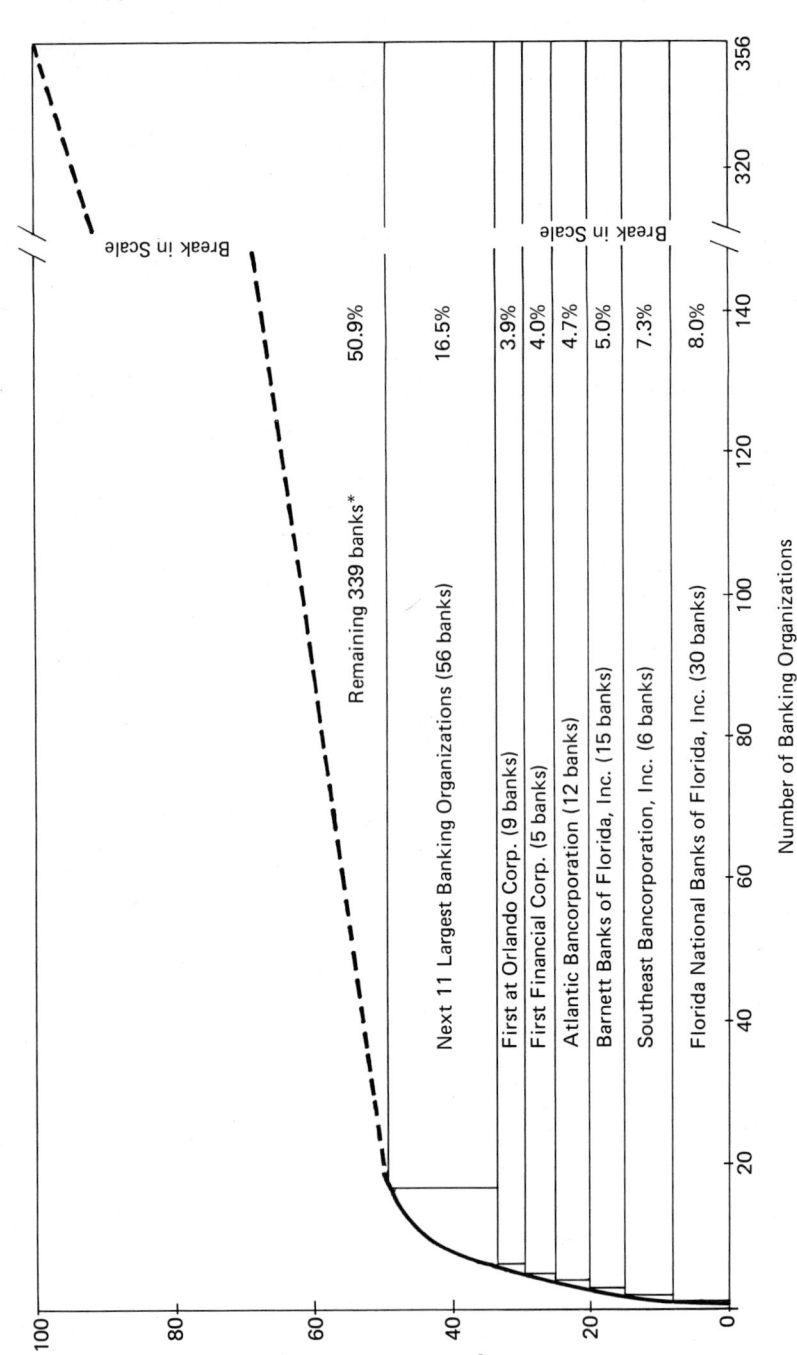

Figure A–4. Holders of Commercial Bank Deposits in Florida—December 31, 1969

*Data by bank unavailable. It is therefore possible that some of the banks included here may hold higher ranks.

Source: "Florida's Bank Revolution," *Florida Trend*, March 1970, pp. 22ff.

Second, the statewide structures do not converge to one or two monolithic banks. Florida and California are both regarded as very competitive banking environments, as is New York City. Unit banks remain, but with a small proportion of the market.

Third, the banking environment in New York State is dominated by New York City. The eight largest Manhattan banks, even if they absorbed the upstate banks entirely, could increase their aggregate size by only about a quarter. By being free to branch within the city (and since 1960 in some of its most populous suburbs), these banks already have enjoyed many of the fruits of branching in a market with more than 10 million people. Their absolute size is greater than any of the statewide systems in Florida or California (except Bank of America).

The upstate banks in New York also have enjoyed relative freedom of branching within their metropolitan markets. Here again, the structure has coalesced toward a group of major competitors in each market surrounded by a collection of smaller banks. For example, the percentage of deposits held by the three largest banks in the Utica-Rome SMSA jumped from 52 percent in 1950 to 81 percent in 1960; in Buffalo, it increased from 75 percent to 92 percent; and in Rochester, from 70 percent to 84 percent.

Both the state authorities and the Federal Reserve Board have imposed competitive limitations on the expansion of bank holding companies. Major competitors in one market may enter another area only through "foothold" acquisitions or *de novo* offices. They may not buy one of the major competitors in that market (see Chapter Four for further discussion of this concept). This explains why the upstate affiliates of the eight large Manhattan banks are all quite small. In the early 1960s several of their proposed upstate acquisitions were rejected by the state on the grounds of reduced competition.

This principle of foothold or *de novo* entry will probably be extended to cover branches, as well as acquisitions, when New York goes to statewide branching in 1976. It seems very unlikely that the state authorities or the Federal Reserve Board (or the Justice Department) would permit Chase Manhattan, say, to buy the largest bank in Rochester or Buffalo. In fact, the state authorities have sought to encourage new (upstate) banking systems that can compete with the New York City banks when they arrive. This was a major reason for inclusion of the four and one half year transition period in the 1971 statewide branching law.[8]

Opinions of Key Individuals and Groups Regarding Branch Banking and the Future of New York State's Banking Industry

For several years now, the most controversial issue among banking industry leaders in New York State has been the expansion of branching powers. Throughout the fifties, large banking organizations, especially those headquartered in New York City, had been pressing for a redistricting so they could follow their customers into the rapidly growing suburbs. Suburban bankers staunchly opposed such entry into their communities and argued that the public was being adequately served in the suburbs. The New York State Banking Department, whose responsibility it is to administer the laws relating to state chartered financial institutions, has held a "middle ground" position. It has sought to preserve and foster viable competition, and it opposes mergers, acquisitions, and branching which would reduce existing or potential competition.

During the years between 1960, when the Omnibus Banking Law granted New York City banks long-sought entry into nearby suburbs, and the enactment of the 1971 Statewide Branching Law, fiercely opposing views regarding the further expansion of branching powers were put forth by representatives of both the large city banks and the smaller suburban banks. Suburban bankers[9] argued that branch banks tend to be impersonal and not as oriented toward the community interest as a home-owned bank. In fact, growth of the community could be retarded because main office personnel housed in distant cities would not have a clear understanding of the needs of the community. When big city banks make decisions, many people in small communities are denied necessary banking services. Furthermore, large banking organizations headquartered in money centers siphon funds from the communities where their branches are located to satisfy the demands of their large corporate customers. The result is a shortage of funds in the communities local branches are supposed to serve, especially during periods of tight money.

The advocates of branch banking say that branch banks are not insensitive to the credit needs of the community. They are prepared to approve all sound loans and in fact can make larger size loans than the small, independent bank. Furthermore, the mobility of funds is enhanced by branching because excess funds are shifted to where the loan demand is greatest. Unit banks, they argue, may make undesirable local loans (in terms of creditworthiness) because they have no other high-yielding outlet for their funds. Branch banks do have alternatives, and if they allocate a lower percentage of their deposits to local lending it is only because they are more selective. Finally, small independent banks actually do divert funds out of the local area in several forms, such as balances on deposit at large and distant city banks; loans to New York City brokers and dealers in securities; and purchases of open market commercial paper or securities issues by out-of-area municipalities, corporations, and the federal government.

The New York State Banking Department feels that local credit needs and the public interest are best served by a competitive network of diverse institutions with different structures, including unit banks and branch organizations. Regional agencies should encourage the chartering of new independent banks to at least partially offset attrition through mergers and acquisitions and promote the development and strengthening of branch banks outside major money market centers.

At the time the 1971 Statewide Branching Law was passed, the superintendent of banks, William T. Dentzer, Jr., promoted the expansion of new bank holding companies to compete with existing ones and the movement of small bank holding companies into new markets. Current decisions made by the Banking Department indicate approval of holding companies that do not eliminate competition between the institutions or affect banking concentration, and that bring to the area a wider range of banking services.

The Banking Studies Department of the Federal Reserve Bank of New York has indicated some likely effects the 1971 Statewide Branching Law will have on the structure of New York State's banking industry. Based on immediate reactions of New York City banks and upstate holding companies, they look for a considerable amount of bank expansion before 1976. In fact, by 1976, when branching throughout the state will be permitted, they expect that the effects of the new legislation may have taken place. A number of holding companies in New York City have already decided to become multibank institutions, and these holding companies will most likely continue to expand on a statewide basis. Upstate banks almost certainly will branch and merge in an effort to protect their markets.

The decline in the number of commercial banks and banking organizations will probably continue. As of late 1971 there were 13 major banking organizations with subsidiaries in more than one district. The New York Fed expects that there may emerge 15 to 20 large statewide organizations with affiliations in most of the major markets throughout the state. However, in view of the goals of New York State's Banking Department, independent banks will continue to exist alongside branch banking systems and holding companies. "History has shown that small- and medium-size banks play a significant innovative role and are important in maintaining a healthy competitive environment. Such banks are often more flexible than very large banks in adapting to local banking needs. Moreover, many banking customers prefer dealing with local institutions.[10] However, it is expected that their share of total state deposits will decline.

The Banking Studies Department feels that the decline in the number of commercial banks and banking organizations will not lessen competition or the number of alternatives available to the public. In fact there should be an actual increase in the number of competitors in communities which formerly fell under the "home office protection" rule and therefore were insulated from outside entry.

CONCLUSIONS

The 1971 statewide branching law is likely to make significant—but not profound—changes in the pattern of banking in New York. Most of the actors are already on the scene and many of the changes have already begun. To recapitulate what we have already said, the characteristics of the banking market in the state are dominated by the financial center in New York City:

1. Eight large banks in Manhattan already hold 78 percent of the state's commercial bank deposits. In absolute size, these banks outrank all except seven other U.S. banks.
2. Seven of these eight banks have already acquired, through a holding company structure, smaller banks in upstate districts.
3. The principal of foothold of *de novo* entry, imposed by both federal and state authorities, will prevent the Manhattan banks from acquiring major upstate competitors. Their expansion must come largely from *de novo* branches.
4. By the same principle it is highly unlikely that these eight banks would be permitted to merge with each other.

The experience of California and Florida suggests that there are no compelling economies which would lead to one or two all-encompassing banks. Rather, the market seems large enough to support a number of competitors, including many small ones. It is worth remembering that New York's banking market is much bigger than California's, so it is likely that New York can support a greater number of large competitors than can California. Also, the state banking authorities have acted to insure that the New York banks will not have the market to themselves.

As the Manhattan banks add upstate branches, New York's banking environment is likely to become much more competitive. Although some of the Manhattan banks could opt out of the upstate competition (as, for example, Morgan Guaranty Trust Co. has chosen not to branch extensively in New York City), that possibility appears unlikely. Most of them have already acquired upstate affiliates which probably will be converted to branches at some time.

To defend themselves, some of the upstate banks are likely to merge (with state encouragement) into larger systems and to expand their own branch networks. The result should be a substantial reduction in New York's population per banking office. How far this phenomenon will continue is a difficult question to answer. The population and the economy of New York State are growing slowly. The state offers much fewer growth opportunities than California or Florida. No bank wishes to operate unprofitable branches and the New York City banks especially will have other opportunities for expansion into nonbanking fields or into international banking. These alternative opportunities, combined with the fact that upstate branching can add at most about 20 percent to their aggregate size, should introduce some restraint (though perhaps not at the outset) in the addition of upstate branches. All in all, it is possible that the advent of statewide branching in 1976 will cause some consolidation and strengthening of upstate banks, much more than a takeover of the state by the New York City banks.

No matter what the effects of the 1971 branching law, New York's aggregate banking market will fall well short of the national growth rate. For a number of years, population and economic activity in the state have grown at a rate considerably below the national average. Also, the growth of commercial bank deposits in New York City has not kept pace with the growth in other Reserve cities. These fundamental trends might cause the more aggressive holding companies to concentrate their energies on faster-growing markets overseas or in nonbanking activities.

NOTES

1. "Home office protected" communities were communities in which some other commercial bank was headquartered. Home office protection did not apply to New York City.

2. Karen Kidder, "Bank Expansion in New York State: The 1971 Statewide Branching Law," Federal Reserve Bank of New York, *Monthly Review,* November 1971. These numbers include banks in all banking districts other than New York City.

3. Ibid., p. 266.

4. There are also 121 mutual savings banks and 179 savings and loan associations in New York.

5. See Figure A-4. One exception to the pattern is Marine Midland Banks, Inc., which has a $1.6 billion bank in Buffalo and several others with deposits over $100 million.

6. Albany, Buffalo, Rochester, Schenectady, Syracuse, and Utica.

7. Charles D. Salley, "A Decade of Holding Company Regulation in Florida," Federal Reserve Bank of Atlanta, *Monthly Review,* July 1970, p. 90.

8. Kidder, p. 273.

9. The views presented here are largely those of Sanford Bush, vice president of First National Bank of Marion, before the New York State Joint Legislative Committee on the Banking Law, Albany, July 17, 1962; Patrick J. Clifford, chairman of Security National Bank in Huntington, before the New York State Joint Legislative Committee on the Banking Law, New York City, November 24, 1969; and Robert H. Fearon, Jr., president and trust officer of The Oneida Valley National Bank and New York State Director of the Independent Bankers Association of America, in "Banking Needs Independent Banks," *Bankers Magazine,* Summer 1974.

10. Kidder, p. 274.

Bibliography

GENERAL REFERENCES AND STATISTICAL WORKS

Baughn, William H. and Walker, Charls E., eds. *The Bankers' Handbook.* Homewood, Illinois: Dow Jones–Irwin, Inc., 1966.

Booz-Allen & Hamilton Inc., Banking Department. *The Challenge Ahead For Banking: A Study of the Commercial Banking System in 1980.* New York: Booz-Allen & Hamilton, 1971.

Federal Deposit Insurance Corporation. *Annual Report*–1972 (1970, 1965, 1960, 1955, 1950, 1945). Washington, D.C.: Federal Deposit Insurance Corporation.

———. *Summary of Accounts and Deposits in all Commercial Banks: National Summary, June 30, 1970.* Washington, D.C.: Federal Deposit Insurance Corporation.

———. *Summary of Accounts and Deposits in all Commercial Banks – June 30, 1972. National Summary.* Washington, D.C.: Federal Deposit Insurance Corporation.

———. *Summary of Deposits in All Commercial and Mutual Savings Banks: June 30, 1973.* Washington, D.C.: Federal Deposit Insurance Corporation, 1973.

Functional Cost Analysis: 1972 Average Banks. Based on Data Furnished by 945 Participating Banks in Twelve Federal Reserve Districts.

"The New Banking." *Business Week* (Special Issue), September 15, 1973, pp. 86–166.

Peretz, David. "Thirty-Five Years of Change for the Financial System." *Futures,* December 1971, pp. 349–356.

Performance Characteristics of High Earning Banks: Functional Cost Analysis–1972. Based on Data Furnished by Participating Banks in Twelve Federal Reserve Districts.

Prochnow, Herbert V. and Prochnow, Herbert V., Jr., eds. *The Changing World of Banking.* New York: Harper & Row, Publishers, 1974.

188 Bibliography

Shapiro, Eli; Solomon, Ezra; and White, William L. *Money and Banking.* 5th ed. New York: Holt, Rinehart and Winston, Inc., 1968.

Shassol, Albert. " '73 Trust Assets Off 8.9% to $297.7 Billion at Top 100 Institutions." *American Banker,* August 20, 1974.

"Total Deposits of 300 Biggest U.S. Banks Rose 20.2% to $531.5 Billion in 12 Months Ended June 30." *American Banker,* Reprint No. 182.

U.S., Board of Governors of the Federal Reserve System. *Annual Report 1973* (1970, 1965, 1960, 1955, 1950, 1945). Washington, D.C.: Board of Governors of the Federal Reserve System.

——. *Bank Holding Companies and Subsidiary Banks as of December 31, 1973.* Washington, D.C.: Board of Governors of the Federal Reserve System, 1974.

——. "Financial and Business Statistics." *Federal Reserve Bulletin,* various issues.

——. *Flow of Funds Accounts, 1945-1972: Annual Total Flows & Year-End Assets and Liabilities.* Washington, D.C.: Board of Governors of the Federal Reserve System, 1973.

——. *Historical Chart Book: 1973.* Washington, D.C.: Board of Governors of the Federal Reserve System, 1973.

——. *Supplement to Banking & Monetary Statistics. Section 6: Bank Income.* Washington, D.C.: Board of Governors of the Federal Reserve System, 1966.

U.S. Department of Commerce, Bureau of the Census. *Statistical Abstract of the United States: 1973.* Washington, D.C.: 1973.

BANK MANAGEMENT ISSUES

Austrian, Caryl. "Massachusetts Bankers Association Votes Major Reorganization by 70-1." *American Banker,* June 28, 1974.

"Average Functional Cost and Revenue for Banks in Three Size Categories, 1966-1969." *Economic Review* (Cleveland), April 1971, pp. 3-22.

Brown, Stanley H. "The Man Who Beat The Rockefeller Bank." *New York,* October 9, 1972, pp. 41-44.

Bryan, Lowell L. and Clark, Simon G. McH. "Unbundling Full-Service Banking." *Financial Executive,* April 1974, pp. 60-66.

Burns, Joseph E. "Compensating Balance Requirements Integral to Bank Lending." *Business Review* (Dallas), February 1972, pp. 1-8.

——. "Bank Liquidity: A Straightforward Concept But Hard to Measure." *Business Review* (Dallas), May 1971, pp. 1-4.

Cacy, J.A. and Bedford, Margaret E. "Commercial Bank Profitability: 1961-71." *Monthly Review* (Kansas City), September-October 1972, pp. 15-24.

"Checking Account Costs—Trends and Composition Among Small Banks, 1966-70." *Business Conditions* (Chicago), October 1971, pp. 2-11.

"Correspondent Banking—1973." *American Banker,* December 17, 1973.

Jessup, Paul F. "Superbanking." *The Bankers Magazine,* Summer 1974, pp. 21-27.

Knight, Robert E. "Correspondent Banking. Part I: Balances and Services." *Monthly Review* (Atlanta), November 1970, pp. 3-14.

———. "Correspondent Banking. Part II: Loan Participations and Fund Flows." *Monthly Review* (Kansas City), December 1970, pp. 12-24.

———. "Correspondent Banking, Part III: Account Analysis." *Monthly Review* (Kansas City), December 1971, pp. 3-17.

———. "The Impact of Changing Check Clearing Arrangements on the Correspondent Banking System." *Monthly Review* (Kansas City), December 1972, pp. 14-24.

Marshall, Robert H. "Competition in Banking." *The Bankers Magazine,* Winter 1973, pp. 81-86.

Mayo, Robert P. "The Challenges for Small Banks." Expansion of Remarks of Mr. Robert P. Mayo, president of the Federal Reserve Bank of Chicago at the Group I Iowa Bankers Association Meeting, Sioux City, Iowa, February 12, 1971. *Business Conditions* (Chicago), March 1971, pp. 10-20.

Nadler, Paul S. "Banking Economic Trends: Banks Must Prepare For Lower Service Charges, Not Higher." *American Banker,* June 11, 1974.

———. "Banking Economic Trends: Liability Mismanagement and Loyalty— Two Factors for Banker Concern." *American Banker,* July 9, 1974.

Piper, Thomas R. *The Economics of Bank Acquisitions by Registered Bank Holding Companies.* Boston: Federal Reserve Bank of Boston, March 1971.

"A Shifting Capital Mix for District Member Banks." *Business Review* (Philadelphia), December 1973, pp. 12-15.

Sotnick, Bart. "First Penn Shrinking Its Correspondent Operations in Move to Improve Profitability." *American Banker,* June 11, 1974.

Warberg, Carla M. "Functional Profitability Varies with Size of Bank." *Business Review* (Dallas), November 1971, pp. 5-11.

BANK TECHNOLOGY AND EFTS

The American Bankers Association, Marketing Division Research Committee. *Direct Pay Deposit, Prearranged Transfers: A Report of the Research Committee, Marketing Division, On a Study Conducted By Booz-Allen & Hamilton and National Analysts.* Washington, D.C.: American Bankers Association, 1974.

The American Bankers Association, The Operations and Automation Division, Research and Planning Committee. *Results of the 1972 National Automation Survey.* Washington, D.C.: American Bankers Association, 1973.

Arthur D. Little, Inc. *An Assessment of Less Cash/Less Check Technology.* A First Phase Report to the National Science Foundation, February 1, 1974. Cambridge, Massachusetts: Arthur D. Little, Inc., 1974.

Atlanta Payments Project. *Automated Clearing Houses: An In-Depth Analysis.* Atlanta: Atlanta Payments Project, 1974.

Booz-Allen & Hamilton and National Analysts. *Marketing Update: Insights into Two Payments System Products—Direct Pay Deposit and Prearranged Transfers.* A Study Conducted for the American Bankers Association. October 1973.

190 Bibliography

Brooke, Phillip. "Electronic Funds Transfer Systems." *American Banker,* Reprint No. 165.

Comments—Regulation J: Nation's Payments Mechanism/Electronic Funds Transfer. Issued for Comment by the Federal Reserve Board 11/19/73. Comments Due 3/8/74.

Doll, Dixon R. "The Telecommunications Industry Outlook and Its Impact on Future Networks." Synopsis of presentation by Dr. Dixon R. Doll, president DMW Telecommunications Corporation, Ann Arbor, Michigan, and Adjunct Faculty Member, IBM Systems Research Institute, New York City. American Bankers Association, 1974 National Operations and Automation Conference, San Francisco, California, May 20, 1974. Mimeographed.

The Federal Reserve Bank of Boston. *Electronic Money—and the Payments Mechanism.* Boston: Federal Reserve Bank of Boston, 1967.

———. *The Payments Mechanism . . . Another Look.* Proceedings of the 47th Annual Stockholders Meeting, October 14, 1971. Boston: Federal Reserve Bank of Boston, 1971.

Fenner, Linda M. and Long, Robert H. *A Check Collection System: A Quantitative Description.* Park Ridge, Illinois: Bank Administration Institute, 1970.

———. *Payment Services.* Park Ridge, Illinois: Bank Administration Institute, 1972.

Fischer, L. Richard. "Legal Implications of a Cashless Society." *Computer,* December 1973, pp. 21–24.

Flannery, Mark J. and Jaffee, Dwight M. *The Economic Implications of an Electronic Monetary Transfer System.* Lexington, Massachusetts: Lexington Books, 1973.

Frost & Sullivan, Inc. *Banking Information Systems—The Checkless Society.* New York: Frost & Sullivan, Inc., November 1972.

Georgia Tech Research Institute. *Research on Improvements of the Payments Mechanism: The Final Report on Phase I, An Analysis of Payments Transactions and Phase II, Payments Flow Data.* Prepared for the Federal Reserve Bank of Atlanta. Atlanta: Georgia Tech Research Institute, Georgia Institute of Technology, 1971.

Harrell, Guy B. "The Automated Banking Facility." Submitted in partial fulfillment of the requirements of The Stonier Graduate School of Banking conducted by The American Bankers Association at Rutgers—The State University, New Brunswick, New Jersey, June 1972.

Lee, Robert E. "Regional Check Processing Centers—An Integral Step to Electronic Payments." Submitted in partial fulfillment of the requirements of the Graduate School of Banking conducted by the American Bankers Association at Rutgers—The State University, New Brunswick, New Jersey, June 1973.

Long, Robert H. *EFTS, Banking and Regulation J.* Park Ridge, Illinois: Bank Administration Institute, 1974.

Long, Robert H. and Fenner, Linda M. *An Electronic Network for Interbank Payment Communications: A Design Study.* Park Ridge, Illinois: Bank Administration Institute, 1969.

Long, Robert H.; Stafeil, Walter W.; and Bergstrom, James. *1972 Survey of the Check Collection System.* Park Ridge, Illinois: Bank Administration Institute, 1973.

Momjian, Dan and Steffen, George W. *On-Line Savings Systems.* Park Ridge, Illinois: Bank Administration Institute, 1970.

NABAC, The Association for Bank Audit, Control and Operation. *An Electronic Network for Check Collection: A Feasibility Study.* Park Ridge, Illinois: NABAC, 1966.

National Data Corporation. *Operating Statement, Nine Months Ending February 28, 1973* (February 29, 1972) and *Prospectus* (February 14, 1973).

"Postal Service Banks on 'Liquidity' Builder." *Financial Trend,* January 14-20, 1972.

Reistad, Dale L. "Payments System Developments in Other Financial Institutions—How Competitors View Their Payments System Role." A presentation to the American Bankers Association's National Automation Conference by Dale L. Reistad, president, Payment Systems Incorporated, New York, May 20, 1974, Fairmont Hotel, San Francisco, California. Mimeographed.

Report of the Automated Clearing House Task Force. Washington, D.C.: The American Bankers Association, January 1974.

"Special Report: Operations/Automation." *Banking,* May 1974, p. 29.

BANKING REGULATION

"Amendment to Regulation Q." *Federal Reserve Bulletin,* December 1973, pp. 921-923.

Baker, Donald I. "Geographic Barriers in Banking." Remarks by Donald I. Baker, deputy assistant attorney general, antitrust division, Department of Justice, prepared for delivery at The Ninth Annual Banking Law Institute sponsored by the *Bankers Magazine* and the *Banking Law Journal.* Mimeographed. Washington, D.C.: Department of Justice, May 3, 1974.

——. "Holding Companies After Hunt." Remarks by Donald I. Baker, director of policy planning, antitrust division, Department of Justice, prepared for delivery at the Annual Meeting of the American Bar Association, Sheraton-Park Hotel, Washington, D.C., August 7, 1973. Mimeographed.

——. "State Branch Bank Barriers and Future Shock—Will the Walls Come Tumbling Down?" Remarks by Donald I. Baker, director of policy planning, antitrust division, Department of Justice, prepared for delivery to Registered Bank Holding Companies—Conference on State Legislation. Mimeographed. Washington, D.C.: Department of Justice, September 10, 1973.

——. "Statement of Donald I. Baker, Director of Policy Planning, Antitrust Division, Before the Committee on Banking and Currency, House of Representatives, Concerning the Recurring Monetary and Credit Crises, September 17, 1973." Mimeographed.

——. "Statement of Donald I. Baker, Deputy Assistant Attorney General, Antitrust Division, Before the Subcommittee on Bank Supervision and Insurance, House Committee on Banking & Currency, Concerning Competitive Issues Presented by Developing Electronic Funds Transfer Technology." Mimeographed. Washington, D.C.: Department of Justice, November 6, 1973.

——. "Thinking Expansively About Bank Expansion." Remarks by Donald I. Baker, deputy assistant attorney general, antitrust division, Department of Justice, prepared for delivery at a joint program of *Bankers Magazine* and

Banking Law Journal. Mimeographed. Washington, D.C.: Department of Justice, December 10, 1973.

"Bank Holding Companies: Operation of Savings and Loan Associations." *Federal Reserve Bulletin,* August 1972, p. 717.

"Bank Holding Company Activities." *Federal Reserve Bulletin,* August 1972, p. 744.

The Banking Law Journal, vol. 90, no. 5, May 1973.

Black, Robert P. *The Federal Reserve Today.* Richmond, Virginia: Federal Reserve Bank of Richmond, 1971.

Brooke, Phillip. "FHLBB Issues Formal Rules for EFTS, First by Any Agency; ABA Raps Move." *American Banker,* June 28, 1974.

———. "Justice Opposes Heavy Fed EFTS Role." *American Banker,* May 20, 1974.

Burnham, David. "Bank Examiner No. 1: Currency Controller Takes Own Medicine." *New York Times,* June 9, 1974, p. F-5.

Burns, Arthur F. "Objectives and Responsibilities of the Federal Reserve System." Excerpt from an address by Arthur F. Burns, chairman, Board of Governors of the Federal Reserve System, at dedication ceremonies for a new building at the Federal Reserve Bank of Minneapolis, September 8, 1973. *Federal Reserve Bulletin,* September 1973, pp. 655-657.

———. "Some Problems of Central Banking." Remarks of Arthur F. Burns, chairman, Board of Governors of the Federal Reserve System, before the 1973 International Monetary Conference, Paris, France, June 6, 1973. *Federal Reserve Bulletin,* June 1973, pp. 417-419.

Byrne, James S. "Performance, Power, and the Public Interest—The Forces of Change Bearing Upon Bank Trust Departments." *American Banker* Reprint Service.

Collins, Charles Wallace. *The Branch Banking Question.* New York: The MacMillan Company, 1926.

Commission on Money and Credit. *Money and Credit: Their Influence on Jobs, Prices, and Growth.* Englewood Cliffs, New Jersey: Prentice-Hall, Inc., 1961.

Conover, Lynn. "Fed Approves BHC Entry Into Retail Insurance Market Over Agent Opposition." *American Banker,* July 8, 1974.

———. "Trust Disclosure Proposal Regulation Gets General Support, Few Reservations." *American Banker,* July 9, 1974.

Dowling, Robert. "Top Court Accepts Potential Competition; Justice Loses on Marine; Connecticut Remanded." *American Banker,* June 27, 1974.

"Fed Shows Concern for Future Competition in Decisions Concerning Southeast Markets." *American Banker,* June 27, 1974.

"Federal Laws Regulating Bank Mergers and the Acquisition of Banks by Registered Bank Holding Companies." *Economic Review* (Cleveland), January 1971, pp. 18-27.

Federal Reserve Bank of Boston. *Policies for a More Competitive Financial System: A Review of The Report of the President's Commission on Financial Structure and Regulation.* Proceedings of a Conference Held in June 1972. Boston: Federal Reserve Bank of Boston, 1972.

Federal Reserve Bank of Richmond. *The Federal Reserve at Work.* Richmond, Virginia: Federal Reserve Bank of Richmond, 1971.

Francis, Darryl R. "Social Priorities and The Market Allocation of Credit." Speech by Darryl R. Francis, president, Federal Reserve Bank of St. Louis, to the College of Business and Industry, Mississippi State University, February 23, 1971. *Monthly Review* (St. Louis), May 1971, pp. 8–13.

Fraser, Donald R. and Rose, Peter S. "The Hunt Commission Report: Implications for Banking." *The Journal of Commercial Bank Lending,* November 1972, pp. 20–27.

Gerloff, Cecilia M., ed. *The Federal Home Loan Bank System.* Washington, D.C.: The Federal Home Loan Bank Board, 1971.

Hutnyan, Joseph D. "Fed Bans Foreign Insurance Underwriting by BHC's; Plans Close Look at Nonbank Growth." *American Banker,* June 21, 1974.

———. "Fed Completing Study of BHC Regulation." *American Banker,* July 1, 1974.

———. "Patman Slates Hearings on BHC Expansion After July 4 Recess." *American Banker,* May 20, 1974.

———. "Washington Bank Notes: Proxmire Will Not Breathe Fire, But His Cool Head Can Be Threat." *American Banker,* June 14, 1974.

———. "Washington Bank Notes: Strong Words on Bank Liquidity On The Hill—There Will Be More." *American Banker,* June 28, 1974.

Kauper, Thomas E; Baker, Donald I.; and Grossman, Barry. "Comments of the United States Department of Justice Before the Federal Home Loan Bank Board in the Matter of Proposed Amendments Relating to Electronic Funds Transfer Through Remote Service Units." Mimeographed. June 24, 1974.

Knight, Robert E. *Federal Reserve System Policies and Their Effects on the Banking System.* Boston: Federal Reserve Bank of Boston, February 1970.

Lawrence, Robert J. *Operating Policies of Bank Holding Companies–Part II: Nonbanking Subsidiaries.* Washington, D.C.: Board of Governors of the Federal Reserve System, 1974.

Lorie, James H. *Public Policy for American Capital Markets.* Prepared by James H. Lorie for submission to the secretary and the deputy secretary of the treasury. Washington, D.C.: Department of the Treasury, 1974.

McCarthy, Edward J. *Reserve Position: Methods of Adjustment.* Boston: The Federal Reserve Bank of Boston, 1964.

"Member Bank Reserve Requirements–Heritage from History." *Business Conditions,* June 1972, pp. 2–18.

Morris, Frank E. "The Need for a Uniform System of Reserve Requirements." An address by Frank E. Morris, president, Federal Reserve Bank of Boston, before the Sixth Annual Commercial Bankers Forum, University of Miami, January 14, 1972. *New England Economic Review* (Boston), January-February 1972, pp. 14–18.

National Banks and the Future: Report of the Advisory Committee on Banking to the Comptroller of the Currency. Washington, D.C.: U.S. Treasury Department, Comptroller of the Currency, 1962.

"The 1970 Amendments to the Bank Holding Company Act: One Year Later." *Business Conditions* (Chicago), December 1971, pp. 2–11.

"One-Bank Holding Companies Before the 1970 Amendments." *Federal Reserve Bulletin,* December 1962, pp. 999-1008.

"Policy Frontiers Among the Multinationals." *American Banker,* June 28, 1974.

"Proxmire Outlines Goals as Chairman." *National Journal Reports,* July 7, 1974, p. 1117.

The Report of the President's Commission on Financial Structure and Regulation. Washington, D.C.: U.S. Government Printing Office, 1972.

"Required Reading: Fed Committee Seeks to Improve Certainty in International Policies." *American Banker,* June 14, 1974.

"Required Reading: Fed Completing Full-Scale Study of Bank Holding Company Regulations." *American Banker,* July 8, 1974.

"Required Reading: Foreign Insurance Underwriting Is Currently Taboo for BHC's." *American Banker,* June 26, 1974.

"Required Reading: Text of ABA Statement to Senate on Financial Institutions Reform." *American Banker,* May 22, 1974.

Robertson, Ross M. *The Comptroller and Bank Supervision: An Historical Appraisal.* Washington, D.C.: The Office of the Comptroller of the Currency, 1968.

Rubenstein, James. "Michigan Hearings Planned On Defining Scope of Loan Production Offices." *American Banker,* July 1, 1974.

"Senator Proxmire's Views on Banking Legislation." *American Banker,* June 27, 1974.

Simon, William E. "Statement of the Honorable William E. Simon, Secretary of the Treasury, Before the Subcommittee on Economic Growth of the Joint Economic Committee, June 26, 1974." *News.* Washington, D.C.: Department of the Treasury, June 26, 1974. Mimeographed.

———. "Statement of the Honorable William E. Simon, Secretary of the Treasury, Before the Subcommittee on Financial Institutions of the Senate Subcommittee on Banking, Housing, and Urban Affairs, Monday, May 13, 1974, 9:45 A.M." *News.* Washington, D.C.: Department of the Treasury. Mimeographed.

Slevin, Joseph R. "Inside the Economy: Fed Denial of Bank-America Bid for Insurance Company Is Warning to Banks." *American Banker,* July 1, 1974.

———. "Inside the Economy: Fed Wants to Find New Ways to Gauge Condition of Banks." *American Banker,* July 2, 1974.

Sparkman, John. "What to Look for in Banking Legislation." *Bankers Monthly Magazine,* January 15, 1973, p. 12.

"Staff Economic Studies." *Federal Reserve Bulletin,* June 1973, pp. 531-532.

Talley, Samuel H. *The Impact of Holding Company Acquisitions on Aggregrate Concentration in Banking.* Washington, D.C.: Board of Governors of the Federal Reserve System, 1974.

U.S., Congress, House of Representatives, Committee on Banking and Currency. *Financial Institutions: Reform and Public Interest.* Staff Report of the

Subcommittee on Domestic Finance, Committee on Banking and Currency, House of Representatives, 93rd Cong., 1st sess., August 1973. Washington, D.C.: U.S. Government Printing Office, 1973.

———. *The Growth of Unregistered Bank Holding Companies– Problems and Prospects.* Staff Report for the Committee on Banking and Currency, House of Representatives, 91st Cong., 1st sess., February 11, 1969. Washington, D.C.: U.S. Government Printing Office, 1969.

U.S., Congress, Senate, Committee on Banking, Housing, and Urban Affairs. *Conversion of Savings and Loan Associations from Mutual to Stock Form.* Hearings before the Subcommittee on Financial Institutions of the Committee on Banking, Housing, and Urban Affairs, United States Senate, 93rd Cong., 2d sess., April 8, 9, and 10, 1974. Washington, D.C.: U.S. Government Printing Office, 1974.

———. *Depository Institutions Amendments of 1974.* Report of the Committee on Banking, Housing, and Urban Affairs, United States Senate to Accompany H.R. 11221, Together with Additional Views. Washington, D.C.: U.S. Government Printing Office, 1974.

———. *Government Deposit Insurance.* Hearings before the Subcommittee on Financial Institutions of the Committee on Banking, Housing, and Urban Affairs, United States Senate, 93rd Cong., 2d sess., March 19, 20, and 21, 1974. Washington, D.C.: U.S. Government Printing Office, 1974.

U.S., Department of the Treasury. *Recommendations for Change in the U.S. Financial System.* Washington, D.C.: Department fo the Treasury, August 3, 1973.

U.S., House of Representatives. *A Bill to Provide Full Deposit Insurance for Public Units and to Increase Deposit Insurance from $20,000 to $50,000.* 93rd Cong., 1st sess., H.R. 11221, in the House of Representatives, October 31, 1973. By Mr. St. Germain, Mr. Annunzio, Mr. Barrett, Mr. Moorhead of Pennsylvania, Mr. Brasco, Mr. Cotter, Mr. Hanley, Mr. Johnson of Pennsylvania, Mr. Moakley, and Mr. Roncallo of New York.

U.S., Senate. *A Bill to Establish a Commission on Electronic Fund Transfers.* 93rd Cong., 2d sess., S. 3266, in the Senate of the United States, March 28, 1974. By Mr. McIntyre, Mr. Bennett, Mr. Brock, Mr. Brooke, Mr. Pell, Mr. Proxmire, Mr. Sparkman, Mr. Tower, and Mr. Williams.

———. *A Bill to Improve the Efficiency and Flexibility of the Financial System of the United States in Order to Promote Sound Economic Growth, Including the Provision of Adequate Funds for Housing.* 93rd Cong., 1st sess., S. 2591, in the Senate of the United States, October 18, 1973. By Mr. Sparkman and Mr. Tower.

Upshaw, William F. "Bank Affiliates and Their Regulation: Part I." *Monthly Review* (Richmond), March 1973, pp. 14–20.

———. "Bank Affiliates and Their Regulation: Part II. *Monthly Review* (Richmond), April 1973, pp. 3–9.

———. "Bank Affiliates and Their Regulation: Part III. *Monthly Review* (Richmond), May 1973, pp. 3–10.

Wiegold, C. Frederic. "Fed Foreign Proposal Seen Threat to New York Role." *American Banker,* June 24, 1974.

Wentz, John and Mazza, Gertrude. "The Acquisitive Bank Holding Companies: A Bigger Role In Mortgage Banking." *Business Review* (Philadelphia), October 1973, pp. 7-8.

BANKING STRUCTURE

Darnell, Jerome C. "Banking Structure: What Does the Future Hold?" *Business Reivew* (Philadelphia), August 1973, pp. 3-9.

———. "Does Banking Structure Spur Economic Growth?" *Business Review* (Philadelphia), November 1972, pp. 14-22.

Hayes, Alfred. "Recent Developments in Banking Structure and Monetary Policy." *New York,* June 1970, pp. 119-123.

McClelland, Edward L. "Concentration Projected to Increase in Texas." *Business Review* (Dallas), February 1973, pp. 7-10.

"Recent Changes in the Structure of Commercial Banking." *Federal Reserve Bulletin,* March 1970, pp. 195-209.

Studies in Banking Competition and the Banking Structure: Articles Reprinted from the *National Banking Review.* Washington, D.C.: U.S. Treasury, The Administrator of National Banks, 1966.

COMPETITIVE ENVIRONMENT OF BANKS

Anderson, Paul S. and Eisenmenger, Robert W. "Structural Reform for Thrift Institutions: The Experience in the United States and Canada." *New England Economic Review* (Boston), July-August 1972, pp. 3-17.

Balles, John J. "Competitive Outlook in Banking." *Monthly Review* (San Francisco), November 1972, pp. 3-10.

Black, Robert P. and Harless, Doris E. *Nonbank Financial Institutions.* Richmond, Virginia: Federal Reserve Bank of Richmond, December 1969.

Brooke, Phillip. "Some S&L's Back, Bank Groups Oppose FHLBB Interstate EFTS Plan." *American Banker,* June 21, 1974.

Carberry, James. "Credit Unions Gain in Members, Money, Make Plans to Expand Their Activities." *Wall Street Journal,* August 19, 1974, p. 22.

Christophe, Cleveland A. *Competition in Financial Services.* New York: First City National City Corporation, 1974.

Federal Home Loan Bank of Boston, *Annual Report 1973.* Boston: Federal Home Loan Bank of Boston.

Federal Home Loan Bank Board. Journal 74 (Special Issue: 1973 Annual Report), vol. 7.

Federal Reserve Bank of Boston. *Number of Institutions Offering N.O.W.'s and N.O.W. Balances,* Boston: Federal Reserve Bank of Boston, monthly issues.

Flannery, Mark J. "Credit Unions as Consumer Lenders in the United States." *New England Economic Review* (Boston), July-August 1974, pp. 3-12.

———. *An Economic Evaluation of Credit Unions in the United States.* Boston: Federal Reserve Bank of Boston, February 1974.

Longbrake, William A. and Cohan, Sandra B. *The NOW Account Experiment.* Washington, D.C.: Federal Deposit Insurance Corporation, 1974.

Oram, George S., Jr. and Trotter, Richard P. "S&L's and EFTS." *News.* Washington, D.C.: Federal Home Loan Bank Board, April 3, 1973.

Roessner, Gilbert G. with Nadler, Paul S. "What S&L's Want NOW." *The Bankers Magazine,* Winter 1974, pp. 59-66.

"An S&L Puts the Teller in the Supermarket." *Business Week,* April 20, 1974, pp. 88-91.

United States Savings and Loan League. *1973 Savings and Loan Fact Book.* Chicago: U.S. Savings and Loan League, 1973.

———. *1971 Savings and Loan Fact Book.* Chicago: U.S. Savings and Loan League, 1971.

Weiss, Steven J. and McGugan, Vincent John. "The Equipment Leasing Industry and the Emerging Role of Banking Organizations." *New England Economic Review* (Boston), November-December 1973, pp. 3-30.

CONSUMER SAVING AND SPENDING

Hendricks, Gary; Youmans, Kenwood C.; and Keller, Janet. *Consumer Durables and Installment Debt: A Study of American Households.* Ann Arbor: The University of Michigan, Institute for Social Research, 1973.

Keen, Howard, Jr. "Household Savings at Commercial Banks: Bigger Slice of a Bigger Pie." *Business Review* (Philadelphia), November 1972, pp. 8-13.

Mandell, Lewis; Katona, George; Morgan, James N.; and Schniedeskamp, Jay. *Surveys of Consumers 1971-72: Contributions to Behavioral Economics.* Ann Arbor: The University of Michigan, Institute for Social Research, 1973.

Morgan, James N., ed. *Five Thousand American Families—Patterns of Economic Progress.* Volume II: Special Studies of the First Five Years of the Panel Study of Income Dynamics. Ann Arbor: The University of Michigan, Institute for Social Research, 1974.

O'Brien, James M. "The Household As A Saver." *Business Review* (Philadelphia), June 1971, pp. 14-23.

"The Pattern of Growth in Consumer Credit." *Federal Reserve Bulletin,* March 1974, pp. 175-188.

Projector, Dorothy S. *Survey of Changes in Family Finances.* Washington, D.C.: Board of Governors of the Federal Reserve System, 1968.

Projector, Dorothy and Weiss, Gertrude S. *Survey of Financial Characteristics of Consumers.* Washington, D.C.: Board of Governors of the Federal Reserve System, 1966.

Smith, James D. *The Concentration of Personal Wealth in America, 1969.* Washington, D.C.: The Urban Institute, 1973.

CORPORATE FINANCING

"Corporate Financing in 1970." *Federal Reserve Bulletin,* January 1971, pp. 1-8.

Davidson, Philip H. "Corporate Financing and Liquidity: 1968-1972." *Monthly Review* (Richmond), November 1972, pp. 12-15.

———. "Corporate Financing in the Sixties." *Monthly Review* (Richmond), September 1970, pp. 6-7.

———. "Liquidity Patterns in Corporate Financing." *Monthly Review* (Richmond), May 1971, pp. 2-5.

"Direct Placement of Corporate Debt." *Economic Review* (Cleveland), August 1970, pp. 18-32.

"Financing Corporate Investment." *Federal Reserve Bulletin,* June 1972, pp. 523-530.

"Recent Patterns of Corporate External Financing." *Federal Reserve Bulletin,* December 1973, p. 837.

Spencer, Roger W. "Strong Credit Demands, But No 'Crunch' in Early 1973." *Monthly Review* (St. Louis), June 1973, pp. 2-10.

Weaver, Mary F. and Fry, Edward R. "Bank Rates on Business Loans—Revised Series." *Federal Reserve Bulletin,* June 1971, pp. 468-477.

ECONOMICS AND FINANCIAL MARKETS

Burgess, B. Gayle and McCabe, James. "The Forgotten Liabilities . . . Capital Notes and Debentures." *Monthly Review* (Richmond), December 1971, pp. 8-10.

Bussmann, Wynn V. and Margolis, Marvin S. "Econometrics—Large Models Aid GNP Forecasters." *Business Review* (Dallas), June 1973, pp. 1-7.

Coldwell, Philip E. "Some Financial Guides from 1970." An address by Philip E. Coldwell, president, Federal Reserve Bank of Dallas, at the Salesmanship Club of Dallas, February 4, 1971. *Business Review* (Dallas), February 1971, pp. 1-5.

"Commercial Paper, 1960-1969." *Economic Review* (Cleveland), May 1970, pp. 15-25.

DePamphilis, Donald M. *A Microeconomic Econometric Analysis of the Short-Term Commercial Bank Adjustment Process.* Boston: Federal Reserve Bank of Boston, April 1974.

Dill, Arnold A. "Maturity of Negotiable CD's at District Banks." *Monthly Review* (Atlanta), March 1973, pp. 34-39.

"Disintermediating Year." *Monthly Review* (San Francisco), February 1970, pp. 44-46.

"Employment Shifts Toward the Service Industries in Major Areas of the Fourth District." *Economic Review* (Cleveland), April 1970, pp. 19-27.

"The Flow-of-Funds Accounts." *Monthly Review* (Richmond), June 1970, pp. 8-12.

Humphrey, Thomas M. "Changing Views of the Phillips Curve." *Monthly Review* (Richmond), July 1973, pp. 2-13.

"Interest Rates, Credit Flows, and Monetary Aggregates Since 1964." *Federal Reserve Bulletin,* June 1971, p. 425-440.

Johnston, Robert. "Commercial Paper: 1970." *Monthly Review* (San Francisco), March 1971, pp. 57-63.

Kaminow, Ira. "How Well Do Economists Forecast?" *Business Review* (Philadelphia), May 1971, pp. 9-19.

Knight, Robert E. "Part II: An Alternative Approach to Liquidity." *Monthly Review* (Kansas City), February 1970, pp. 11-22.

———. "Part III: An Alternative Approach to Liquidity." *Monthly Review* (Kansas City), April 1970, pp. 3-12.

———. "Part IV: An Alternative Approach to Liquidity." *Monthly Review* (Kansas City), May 1970, pp. 10-18.

Mayo, Robert P. "Rebuilding America's Liquidity." Remarks of Robert P. Mayo, president of the Federal Reserve Bank of Chicago, before the Investment Analysts Society of Chicago, February 4, 1971. *Business Conditions* (Chicago), May 1971, pp. 2-8.

McCracken, Paul W. *Inflation: The Program.* Paper presented at the American Bankers Association Symposium On Inflation, Washington, D.C., July 18, 1974. Mimeographed.

The New York Stock Exchange. *The Capital Needs and Savings Potential of the U.S. Economy: Projections Through 1985.* New York: The New York Stock Exchange, Inc., September 1974.

Quint, Michael. "Citicorp Triples Size of Its Floating-Rate Note Proposal, Points to Strong Demand." *American Banker,* June 28, 1974.

"Revised Series on Bank Credit." *Federal Reserve Bulletin,* August 1968, pp. A-94-A-97.

Scanlon, Martha Strayhorn. "Changes in Time and Savings Deposits at Commercial Banks: April-July 1973." *Federal Reserve Bulletin,* October 1973, pp. 724-730.

Schadrack, Frederick C. and Breimyer, Frederick S. "Recent Developments in the Commercial Paper Market." *Monthly Review* (New York), December 1970, pp. 280-291.

Schulkin, Peter A. "Recent Developments in the REIT Industry." *New England Economic Review* (Boston), September-October 1972, pp. 3-12.

Scott, John W. "Comparative Asset Structures of Selected Financial Institutions." *Monthly Review* (Richmond), October 1971, pp. 15-19.

"Staff Economic Studies. Study Summary. The Determinants of a Direct Investment Outflow with Emphasis on the Supply of Funds." *Federal Reserve Bulletin,* June 1973, pp. 403-404.

Stahl, Sheldon W. "The Service Sector—Where the Action Is." *Monthly Review* (Kansas City), March 1970, pp. 3-11.

Stahl, Sheldon W. and Harshbarger, C. Edward. "Free Enterprise Revisited— A Look at Economic Concentration." *Monthly Review* (Kansas City), March 1973, pp. 10-16.

"State Projections of Income, Employment, and Population to 1990." *Survey of Current Business.* Washington, D.C.: U.S. Department of Commerce, April 1974, pp. 19-45.

U.S., Department of Commerce, Domestic and International Business Administration. "Banking and Securities." In *U.S. Industrial Outlook 1973 with Projections to 1980.* Washington, D.C.: U.S. Government Printing Office, 1973, pp. 411-417.

200 Bibliography

———. "Life, Property and Liability Insurance." In *U.S. Industrial Outlook 1973 with Projections to 1980.* Washington, D.C.: U.S. Government Printing Office, 1973, pp. 419-423.

U.S., Department of Labor, Bureau of Labor Statistics. *The U.S. Economy in 1985: A Summary of BLS Projections.* Washington, D.C.: U.S. Government Printing Office, 1974.

Vojta, George J. *Bank Capital Adequacy.* New York: First National City Bank, 1973.

Willis, Parker B. *Federal Funds Market: Origin and Development.* Boston: Federal Reserve Bank of Boston, 1970.

Wilson, Ruth and Johnston, Verle. "Searching for Liquidity." *Monthly Review* (San Francisco), August 1970, pp. 164-167.

INTERNATIONAL BANKING

"The EEC and U.S. Agriculture." *Business Conditions* (Chicago), Federal Reserve Bank of Chicago, February 1970, pp. 6-10.

"The Eurodollar Market: Part I: The Anatomy of a Deposit and Loan Market." *Economic Review* (Cleveland), March 1970, pp. 3-19.

"The Eurodollar Market: Part II: Interest Rate Relationships." *Economic Review* (Cleveland), April 1970, pp. 3-18.

"The Eurodollar Market: Part III: Some Implications." *Economic Review* (Cleveland), May 1970, pp. 3-14.

"The Expanding Edge Act Subsidiaries." *American Banker,* April 17-23, 1973.

Friedman, Milton. "The Euro-Dollar Market: Some First Principles." *Monthly Review* (St. Louis), July 1971, pp. 16-24.

Hoffman, Diether H. "German Banks as Financial Department Stores." *Monthly Review* (St. Louis), November 1971, pp. 8-13.

Klopstock, Fred H. "Foreign Banks in the United States: Scope and Growth of Operations." *Monthly Review* (New York), June 1973, pp. 140-154.

Leimone, John E. "Banking in a Developing Economy: Latin American Patterns." *Monthly Review* (Atlanta), November 1970, pp. 154-160.

Lemmon, Douglas H. "Edge Corporations: A Microcosm of International Banking Trends." *Monthly Review* (Richmond), September 1973, pp. 15-16.

Tuke, Anthony Favill. "Organizing for Global Banking." *The Bankers Magazine,* Fall 1973, pp. 37-41.

Wiegold, C. Frederic. "Mitchell Sees Fed Setting Rules on U.S. Banks Abroad Soon." *American Banker,* June 11, 1974.

APPENDIX—BANKING IN NEW YORK, CALIFORNIA, AND FLORIDA

Albright, Harry W., Jr. "Address of Harry W. Albright, Jr., New York State Superintendent of Banks, before the 80th Annual Convention of the New York State Bankers Association." Mimeographed. New York: New York State Banking Department, June 6, 1974.

Fearon, Robert H., Jr. "Banking Needs Independent Banks." *The Bankers Magazine,* Summer 1974, pp. 29-33.

Florida Bankers Association. *Florida Banking Structure.* Orlando: Florida Bankers Association, 1974.

"Florida's Bank Revolution." *Florida Trend,* March 1970, p. 22.

Horton, Joseph J., Jr. "Florida Banking." *Dimensions,* December 1969, pp. 10-14.

Kidder, Karen, "Bank Expansion in New York State: The 1971 Statewide Branching Law." *Monthly Review* (New York), November 1971, pp. 266-274.

Kohn, Ernest and Carlo, Carmen J. *The Competitive Impact of New Branches: A Summary Report.* New York: New York State Banking Department, 1969.

———. *Potential Competition: Unfounded Faith or Pragmatic Foresight?* New York: New York State Banking Department, 1970.

Kohn, Ernest; Carlo, Carmen J.; and Kaye, Bernard. *Meeting Local Credit Needs.* New York: New York State Banking Department, 1973.

New York State Bankers Association. *Profile: Commercial Banks, New York State, At Year End 1973.* New York: New York State Bankers Association, 1974.

Rose, Peter S. and Fraser, Donald R. "State Regulation of Bank Holding Companies." *The Bankers Magazine,* Summer 1974, pp. 42-48.

Salley, Charles D. "A Decade of Holding Company Regulation in Florida." *Monthly Review* (Atlanta), July 1970, pp. 90-97.

Treiber, William F. "The Changing Banking Scene." *Monthly Review* (New York), June 1972, pp. 135-139.

Index

ACH: automatic clearing house, 141
agriculture, 24, 25, 110
Alcoa, 71
American Express: and EFTS, 142-152
antitrust, 113; history of, 162
Arabs: and capital-to-deposit ratios, 48; petrodollars and effects on loans/investments, 14
assets: composition change, 42; and economies of scale, 71; foreign banking, 93; growth rate, 36; and household patterns, 61; management, 20; and rate of return, 16; risk and equity, 48

balance-of-payments, 14
Bank Holding Company Act, 71, 112; content of, 120
Bank Merger Act of 1960, 10, 113
Bank of Tokyo Trust Co., 94
Bank Wire: on EFTS, 142-152
Bankers Trust Co., 167
Banking Act of 1935, 9
banking: and asset management, 21; attitude toward and reform, 128; characteristics of commercial banks, 76-79; commercial banks defined, 2; commercial banks and Hunt Commission, 96-102; commercial bank services, 68; costs and services, 106; equity, 48; foreign banks, 93; growth, 30; history of, 6; industry defined, 1; industry structure, 139; New York state, 170; postwar developments, 33; profit, service and operating costs, 161; and quantity theory of money, 20; resistance of to innovation, 155; safety, 112; states and bank charters, 6; statewide structure, 123; trust departments, 71; trust management recommended by Patman, 103; use of and bank cards, 71
bond: issues and holding company, 46
branching, 114; controversy, 181; defined, 9; description, 119, 120; and industry structure, 173; in New York, 166; restraints, 160

California, 93, 118; branching, 160; New York and Florida banking profile, 173-178
capital formation, 53
certificates of deposit (CD), 41, 70
Chase Manhattan Bank, 71, 167
checking, 14; and technology, 132
Chemical Bank, 167
CIT Financial Corp., 91
Clayton Act, 113
competition: for banks, 83; and branching, 103-105, 120; branching controversy, 181-183; consolidation and merger, 10; and EFTS, 138; consolidation and merger, 10; and EFTS, 138; in Florida, New York and California, 181; liability management, 72; mortgage banking, 90; nature of in banking, 66; thrifts, banks and finance companies, 157; underside of reform, 126-128
commercial paper: growth of, 90; market, 55
Commission on Money and Credit, 95, 162
Committee for Economic Development, 95
Consumer Credit Protection Act, 103
consumers: finance companies, 93; goods and household growth, 57; lack of goods, and bank balances, 17
corporations: equipment leasing, 56; financial management, 53

203

204 Index

Council of Economic Advisors, 126
credit: alternative sources, 84; consumer market, 103; during World War II, 20; in intermediary, 2; mortgages, 82; reforms, 126; total — extensions, 21
credit unions (CU), 72, 74; characteristics, 76-79; and Hunt Commission proposals, 96-102
currency: and definition of money, 15

debt: growth of, 33; in intermediary, 2
Dentzer, W.T. Jr., 183
deposits: cost of, 49; decline of demand deposits, 53; demand, 16; growth rate, 36; interest on demand deposits, 52; modes of, 4; and new reserve funds, 21; ownership pattern change, 41; ratio to bank capital, 33; and reserve volume, 21; safety, 8; and technology, 138
depreciation, 52
Depression: bank holiday and legislation, 9; and regulatory structure, 95
disintermediation, 159; defined, 80; Federal Home Loan Bank Board, 128

EFTS (electronic funds transfer systems), 75, 128; and policy generation, 114; services, 140
exports, 14
equity: debt funds, 36; issues, 56

Farmers Home Administration, 116
Federal Bank Holding Company Act, 166
Federal Deposit Insurance Corporation (FDIC), 6; and foreign banks, 94; history of, 111
Federal Funds, 18; extensive use of, 46
Federal Home Loan Bank System, 75, 117, 163; and EFTS, 154
Federal Land Banks, 116
Federal National Mortgage Association, 117, 128, 163
Federal Open Market Committee (FOMC), 15
Federal Reserve Banks, 5, 31; borrowing, 46; growth rate, 33
Federal Reserve Board: aggregate commercial bank asset/liabilities, 61; and CDs and interest rate increase, 48; decisionmaking, 158; and holding company, 114; money supply and bank credit, 110; and Patman House Committee, 103
Federal Reserve System: credit expansion, 17; history, 8; holding company, 123; and Hunt Commission Report, 96-102; and technology, 133

Federal Savings and Loan Insurance Company, 117
Fedwire, 135
finance companies, 84, 86-89; in Consumer Credit Protection Act, 104
First Federal Savings and Loan Association, 75
First National City Bank, 142-152, 167, 170; and EFTS, 153
Fisher, John F.: on EFTS, 142-152
Florida: holding companies, 160; New York and California banking profile, 173-178
Franklin National Bank, 48, 112
funding: liability management, 72; shortages, 159; source development, 33; source innovation, 45

G.E. Credit Corporation, 91
General Motors Acceptance Corp., 55
Germany, 22
Girard Trust Corn Exchange Bank, 10, 113
Glass-Steagall Act, 9
GNP, 22; and demand deposits, 159; growth and fund demand, 63; and money velocity, 16
government: bank charters, 5; bonds, 8; Comptroller of the Currency and leasing, 71; and disintermediation, 82; Hunt Commission proposals, 96-102; Justice Dept., 10; Justice Dept. and EFTS, 142-152; Justice Dept. and statewide banking, 125; Justice Dept. suits, 113, 114; and MSBs, 74; regulation complaints, 95; regulation and specialization, 104; sector and job supply, 28; state and local, 57; and strategy of monetary policy, 110
Great Britain, 22
growth: banking industry, 30; of CDs, 45; and competition for deposits, 41; state and local, 57

Hill, R.D.: on EFTS, 142-152
Hock, D.W., 142-152
holding companies: and commercial paper, 46; floating rate bonds, 81; mortgage banking, 90, 91; and nonbanking services, 49; origin, 10; regulations, 120-123; and regulatory trends, 104; and statewide banking, 116
House Committee on Banking and Currency, 103
household: asset pattern, 61; and commercial banks, 68; and consumer debt, 57
housing: mortgages, 57
Hunt Commission Proposals, 95-102; recommendations, 126, 127

imports, 14
inflation, 159; and interest rates, 49
innovation: industry and balance, 162
interest: and deposit change, 16; rates and indebtedness, 52; rate equalization and Hunt Commission proposals, 96-102; rate rise, 31; rates and war period, 17
intermediation, 68; defined, 2
investment companies: outlined 86-89; postwar pattern, 30
Iowa: holding companies, 123
Iran, 22

Japan, 22
Joint Center for Urban Studies, 61
Justice Dept. *See government.*

labor force, 24
leakage, 14
leasing: as alternative credit course, 94; and bank control, 71
lending: market analysis, 84; and mutual savings banks, 74; practices, 4
liabilities management, 20, 160
life insurance companies: characteristics, 86-89
liquidity: concept of velocity of circulation, 15; and corporate positions, 53; government security holdings, 42; and money velocity increase, 63; risks and protection, 158; U.S. Treasury bills, 16
Lloyds Bank, 94
loans: consumer, 91; Federal Funds, 18; and foreign banking, 94; market share, 158; short-term corporate, 56

McFadden Act, 1927, 119
manufacturing, 26
Mellon National Bank, 71
Mississippi: holding companies, 123
Missouri: holding companies, 123
Mitchell, George W.: on EFTS, 142
money: circulation and concept of velocity, 15; commercial paper market, 56; corporate financial management, 53; fractional reserve banking, 13; income velocity, 17; investment pattern, 30; quantity theory of, 20; reduced liquidity and money velocity, 63; shortages, 159; supply and GNP, 41; supply and price level, 18; U.S. Treasury bills and liquidity, 16; velocity decline, 17
Morgan Guaranty Trust Co., 71, 170
mortgages: and disintermediation, 82; and Hunt Commission Proposals, 96-102; market and innovation, 163, 164; and need for reform, 128; reforms, 126; and thrifties, 72
mutual savings banks (MSB)72-74; characteristics, 76-79; in Consumer Credit Protection Act, 103; Patman House Committee proposals, 103

National Bank Act of 1864, 118
National Banking System, 6
National Commission on Consumer Finance, 126
National Commission on Electronic Fund Transfers, 154
New Hampshire: branching, 119
New Jersey: branching, 119; holding company, 123
New York: banking profile, 173-178; City, 93; branching, 119; history, 165; state, 118
Nixon, R.M., 95
North Dakota, 118
NOW accounts, 52, 75; and reform, 126

Occidental Life Insurance Company, 115
Omnibus Banking Act, 167

Patman, Wright, 103
pension funds: characteristics, 86-89
Philadelphia: mergers, 10; —National Bank, 10, 113
point of sale (POS): concept of, 138
population: household spending patterns, 57; shift and age distribution, 22
Presidents Commission on Financial Structure and Regulation. *See The Hunt Commission.*
public policy: adequate bank capital, 64; bank safety and liquidity, 158; and bank technology, 137; and consumer protection, 127; and EFTS, 153; and reform, 126; and safety regulations, 110

reform: public pressure, 127
regulation, 7; complaints, 95; EFTS and Comptroller of the Currency, 154; federal, 109; and Hunt Commission, 127
reserves: concept of fractional reserve banking, 14; and Feds control, 15; and Fed requirement, 36
resource allocation, 127
restrictions: and disintermediation, 82
Reynolds, John: and EFTS, 142-152
Roosevelt, F.D., 9

security repurchase agreements (RP), 41
savings and loan association (S&L), 73, 74; characteristics, 76-79; in consumer credit

Protection Act, 103; Hunt Commission, 96-102; lending specialization, 4; Patman House Committee Proposals, 103
Sears Roebuck, 91
securities: and Federal Reserve Banks, 17; liquidation for expansion, 41; long-term, 20
services, 26; and EFTS, 138; flexibility, 155
Small Business Administration, 117
SPC (switching and processing center), 153
Statewide Branching Law, 165, 182
Stephens Act, 166
strategy: CD interest rate rise, 48; commercial paper market, 56; and competition, 103-106; inventory policy, 52; production and acquisition, 2; reforms, 126
Strunck, Norman, 142-152
Student Loan Marketing Association, 117
suburbs: and investment pattern, 30
Sumitomo Bank of California, 94

taxes, 17; law and LIFO inventory accounting, 52; uniform treatment and Hunt Commission Proposals, 96-102

technology: and banking overview, 131-135; privacy of information, 140; regulation and commissions, 154, 155
Texas: holding company, 123
thrifts: institutions and attitude toward reform, 128; competition, 160, 161; institutions, 72; and Patman House Committee, 103; and restrictions, 82; restrictions and regulatory favors, 117; and technology, 140. *See also mutual savings banks, credit unions, savings and loans.*
Transamerica Corporation, 115
transfers: loans and investments, 21
Transmatic Money Service, 75
Treasury Bills, 31

U.S. v. Philadelphia National Bank, 113, 114

Vermont: holding companies, 123
Virginia: branching, 119

West Virginia: holding companies, 123

Xerox Corporation, 71

RARY OF DAVIDSON